Poe and the Subversion of American Literature

Poe and the Subversion of American Literature

Satire, Fantasy, Critique

Robert T. Tally Jr.

Bloomsbury Academic
An imprint of Bloomsbury Publishing Inc

B L O O M S B U R Y
NEW YORK • LONDON • NEW DELHI • SYDNEY

Bloomsbury Academic
An imprint of Bloomsbury Publishing Inc

1385 Broadway	50 Bedford Square
New York	London
NY 10018	WC1B 3DP
USA	UK

www.bloomsbury.com

Bloomsbury is a registered trademark of Bloomsbury Publishing Plc

First published 2014
First published in paperback 2015

Library of Congress Cataloging-in-Publication Data
A catalog record for this book is available from the Library of Congress.

ISBN: HB: 978-1-6235-6427-8
PB: 978-1-5013-0929-8
ePub: 978-1-6235-6970-9
ePDF: 978-1-6235-6920-4

Typeset by Fakenham Prepress Solutions, Fakenham, Norfolk NR21 8NN
Printed and bound in the United States of America

In Memory of a Little Black Cat,
and for Reiko

Contents

Acknowledgments

My life and work have been inexpressibly enhanced by both of those to whom this book is dedicated: a little black cat, who was sagacious to an astonishing degree, perfect and cute, and Reiko, whose beauty, intelligence, and powers of inspiration are about all she has in common with many of Poe's best known heroines, thank goodness. Peripety occasionally works to one's advantage, and I am extremely fortunate to have had the rays of my destiny gather into focus as they have. Much of this owes to the vital influence of these beloved dedicatees.

There are many others I would like to acknowledge. My colleagues at Texas State University have been extremely generous and encouraging, and I have benefitted from our conversations about Poe, literary criticism and history, American Studies, and literary and cultural studies more generally. I would especially like to thank Michael Hennessy and Ann Marie Ellis, whose support for me in their roles as departmental chairperson and college dean has gone above and beyond the duties of those offices. My students have often been thoroughly exasperating, but their wit, enthusiasm, and curiosity have never failed to help replenish my reserves of the same, making my own work better and more enjoyable along the way. I would particularly like to thank Abigail Brown, Andrea Diaz, Julia Eddington, Chelsey Hauptrief, Daniel Keltner, Whitney May, Jaime Netzer, Richard Santos, and Tyrica Terry for their thoughtful contributions. Prior to my arrival in Texas, I had mentors and teachers whose intellectual energy and patient, engaged pedagogy disclosed new critical vistas and continue to inform my work, often in subtle and unseen ways, but almost always in profoundly productive ones. Of these, I would like to thank Jonathan Arac, whose example as a teacher and scholar informs all of my own efforts, and whose contributions to literary history have so influenced my own reading and thinking. Also, I could give through quotations or references no idea of the degree to which Paul A. Bové has contributed to my intellectual and professional formation as a literary critic, scholar, and teacher. Some of my early and informal empirical research in amateur Poe Studies was aided by the resources, human and otherwise, of the Hideaway, Tune Inn, College Inn, Down Under, and Raccoon Lodge. Before and during nearly all of this, my brothers, in-laws, parents, and grandparents were there for me. Additionally, *les sœurs pantalons* have on an almost daily basis endeavored to illustrate Voltaire's maxim, *tout les chats sont bon, hors le chat ennuyeux.*

A number of the arguments in this study found their form, sometimes tentatively and unexpectedly, through my interactions with others in a community of scholars of Poe, American literature, or literary studies more broadly. Early versions of parts of this book were first presented in the form of conference papers for panels at annual meetings of the American Literature Association, the Modern Language Association, and the South Central Modern Language Association. Several such panels were sponsored by the Poe Studies Association, and I am especially grateful to the many devoted scholars, critics, and enthusiasts who make that organization such an effective and enjoyable site for spirited discussion and fellowship. Among them, I should thank Professors Amy Branam, Susan Amper, John Gruesser, and Susan Elizabeth Sweeney for organizing the panels on which I appeared. Also, I want to thank my co-panelists, as well as the many attentive and engaged scholars in the audience, whose insights, questions, and comments have certainly improved my initial thoughts. I wish to give special thanks to the Edgar Allan Poe Society of Baltimore for their indefatigable efforts to preserve and promote serious scholarship as well as general enthusiasm for Poe's life and works.

Portions of Chapters 3, 4, and 7, in much earlier versions, appeared as "The Poetics of Descent: Irreversible Narrative in Poe's 'MS. Found in a Bottle,'" in Benjamin Schreier, ed., *Studies in Irreversibility: Texts and Contexts* (Newcastle-upon-Tyne: Cambridge Scholars, 2007); "The Nightmare of the Unknowable, or, Poe's Inscrutability," in *Studies in Gothic Fiction* Vol. 1, no. 1 (2010); and "How Utterly Thou Hast Murdered Thyself: Poe's Comedic Double-Take in 'William Wilson,'" in Christian Hoffstadt and Sabine Müller (eds), *Doppelgänger, Polygänger, Alter Egos* (Bochum/Freiburg: Projekt Verlag, 2012), respectively. I gratefully acknowledge the editors and publishers. I am also appreciative of the anonymous peer-reviewers, whose careful reading and constructive criticism of earlier forms of the manuscript helped to make the final version much better than it could have been without them. Needless to say, perhaps, any flaws, errors, omissions, loose threads, double entendres, bad puns, improperly interred bodies or insufficiently unearthed ones, and almost all of the words, are my responsibility alone.

Introduction: A Poetics of Descent

A rhetoric of ascent looms large in the discourse of American literary studies. This rhetoric can be heard in the ideological commitment to such imagery as the heavenward, or, at least, progressive, march of a chosen people, a favored trope undergirding "the Puritan origins of the American self," in Sacvan Bercovitch's phrase, and in the famously optative mood of F. O. Matthiessen's "American Renaissance" writers, as well as in the promise of the "American Century" announced by Henry Luce in the 1940s. The same rhetoric breathes life into the pervasive, but often dubious, sense of consistently upward mobility, where individuals and groups elevate themselves in a socio-economic sphere, as if by fate or perhaps by a sort of manifest destiny, notwithstanding the all-too-clear and common-sense apprehension that such mobility cannot be unidirectional, and that it is just as easy to fall in social rank and economic class as it is to rise. This rhetoric animates the discourse of the "inevitable" ascension of the nation to the top of the global hierarchy in a geopolitical, sometimes also military and economic, organization of the world system. The rhetoric of ascent resounds in the belief-system of a well-nigh religious American Studies as it established itself as a disciplinary field in the 1940s and 1950s, and can be heard equally loudly, although formulated negatively, in those various, more recent jeremiads lamenting America's "fall," its betrayal of the true calling of Winthrop's city upon a hill, for instance, or its descent from its lofty ideals into the morass of *Realpolitik*. As a distinct but inextricable part of the interdisciplinary project of American Studies, the institution of American literature has been shaped by and has actively contributed to this national rhetoric, whether in identifying and promoting those writers who are thought to embody it through processes of canon-formation, or in interpreting texts and history in such a way as to foreclose on alternative visions, wittingly or otherwise. By positing something like a distinctively national literary tradition, American literature participates in this nationalist rhetorical and allegorical program.

In this study, I argue that the nomad thought discernible in the works of Edgar Allan Poe subverts American literature through an assiduously satirical and critical mode of fantasy. By *subversion*, I am not referring to an oppositional political project, although one could argue for such an express or implied resistance to American national culture in Poe's writings.[1] Rather, I have in mind an almost geological meaning: Poe undermines the project of American Studies, playfully eroding its foundational assumptions. Although Poe is in some ways a central figure in the literary history of the United States, and he remains among the most popular authors born in the U.S., Poe's work resists incorporation into the national self-image. Indeed, Poe savages that imaginary America by means of a satirical, fantastic, and critical approach that he uses to subvert both the actually existing customs and practices of nineteenth-century American life and the ideological foundations of what will become the field of American literary studies of the twentieth century and beyond. In contrast to the rhetoric of ascent, Poe formulates a poetics of descent, which operates as a critique of all things lofty. It is a mode by which to "take things down," to bring the highfalutin conceits back down to the level of the street or even lower, to plunge such grand ideals into the muck and mire of material culture. Poe's satirical fantasy opposes the optative state philosophy of American Studies, but not by arguing that the city upon the hill has become a lowly town in a swamp, a place in need of elevation. Rather, Poe does so by puncturing the national rhetoric itself, by playfully poking holes in it, by revealing that both the city and the hill are chimeras, by making a mockery of these pretensions and aspirations.

Poe's critique of the idealized language of American national narrative also extends to the ideological and philosophical airiness that so many Americans of his day affected. This is most clearly audible in Poe's attacks on transcendentalism and the New England clique, but it is also present in his satires of various kinds of Platonism, including those that are sometimes attributed to him. Although it is not uncommon for literal-minded scholars to think of Poe as himself a Platonist, who extols the pure, ideal forms of Beauty or Art or what have you, Poe is more apt to make fun of such philosophizing, as for example in "Berenice," where the narrator's obsession with Berenice's teeth is a send-up of Platonic forms, hilariously invoked in the motto, *tous ses dents etaient des idées.*[2] Poe's writing satirizes the then dominant, and still influential, pneumatic rhetoric in the public culture of the United States of his era and in the ideology of the American Studies of the following century. Poe's writings thus exert a countervailing force, opening spaces for exploring an alternative literature no longer tethered to the myths and symbols of a national narrative.

As a great deal of recent criticism has made clear, and contrary to some of the most famous, popular images of the man, Poe does not "rise above" the material world in which he lives and works, but partakes of it, often as a willing and astute participant in the most mundane aspects of everyday life in the first half of the nineteenth century. Although he was certainly dogged by poverty throughout much of his adulthood, Poe was not a starving artist, out of touch with the crassly commercial realm of bourgeois American life, as Charles Baudelaire had characterized him, but was acutely in tune with the ways of the world in his own time and place. Poe uses the elements

---

[1] For the now classic and still important study of implicit or explicit political critique in antebellum American literature, see David S. Reynolds, *Beneath the American Renaissance.*
[2] Poe, "Berenice," *Poetry and Tales*, 231.

of his "low" humor and street-smarts to make deliberate sport of the rhetoric which predominates the nationalist discourses of the day. Recent studies, such as Terence Whalen's *Edgar Allan Poe and the Masses*, Meredith L. McGill's *American Literature and the Culture of Reprinting, 1834–1853*, or J. Gerald Kennedy and Jerome McGann's *Poe and the Remapping of Antebellum Print Culture*, have demonstrated the degree to which Poe remained well situated within the mainstream material culture, but I would argue that this does not make him representative of his time and place so much as it made possible his pointed critique of American society and of the dominant narrative that undergirded its nascent identity as an identifiably national culture. During the 1830s and 1840s, Poe was very much a part of the burgeoning national culture that was emerging and consolidating itself, yet he also remained aloof from it, in part through the critical distance he maintained as part of his professional calling and in part owing to the exigencies of his own daily life. As I argue in Chapter 1, Poe's satirical and fantastic critique of U.S. national culture in his own day, as well as of the ideological underpinnings of a twentieth-century American Studies, emerges in the form of mysteriously comical subterranean noises, rather than as revolutionary fusillades or detailed critical treatises. Poe's laughter is subtle and profound.

In arguing that Poe's nomad thought places him outside of and athwart the national traditions of American literature, I do not necessarily mean to endorse the by now dubious claim of early and mid-twentieth-century Americanists who remained under the influence of specious, largely incomplete or sometimes biased biographical criticism of Poe. Poe's own words—or, rather, those of his typically romantic narrators in his poems and tales—situated him "out of space, out of time,"[3] and this led many literary critics and historians, as well as nearly all fans of Poe, to embrace the proposition that Poe could not fit within the literary culture of the United States. Most notorious, perhaps, was Matthiessen's decision to omit Poe from his field-establishing study, *American Renaissance*, although it should be noted that Matthiessen did pen a long, largely sympathetic entry on Poe for *The Literary History of the United States* (1948). Recent scholarship has rightly disabused us of the false image of Poe the romantic outsider, focusing attention on Poe's savvy awareness and deliberate manipulation of various literary conventions and practices in his era. In his introduction to the aforementioned *Poe and the Remapping of Antebellum Print Culture*, Kennedy notes that the contributors to that volume aimed at "remapping" American literature, not by replacing one set of coordinates with an equally problematic set, but by re-envisioning the terrain to be mapped entirely. As Kennedy puts it,

> participants in the project wished to avoid a mere re-centering of antebellum print culture—famously conceived by F. O. Matthiessen in *American Renaissance* (1941) to revolve around Emerson, Hawthorne, Melville, Thoreau, and Whitman on an axis from Boston to New York—that would position Poe at the crux of another fixed national cartography. We wished instead to remap the space of antebellum print culture horizontally, not from a top-down, hierarchical perspective that

[3] See Poe, "Dream-Land," *Poetry and Tales*, 79.

would re-inscribe literary preeminence. Poe would figure not as the unrecognized Master Genius, but rather as a shrewd, peripatetic author-journalist whose circulation in what he called "Literary America" epitomized the ploys and practices of a horizontal culture of letters sustained by proliferative redistribution.[4]

As will become clear in the pages that follow, my argument aligns with this view of Poe as a canny participant in and observer of a dynamic national marketplace for literary productions in the 1830s and 1840s. However, I also see in Poe's opposition to the literary nationalism, as well as to the regional provincialism, of his time a scarcely disguised critique of the project of American literature itself. The early Americanist critics were thus correct, if not always for the right reasons, in viewing Poe as lying outside the main currents of American thought. Poe's nomadism, as I characterize it, opposes and undermines any national literary tradition in advance of its formation. As Poe put it in his "Exordium to Critical Notices," no "true literature" could possibly be national, for "the world at large" is "the only proper stage for the literary *histrio*."[5] Poe's call for a world literature, somewhat like Goethe's a bit earlier, would signal his anticipatory break with the emerging national tradition into which he has never really quite fit.

Poe's career is marked by both constant movement and reversals of fortune, peripatetic wandering and *peripeteia*. One of the more interesting collateral aspects of this constant reversal of fortune and perpetual motion is that Poe's writing career does not really develop according to the *Bildungsroman*-styled unfolding of a poet's maturation or to the professional craftsman's honing of techniques as he moves from apprentice to journeyman to master. To take what may seem at first an obvious example, with the exception of his early poetry (and, even there, one could make an argument to the contrary), Poe's personal history as a writer does not really have recognizable stages of development, of the sort that typifies the careers of a Nathaniel Hawthorne or a Herman Melville. The young Hawthorne produced vibrant sketches and excellent short tales, plus a good deal of "hack work," before his emergence as a *littérateur* to be reckoned with after *The Scarlet Letter* is published in 1850. Melville's career is sometimes neatly divided among his various, somewhat discrete, stages: his early, largely nonfictional personal narratives of 1846–1850, the tumultuous period in which he wrote *Moby-Dick* and *Pierre*, his magazine writing period from 1853 to 1856, his long "silence" between 1857's *The Confidence-Man* and the end of his life, during which he wrote relatively little, and that mostly self-published poetry, and then the posthumous discovery of "Billy Budd," the publication of which inaugurated the Melville Revival of the 1920s and, arguably, helped launch the interdisciplinary field of American Studies itself.[6] In contrast, and owing in part to the perceived requirements of the magazine and book-publishing industry, notably the aforementioned "culture

---

[4] Kennedy, "Introduction," in Kennedy and McGann, eds, *Poe and the Remapping of Antebellum Print Culture*, 2.

[5] Poe, "Exordium to Critical Notices," *Essays and Reviews*, 1027.

[6] See Clare L. Spark, *Hunting Captain Ahab: Psychological Warfare and the Melville Revival*. On the coincidence, if not complicity, between the Melville Revival and the emergence of American Studies, see Spanos, *The Errant Art of* Moby-Dick, especially 2–23.

of reprinting," Poe reworked and republished even his earliest materials throughout his career. Many of his early tales appeared in several magazines and books during Poe's lifetime. Often Poe made substantial revisions to the various editions, as with his "Loss of Breath," which was first published in 1832 as "A Decided Loss" and appeared in five different versions during Poe's career. To take another example, "MS. Found in a Bottle"—first published in 1833 and republished in one form or another five more times, each with slight modifications to the text, between then and 1850—included a new note for its "final" form, the 1850 edition of *The Works of the Late Edgar Allan Poe*. In other words, with Poe, even the "early" writings may also represent the "later" Poe. Of course, detailed textual analysis can reveal fascinating information about these changes, and a sensitive reading of the variations can tells us a great deal about Poe's own life and times, as well as about the characteristics of the reading public and the demands of the literary marketplace of the day.[7] However, except for the discussion of Poe's biography in Chapter 2, this study does not really follow a chronological narrative trajectory. Although my approach is certainly not synchronic, I think Poe's work invites impossible attempts to say everything at once, and that this can lead one on a rather circuitous path, where repetitions occasionally encounter the odd *non sequitur*, and the most familiar objects suddenly appear terrible and strange, humorous or grotesque.

Few nineteenth-century writers have had their lives so thoroughly intertwined and confused with their works as Poe. Indeed, Poe's mythical life story wields far more power than the true biography, and this myth is largely responsible for the fascination with, and canonization of, Poe's writings. One of the most noteworthy features of Poe's biography is his nearly constant movement or, to speak only somewhat metaphorically, his nomadism. From infancy until his death, Poe never lived in one place for more than a few years, and his peripatetic life was filled with reversals of fortune that seemed to keep him on the move. Although an apparently constant movement or migration was part of the national self-image in the United States in the nineteenth century, Poe's nomadic movements actually set him apart from the mainstream of American life. For all the discussion of social mobility in that era, the real direction of all of this hustle and bustle was toward settlement, and Poe was completely unable, and likely unwilling, to settle. Poe's wanderings among the great cities of the Eastern seaboard are always remarked upon by biographers and critics, but rarely are they viewed in light of his definitive break with the American national culture, in both his own time and in the image produced later. To borrow Gilles Deleuze's well known distinction, Poe's nomad thought opposes the state philosophy of national narrative. Poe was a nomad in a nation of settlers, a subtly disruptive force in the emerging spaces of American culture. Poe's life and works figure forth a disquieting image just visible beneath the surface of the new national experience of his era, and present

---

[7] My study of Poe does not go into great detail about these differences, but I am extremely grateful for the important work does by such trailblazing and painstaking scholars as Thomas Ollive Mabbott, who have performed such an invaluable service to literature and history.

a radically different iconography from the national image-repertoire mobilized by American Studies a hundred years later.

Wandering back and forth among the great American cities of Boston, Richmond, Baltimore, New York, and Philadelphia, Poe in his peripatetic life aptly registers a corresponding element of his poetics and his work. A nomadic movement animates much of his writings, whether in the physical travels of individuals to distant regions unknown (like Arthur Gordon Pym, Julius Rodman, or Hans Pfaall), in the movements of characters (such as the man of the crowd and his dogged pursuer, the two William Wilsons, or the narrators of "Ligeia" or "The Fall of the House of Usher"), or in the pervasive nomadism of Poe's own thought (as in his theory of perversity in "The Philosophy of Composition," "The Imp of the Perverse," or "The Black Cat"). Yet, unlike many personal narratives in mid-nineteenth-century American literature, Poe's voyages lead less to knowledge and conquest, than to greater mysteries and insecurity. Poe's work thus undermines not only the famously optative mood of the American Renaissance, but also the principal purpose of personal narrative, which frequently fostered ideological programs of national expansion, both territorial and spiritual. Poe's perversity (literally, a "turning away") expresses the nomadic rejection of the norm while also exploring territories of the unthought and unrepresented. In this, Poe's "thought from the outside," as Michel Foucault might put it,[8] reveals itself as a powerful and unsettling counter-argument to the prevailing nationalist philosophy of his epoch.

In his literary historical analysis of narrative forms in nineteenth-century American literature, Jonathan Arac identifies four genres (national, local, personal, and literary narratives) that emerged, proliferated, and competed with one another during the epoch spanning 1820 to 1860.[9] Poe's work fits rather uneasily within Arac's typology, for, although Poe arguably made use of the characteristics of all four genres, none of his various narratives seem representative of any. Among the narrative forms most associated with movement and with exotic encounters, personal narratives dominated American literature in the era in which Poe was establishing himself as a writer and critic. Personal narratives, whose plots generally followed a simple descent-and-return trajectory, told the story of an individual's experiences in what the readers would recognize as an unfamiliar environment, be it a foreign land, a lower class, a wilderness, or what have you. In the case of slave narratives, several of these exotic experiences were combined with the matters of race and politics to make the narrative all the more extraordinary and yet topical. The return of the traveler to the mainstream world of the narrative's audience functioned as a symbol of conquest and domestication, where novel and foreign experiences came to be known and thus to be rendered safe for readerly consumption. In a number of works—most thoroughly visible in *The Narrative of Arthur Gordon Pym*, but also in such pieces as "The Unparalleled Adventure of One Hans Pfaall" or "The Journal of Julius Rodman"—Poe produced personal narratives; or perhaps it might be more accurate to say that he

---

[8] See Foucault, *Maurice Blanchot: The Thought from Outside*.
[9] See Jonathan Arac, *The Emergence of American Literary Narrative, 1820–1860*.

engaged creatively with this form, partly in order to lampoon it. As early as 1833, in one of his first tales published as a professional writer, Poe conceived of a personal narrative of voyage and discovery, which, contrary to the format and function of most personal narratives, involved no return. Without the narrator's return to the metropolitan center, the place occupied by the reader, the tale's exoticism is enhanced, as the unfamiliar experiences remain inexplicably foreign. In Chapter 3, I look at the irreversible narrative of "MS. Found in a Bottle" especially, and discuss the ways in which Poe uses the personal narrative form to undermine the claims of knowledge that this genre normally encouraged and made possible. I argue that Poe's refusal to supply a comforting return or homecoming of the narrator, along with his proffering of mystical discovery in lieu of an actual pseudo-scientific report from the fringe, operate in such a way as to criticize the nationalist ethos of most nineteenth-century personal narratives. Poe's satirical and altogether fake personal narrative sweeps the legs out from under this narrative form, thus also undermining a key ideological device of the incipient discourse that would come to be re-characterized and promoted by the field of American Studies.

Returning to several of Poe's famous and popular tales in Chapter 4, I focus on the theme of terror or horror, with which Poe is perhaps most closely associated by his legions of twentieth- and twenty-first-century fans. As with his critique of the quasi-scientific pretensions of the personal narrative genre, Poe's peculiar use of "tales of terror" makes clear that the most horrifying aspect is the unsettling sense of not knowing. That is, the reader experiences a fear of, not merely the unknown, but the unknowable. For example, Poe begins and ends his enigmatic study of the man of the crowd with the phrase, "it does not permit itself to be read." The same observation might apply to much of Poe's own work, in which a kind of inscrutability subtends the very mode of reading. One might say that Poe's work actively defies interpretation, at times subtly and at others overtly undermining the reader's assumptions that the story's "meaning" will reveal itself. In some mysteries, like the Dupin trilogy or "The Gold-Bug," Poe is willing to offer an explanation. But more often than not, Poe's texts frustrate the desire for comprehension. For instance, "MS. Found in a Bottle" drama-tizes the unnamed narrator's thrill of "discovery" as he descends into the unknown and unknowable, but at the end of the narrative he knows very little, and can report even less, of what he has discovered. In other purported tales of terror, such as "Ligeia," "The Fall of the House of Usher," or "The Black Cat," Poe deliberately puzzles his readers, leading them to imagine a stable meaning that then will not hold. I argue that the horror of Poe's tales lies not in a particular fright, but in a general mood of uncertainty. Again and again, Poe presents the arcane, exotic, otherworldly, unique, but he refuses to play the anthropologist, explicating the unknown and bringing it into a safe and familiar intellectual archive. Poe's texts present something that does not let itself be read. Rather than offering a puzzle like a crossword or a Sudoku where one takes pleasure in figuring it out, Poe insists on the insoluble puzzling. This puzzlement relates to the reading experience as well. The inscrutability of these tales lies at the heart of the reading. We, like Poe's narrator in "The Man of the Crowd," can marvel at the enigma before us, but we cannot understand. It may be that this is for the best; as that narrator concludes, "perhaps it is one of the great mercies of God that '*er lässt sich nicht lesen*.' "[10] This, too, may be part of Poe's irreverent practical joking, as the reader who was so intent on solving the mystery ultimately is left, like the narrator, entirely in the dark.

Poe's perversity with respect to epistemology informs his literary theory as well, particularly in his view of the relationship between the writer and the reader, which itself turns on a question of genre. As Arac has pointed out, audiences in Poe's own day were frequently perplexed by his stories, as they found it difficult to discern just what they were reading and how to approach it. Frequently there arises the question of whether the readers themselves were the butt of some authorial joke, which is clearly the case in a practical joke like "The Balloon-Hoax," the coy "Editor's Note" in the republication of "The Facts in the Case of M. Valdemar," or even in farcical burlesques like "The Angel of the Odd." But such prankishness may often also operate in writings taken more seriously by their initial audience and by readers today, such as "The Pit and the Pendulum," "William Wilson," or even nonfiction like "The Philosophy of Composition." Poe's theory of the *single effect*, closely tied to his argument in favor of short stories and brief poems over novels and epics, betrays an almost antagonistic relationship between an author and his readership. The reader must be captured, captivated, and manipulated by the writer. Poe imagines his own works as apparatuses of capture, as I discuss in Chapter 5. In a variety of works, Poe refuses to establish a familiar identity with which the reader may identify, such as the Adamic American figures of national narratives, but instead Poe invokes a fantastic and unsettling presence, half-familiar but still strange, that causes the reader to doubt even that which she or he thought was known. Poe's own literary theory, then, is imbued with the spirit of the perverse.

Poe's tales of terror, of the grotesque and arabesque, frequently posit the unknown or unknowable as the most truly horrifying phenomenon. But this frustration or perplexity also extends to the audience. As Arac has pointed out, "Poe's work provoked a fundamental uncertainty in response. Was he serious? Should his readers be serious? The problem is one of genre: What kind of work is this?"[11] Poe's meditation on the inscrutable goes a step further in his analysis of "the spirit of perversity," which the narrator of "The Black Cat" calls "this unfathomable longing of the soul to *vex itself*." The spirit of perverseness disrupts the Cartesian certitude of the ego, and, as Poe points out in "The Imp of the Perverse," that the only reason science has overlooked this *primum mobile* of the human soul is "the pure arrogance of the reason."[12] Poe's critique of rational inquiry, of the system of classification in psychology and philosophy that renders the text (in this case, the human subject itself) unknowable, might be compared to the Foucauldian exposition of unreason and the Deleuzian analysis of the encounter with stupidity. With perverseness, Poe imposes an uncertainty principle on the agent and the author, as well as on the subject and the text.

---

[10] Poe, "The Man of the Crowd," *Poetry and Tales*, 396.
[11] Arac, *The Emergence of American Literary Narrative*, 68.
[12] Poe, "The Black Cat," *Poetry and Tales*, 599; Poe, "The Imp of the Perverse," *Poetry and Tales*, 826.

Poe's satirical critical theory thus opposes itself to the more hopeful or progressive views of the science and literature of the American Renaissance. In his playful use of genres, as I examine in Chapter 6, Poe calls into question not only our ability to know but also the ways in which we hope to make sense of things. Here he pushes the basic forms of literature to unforeseen extremes, allowing perversity itself to become the prime mover in human endeavor. Of course, this also means that a central figure of the American national project, the individual human subject endowed with freedom— whether as an "American Adam," the "rugged individualist," the liberal free-market participant, or the like—is put into a very precarious and untenable position. As with the terrifying absurdity or absurd terror of "William Wilson," the sovereign subject is shown to be utterly vexed.

Unlike other famous travelers who wrote popular and influential narratives based on their experiences, Poe himself never voyaged to the South Pacific (like Melville), ventured along the Oregon Trail (like Francis Parkman), or spent a couple of years bivouacking in a shack by Walden Pond (like Henry David Thoreau). Poe did have an intimate familiarity with another kind of space, which in its own way seemed nearly as exotic as those others. I refer to his status as perhaps the first recognizably urban writer in American literature and to his knowledge of the paradoxically bewildering spaces of the city. Poe is obviously not the first to live in cities, nor is he the first to move among them. But Poe is the most significant antebellum writer to be *of* the city, to have his work deploy and exude a kind of urban substance that informs his tales, many of which appear on their face to be hardly urban at all. One feels aspects of the urban atmosphere vividly even in such ostensibly nonurban tales as *The Narrative of Arthur Gordon Pym* or "The Fall of the House of Usher," perhaps even more so than in tales like "The Man of the Crowd" or "The Murders in the Rue Morgue" which are set in major metropolises. In Chapter 7, I look at Poe's role as a "connoisseur of cities," to use Scott Peeples's phrase. Poe's ambiguous relationship with the city informs much of his work, and the "world of strangers" he inhabits presents a striking counter-image to the national image repertoire of nineteenth-century panegyrics written in the optative mood, and of twentieth-century American Studies, with its often profoundly pastoral vision of Virgin Lands and errands into the wilderness. Poe is "at sea" in the city, and the urban acceleration of social motion stresses the maelstrom-like effects of the changing environment on the national self-image of the United States. Winthrop's utopian city on the hill becomes, for Poe, an Atlantis, sinking among and beneath the waves. As the national mission required readers to repress memories of such a fallen city in its heavenward, progressive march, Poe's poetics of descent celebrates the terrors of the fall. And yet it does so with a wry smile, the culmination of the diddler's scheme, as Poe asserts in "Diddling Considered as One of the Exact Sciences."

As with his penchant for practical joking, hoaxing, or diddling, Poe's perverse literary theory finds its most fertile ground in the literary practices associated with satire, humor, and fantasy. Though he remains best known to the greater reading public as an author of horror or mystery, Poe's laughter is what really enchants, and ultimately haunts, the conscientious student of his overall *oeuvre*. In his more ludicrous writings, Poe highlights those elements that proceed, as he suggests in his theory of the imaginative faculties, from the imagination, to the fancy, to fantasy, and on to humor. The otherworldliness of Poe's stories is often, perversely but appropriately, a mark of his worldliness, inasmuch as the most *outré* tales speak more directly to his readers' imaginations than tales in the supposedly realistic mode could. Poe's alterity makes possible an ultimately more effective representation of the real world of which he is viscerally a part. In Chapter 8, I argue that Poe's satirical fantasy, his grotesque and arabesque writings, may exceed the boundaries of taste, but they can also approach the precincts of the truth, precisely because of the otherness Poe is willing to countenance. Like that vision of Epicurus made famous in Lucretius' *De Rerum Natura*, Poe ventures *extra mœnia flammantia mundi* ("beyond the flaming walls of the world") to find the more "real" reality, unavailable to those whose imaginations and senses of humor are more rigidly circumscribed. In his harlequinesque oddness, Poe manages to get the last laugh.

Finally, in the conclusion, I examine one of Poe's most celebrated themes as a way of estimating his lasting influence in American literary studies, for better or for worse, and I suggest that his subterranean sounding of the underside of the American national literary tradition still resonates in the post-American century to which we now belong. Premature burial is a recurrent theme in Poe's tales of terror, whether the interments appear accidental (as in "Berenice" or "The Fall of the House of Usher"), intentional ("The Cask of Amontillado" or "The Pit and the Pendulum"), mystical ("Ligeia"), mistaken (*The Narrative of Arthur Gordon Pym*), comical ("Loss of Breath" or "The Premature Burial"), or even reversed, as "The Facts in the Case of M. Valdemar," in which the living corpse probably *should* have been given a proper burial. Premature burial also functions as an apt metaphor for Poe's own career and reputation. Early on in his career, Poe's work was itself in danger of being figuratively buried alive. For example, in rejecting Poe's proposed *Tales of the Folio Club*, one publisher concludes that "[n]othing is more difficult, in regard to literary reputation, than to overcome the injurious effect of a first failure."[13] Buried and exhumed again and again, Poe's reputation waxed and waned throughout his lifetime. Rufus Griswold's 1849 hatchet job in his "Ludwig" obituary and the subsequent *ad hominem* mythologizing damaged Poe's personal reputation even as it elicited vociferous defenses from Poe's admirers. However, even these defenders of Poe clouded his reputation with a powerful mythologizing. Baudelaire's representation of Poe as a *poète maudit*, for instance, was unquestionably intended as a wholly laudatory characterization, but it helped to render Poe a mere stereotype. Critical treatments in the twentieth century contributed to Poe's shifting posthumous reputation, as such influential scholars as T. S. Eliot, R. P. Blackmur, and Harold Bloom were sometimes dismissive, while psychoanalytic criticism, French poststructuralism, and the popular culture elevated Poe's work to ever greater canonical heights. It is as if the metaphorical Poe, like the narrator of "The Premature Burial," shrieks from his erstwhile tomb, demanding to be set free after each unjust interment. But, as in that narrator's predicament, it may also be one great joke, as the putative terror turns out to be unfounded, becoming merely the

[13] See Thomas and Jackson, *The Poe Log*, 169.

stuff of dockside ribaldry and tawdry laughter. Using the figure of premature burial, I discuss Poe's reputation and lasting effect on literary criticism and theory, and make the case that Poe's subterranean noises continue to trouble the sleep and dreams of American literature.

Poe's subversive laughter sounds altogether different in the light, or perhaps the twilight, of the twenty-first century's reconfiguration of American literature. The proleptic critique of the project of American Studies from within or from below makes Poe's nomad thought all the more interesting in an era that has become increasingly skeptical of the rhetoric of ascent in American or in world literature. In the "post-American literature" of the twenty-first century, the perennially displaced poet-critic-*littérateur* may be better suited for our own age of globalization and exile than he could have been in either his own time of fervid exertion in "Literary America" or during the heyday of American Studies as a disciplinary field. Like Melville, Poe was able to imagine a post-American world system in which the nation was no longer the dominant or organizing cultural force. But, unlike Melville, Poe does not so much embrace the global or multicultural diversity as he calls into question and condemns the organizational project altogether. Where one vision conceives of and strives for a kind of postnational Utopia, the other laughingly and good-naturedly bids adieu to the evanescing vistas of Atlantis.

In the end, I view Poe not as a representative American writer, an eccentric American writer, or even as an un-American American writer, but as a force from below that can challenge us to rethink the field of American literary studies that seeks to contain, embrace, or exclude him. Poe's work does not symbolize the best or the worst or even the middle ground of literary culture in the United States, in his day or in ours, but neither does it have nothing to say. Literary critics, who are often engaged in the quasi-scientific inquiries and political debates internal and external to our disciplinary formations, may do well to investigate the nature and origins of these subterranean noises, to pry open the crypt of Poe's work once again, and to try to figure out just what he thinks is so damned funny.

1

Subterranean Noises

In one of his earliest tales, a burlesque or grotesque *bizarrerie* in which the narrator suddenly finds himself all-too-literally breathless, Poe takes the opportunity to skewer the national, political, and scientific pretensions of the contemporary culture in the United States. At what might be considered the climax of "Loss of Breath," the narrator and protagonist, Mr. Lackobreath, regains his lost voice after entering into a contractual transfer agreement with Mr. Windenough, with whom he had been prematurely "interred in a public vault." Still locked in their underground tomb, they had little trouble "effecting an escape from the dungeons of the sepulchre," for "[t]he united strength of our resuscitated voices was soon sufficiently apparent. Scissors, the Whig editor, republished a treatise upon 'the nature and origin of subterranean noises.' A reply—rejoinder—confutation—and justification—followed in the columns of a Democratic Gazette. It was not until the opening of the vault to decide the controversy, that the appearance of Mr. Windenough and myself proved both parties to have been decidedly in the wrong."[1] Here Poe punctuates his wildly extravagant tale by way of a send-up of the hackneyed and irresponsible manias for science or pseudo-science in the form of the republished treatise, and Poe pokes fun more directly at the partisan politics of both knowledge and culture. Notably, the Democratic Gazette's responses to the Whig editor's publication of that treatise include both confutations and justifications, and Poe cannot help but point out that, whatever each party presumed to know about the topic, the evidence eventually discovered underground proved all to be ignorant of the truth. Poe's mockery of the contemporary scene is thus complete. Poe's subterranean noises resound in opposition to the dominant cultural discourses circulating above.

This early tale contains a number of the elements recommended by the fictionalized Mr. Blackwood in Poe's 1938 satire "How to Write a Blackwood's Article," including the detailed description of grisly near-deaths, a first-hand account of being hanged, and a premature burial. Indeed, "Loss of Breath," which Poe called in its subtitle "A Tale Neither In Nor Out of Blackwood," is a spoof of the sort of sensational writing popular at the time, in such magazines as *Blackwood Edinburgh Magazine* or, indeed,

---

[1] Poe, "Loss of Breath," *Poetry and Tales*, 158, 162–3.

of the ones Poe himself edited or wrote for. As Poe explained in a famous 1835 letter to Thomas W. White, editor of *The Southern Literary Messenger*, in less sensational but otherwise similar language to that of his satirical Mr. Blackwood, "[t]he history of all Magazines shows plainly that those which have attained celebrity were indebted for it to articles" whose nature consisted of the following: "the ludicrous heightened into the grotesque: the fearful coloured into the horrible: the witty exaggerated into the burlesque: the singular wrought out into the strange and mystical."[2] The satire and fantasy on display in a tale like "Loss of Breath" is thus typical of Poe's aesthetic and commercial mode of writing, and such works are crucial to Poe's critique of the national culture and literature of his era. The scene in Mr. Lackobreath's ridiculous tomb is emblematic of Poe's humorous and extravagant send-up of American society more generally.

Undercurrents of American thought

Poe's mode of satirical fantasy, drawn from the relatively low comedy and the poetry of the urban street as opposed to the lofty peaks of a romantic sublime which it playfully deployed, functioned in such a way as to criticize his contemporary American civilization as it was forming itself ideologically through the combined political and cultural nationalism in the early to mid-nineteenth century. This program of cultural nationalism is closely tied to what, in the twentieth century, became known as the American Renaissance, and its project formed the foundations of much of American literary studies more generally. The work of Edgar Allan Poe has always sat rather uneasily within this tradition, and more often than not in literary histories Poe has remained an anomaly within American literature. Poe's humor, which frequently involved hoaxes, practical jokes, or what he referred to as "diddling," in addition to traditional forms of comedic writing, derives its force from a profoundly critical sensibility. Poe's fiction, I argue, is fundamentally anti-American, in the sense that it was crafted in opposition to the national self-image in formation in the United States during the early to mid-nineteenth century. Moreover, by opposing the elements that would later be identified as its distinctive myths and symbols, Poe's critique anticipates the nationalist cultural project of twentieth-century American Studies, and Poe subverts this project in subtle, and sometimes not so subtle, ways throughout his overall body of writings. Here I mean *subversion* not so much in the overtly political sense—Poe is no revolutionary, after all—as in the almost geological sense of undermining or eroding the foundations of a nationalist cultural program. In this case, "subversion" retains its more literal or etymological meaning of "going under." It is very much akin to Friedrich Nietzsche's conception of *Untergang* as it is used in *Thus Spoke Zarathustra*, which Nietzsche posits as a counterpoint to the Platonic rhetoric of ascent. In this broader sense, the word is also suggestive of both shipwreck and premature burials, recurring motifs throughout Poe's career. As I argue, this figurative

[2] Poe, "To Thomas W. White" (April 30, 1835), *The Letters of Edgar Allan Poe*, 57–8.

subversion takes on different forms in the course of Poe's life and work, as well as in the afterlife of Poe's influence on American literary studies over the past 160 years. The unquestioned popularity of Poe's writings, along with the much-debated critical assessments of their aesthetic merit, may in the end also be part of Poe's joke. As with the Whig and Democratic editors spoofed in "Loss of Breath," twenty-first-century readers might also mistake the nature and origins of Poe's subterranean noises, confusing his critical laughter with our own good humor and comfort.

"Loss of Breath" offers a nice encapsulation of many of the themes Poe raises in his subversion of American literature. First appearing as "A Decided Loss" in 1832, revised, substantially expanded, and ultimately published six times during Poe's life, "Loss of Breath" on its face would seem to be a spoof of the ever-popular personal narrative, in which a first-person narrator recounts exotic travels to unfamiliar territories, or bizarre experiences beyond the pale. To "lose" one's breath (literally!), and then to be crushed on a crowded stagecoach, dissected by medical students, later hanged as a criminal, and finally buried in a tomb where one converses with the dead, just to name a few of Mr. Lackobreath's adventures, would all certainly be considered exotic or bizarre. Throughout the tale, Poe playfully lampoons the pretensions of scientific knowledge, as in the aforementioned the republication of treatises concerning subterranean noises and also in the laughable use of "a new galvanic battery" as part of the vivisection performed by the physician and apothecary ("who is really a man of information").[3] Poe allows this burlesque tale to poke fun at the claims of knowledge in general, and this satire thus undermines an important aspect of the era's popular personal and national narratives, so many of which involved voyages of actual discovery or at least quasi-scientific researches into the unknown. Poe spoofs the quest for knowledge—for example, Mr. Lackobreath "could not help feeling deeply interested" in the experiments being performed upon his still living, if not breathing, self—while highlighting the absurd and inexplicable. The horror of such inscrutability or unknowability is mitigated by the whimsical tone of the story, but the unsettling experience of "living death" also introduces that admixture of terror and humor that Poe made a hallmark of nearly his entire *oeuvre*.

Nor is even the urban atmosphere of "Loss of Breath" accidental, as the jostling of persons in crowded carriages, the masses witnessing the execution, and the popular press speculating on underground sounds all feature prominently. Although the exact setting of the tale, as with so many of Poe's tales, remains unknown and unmapped, Mr. Lackobreath is a hilariously cosmopolitan character. Had the narrator found himself out of breath on a rural farm or even in a small town, the story would be quite different. Poe is well known as being among the first markedly "urban" authors in American literature, and the satire of "Loss of Breath" plays also upon the burgeoning anxieties associated with the transition from a largely rustic to an increasingly metropolitan society. Above all, perhaps, "Loss of Breath" is a satire of literature and the literary marketplace, much like "How to Write a Blackwood's Article," as Poe levels his sharpest critical comments at the very readers who are presumably enjoying his

---

[3] Poe, "Loss of Breath," *Poetry and Tales*, 156.

work. Poe's perverse literary theory and practice attempts to captivate the audience, to wield power over it, and eventually to have the readers hoist themselves with their own petards, which is to say, with their own irrational excitement over and insatiable desire for such fantastic literary fare. Finally, the intertwinement of satire and fantasy in "Loss of Breath" can be said to represent Poe's overall critical project, in which sardonic laughter and *outré* imagery combine to puncture the pneumatic and triumphalist rhetoric of ascent in American national culture at a historical moment characterized by such ideological forces as Emersonian self-reliance and national Manifest Destiny. Similarly, Poe's satirical fantasy undermines the myths and symbols of twentieth-century American Studies, which have included different variants of an exceptional individual (the American Adam), an exemplary scene (a Virgin Land), and a providential mission (an Errand into the Wilderness),[4] none of which find much support in a tale like "Loss of Breath," which features an extraordinary, atypical individual traversing a well-trodden social space in pursuit of more-or-less ridiculous ends. In its renunciation of these nationalist images, Poe's satirical fantasy suggests new directions for literary studies in a post-American century, in which alterity and estrangement, rather than recognizable identity, might present more suitable categories for cultural criticism. In what might be referred to as Poe's subterranean noises, a representative sample of which can already be seen more or less in Poe's farcical little tale originally written in 1831, at the very beginning of his career as a professional writer and critic, we can discern Poe's satire, fantasy, and critique of American culture and literature throughout his life and work.

I do not mean to suggest that "Loss of Breath" should be read as some sort of allegory of Poe's career or of mid-nineteenth-century American culture. However, Poe's mocking and playful tone here does establish a voice from outside or beneath the main currents of American thought, to use the title of the classic study in which V. L. Parrington glancingly referred to Poe as an "enigmatical figure." Parrington adopted the then standard line of seeing Poe as a dreamer and artist, out of step with the bustling commercialism and "bumptious middle-class enthusiasms" of his era, who "came to shipwreck on the reef of American materialisms."[5] Parrington's *Main Currents of American Thought* (1927) was an early instance of tradition-forming and canon-building in what would become the field of American literary studies. Both in this particular work and in the field as a whole as it has developed and thrived in the decades since Parrington, Poe's position as a canonical figure within American literature has always been anomalous. On the one hand, Poe's writings were quite well known in his own time, and he became legendary and infamous in the years after his death. In the minds of his legions of admirers as well as those of many of his detractors, Poe himself became a Poe-esque fictional character, a half-mad, intoxicated dreamer and outcast, "out of place, out of time." Whether denounced by former friends like Rufus Griswold or celebrated by ardent enthusiasts like Charles Baudelaire, *this* Poe

---

[4] These comprise the "image-repertoire" of American national narrative, according to Donald E. Pease; see note 12, below.

[5] Parrington, *Main Currents of American Thought*, vol. II, 58.

captured the imaginations of readers worldwide. On the other hand, Poe's eccentricity and artifice make his writings appear awkward, unnatural, even unfathomable, and the ambiguities of Poe's life and work have sparked animated debates as to Poe's proper place, in American literature or in the humanities more generally, among scholars and amateurs alike. Such cultural taste-makers as Henry James, T. S. Eliot, and, more recently, Harold Bloom have been dismissive of Poe's writings and of his claim to literary greatness, while others like George Bernard Shaw, D. H. Lawrence, and Jacques Derrida have found supreme value in Poe's work. Most teachers can certainly vouch for the fact that Poe remains extremely popular with students, but these readers are often as smitten with the reputedly tortured soul of the author as they are with the plots and imagery of the tales or poems themselves. Scott Peeples has argued persuasively in *The Afterlife of Edgar Allan Poe* that the mythic Poe, though unreal, may be as valuable as the actual Poe who is but tenebrously visible beneath the accumulated layers of real-and-imagined discourses piled upon him as a cultural signifier. "But this aura of mystery was good for business," Peeples observes, "and it created an open field for speculation about the 'real' Poe even as it made the possibility of finding him more remote."[6] Popular but despised, the loftiest aesthete who was also the most scurrilous of "tabloid" journalists, a romantic genius and shameless huckster, irrevocably canonized yet an outsider to the tradition, Poe is a savage anomaly in American literature.

In the past few decades, scholars and biographers have corrected this compelling yet largely fictional narrative and image of Poe, rescuing him from the calumnies of Griswold and his ilk, but also sparing him from the oversimplifications and idealizations of Baudelaireans and the Goth fan following. Recent scholarship has located the historical Poe more or less at the very center of the dynamic social milieu of the United States in the 1830s and 1840s.[7] Contrary to the image of the Byronic aristocrat, the shabby genteel lost in a crass, bourgeois society to which he does not belong, or the artiste living the life of the mind, "out of place, out of time,"—that is, the figure partly favored and promoted by Baudelaire, for instance, but also the one cherished by most causal readers and students—Poe appears to have been an extremely savvy, business-like, and worldly editor and publisher. Poe clearly knew the literary marketplace well, and he navigated the emerging and shifting commercial currents with sometimes uncanny efficiency and acumen. For example, Mark Canada notes how Poe both criticized and exploited the booming interest in newspapers, using the mania for breaking news and the latest trends to help promote his publications. In his hoaxes ("The Balloon-Hoax," most notoriously), mysteries (e.g. "The Mystery of Marie Roget" was a "fictional investigation" of the recent Mary Rogers murder case), actual reportage (such as his "Doings of Gotham" series), and satire (as in the gossipy news-gathering of "The Man Who Was Used Up"), Poe demonstrated a mastery of the newspaper techniques and audiences of the day. Moreover, as he apparently had every right to brag about, Poe increased the circulations of every periodical he was

---

[6] Peeples, *The Afterlife of Edgar Allan Poe*, 24.
[7] See, e.g. Stuart Levine, "Poe and American Society."

associated with, and he had an acute and instinctive understanding of the topics, themes, styles, and narrative forms that readers craved. It is a picture quite different from that of the forlorn dreamer and otherworldly aesthete, but Poe proved to be a top-notch magazinist, keeping his finger firmly on the pulse of the public's ever-shifting and fickle tastes.

Poe's career presents clear evidence that being successful and earning a good living do not go hand in hand, but it was also his extreme bad fortune that his most productive period as a writer coincided with an all too real economic depression following the Panic of 1837 and arguably running until the start of the Mexican–American War in 1846. Poe proved that he understood the business of publishing by dramatically increasing the circulation of the journals he edited. Further, the success of those periodicals undoubtedly owes more than a little to Poe's own tales, poems, reviews, and other writings published in them. In fact, given the degree to which Poe managed to satisfy the desires of the reading public, given his ability to produce the types of stories and poems the public craved, and given his dexterity in manipulating audiences with actual hoaxes or with more subtle forms of satire, one could argue that Poe is actually the representative writer of his era, a person very much of his own time and place. In a word, far from being the great outsider of American literature, Poe might be seen as an inside presence, standing right at the heart of the American scene. And yet, even in his timely situatedness in a particular moment and setting of American social and literary history, Poe remains anomalous. In his own time, Poe was not recognized as central to or representative of any emergent national literature, and, for the generations that followed, Poe's eccentricity was his calling card. When American literature as a disciplinary field emerged in the early and mid-twentieth century, Poe was a paradoxical presence: too important not to be included in a canon of an American literature, but too un-American to be a representative author within that tradition.[8] As such, Poe maintains a unique position in American Studies. Poe unavoidably belongs to an American literature, but he is also an unsettling presence that subverts it. He is a mocking voice audible from just beneath the high tones of the national theme. If Poe is no longer a figure wandering "out of place, out of time," he is still difficult to pin down.

The man of the street

Poe was also famously a man on the move, who lived at one time or another in every major city along the Atlantic coast of the United States, but never for more than a few years in any one place. Yet for all of his wanderings, both in the "real world" of the United States in the nineteenth century and in the literary life of the mind explored

---

[8] This "un-Americanness" might be considered with respect to either his politics (anti-egalitarian and anti-democratic) or his styles (his "Germanism," for instance), but Poe certainly did not suffer the fates of Hawthorne, Melville, Whitman, and Twain in becoming exemplary or even essentially "American" writers.

and extrapolated through his diverse writings, Poe is often depicted as an underground man, who, like Fyodor Dostoevsky's version of the type, somehow represents his time and place by not fitting easily into either. The outsider who is nevertheless right in the middle of the room, this Poe is really a central figure of American literature while, simultaneously, not seeming to belong in it at all. In his excellent study *Poe, Death, and the Life of Writing*, J. Gerald Kennedy terms his discussion of Poe's premature burials "Notes from the Underground,"[9] and this evocative label is suggestive of Poe's entire career with respect to American literary and cultural studies. Characterized as "the lost soul of the American tradition" by Donald E. Pease,[10] Poe has never sat easily within the variously imagined traditions of American literature.

In another, still influential view, Poe might be said to represent a counter-tradition within American civilization. As Harry Levin put it in *The Power of Blackness* (1958), when the American "national credo [...] seems more and more self-evidently composed of eupeptic half-truths," it only makes sense that "our most perceptive minds have distinguished themselves from our most popular spokesmen by concentrating upon the dark other half of the situation, and their distinctive attitude has been introspection, dissent, and irony."[11] In Poe's case, however, this concentration upon the "dark other half" of American culture did not really forego the satirical and critical approaches to the light half. That is, Poe's work does not just ignore or even resist the lighter side of American culture, but actively lampoons it, if sometimes only subtly.

In the end, Poe belongs wholly to neither side of the divide; he is neither a straightforwardly American writer who exemplifies this or that aspect of a distinctively national character, nor is he the consummate outsider. Poe is representative of something, but unlike such other dark Romantics or humorists as Nathaniel Hawthorne, Herman Melville, perhaps Mark Twain, or other sundry figures in nineteenth-century American literature, neither Poe nor any of his characters is really considered representative of some vision of the national identity. Poe's writings do not really depict any Virgin Land, American Adam, or Errand into the Wilderness, elements in the "image-repertoire" of American national narrative, as Pease has called it.[12] Some readers have followed Baudelaire in questioning whether Poe belongs to American literature at all. At times, Poe appears to represent a sort of anti-American literature. As far as American Studies has reconstituted the narrative of the national image-repertoire, and despite his facility in navigating the protean social organization of his own era, Poe usually appears to exist "outside of the main currents of American

---

[9] Kennedy, *Poe, Death, and the Life of Writing*, 32–59.

[10] Pease, *Visionary Compacts*, 158.

[11] Levin, *The Power of Blackness*, 6–7.

[12] Pease, "National Identities, Postmodern Artifacts, and Postnational Narratives," in Pease, *National Identities and Post-Americanist Narratives*, 3–4. As Pease acknowledges, the terms are oversimplifications, of course, but they are also titles of three majors works—R. W. B. Lewis's *The American Adam*, Perry Miller's *Errand into the Wilderness*, and Henry Nash Smith's *Virgin Land*—all published during the foundational period of academic American Studies in the 1950s, and the language continues to resonate in both scholarly discourse and, even more so, political rhetoric in public discourse in the United States in the twenty-first century.

thought."[13] Perhaps it would be better to say that he operates somewhere beneath them.

Poe's pronouncements upon the banalities of American culture emerge as a voice from below, a subterranean presence that at all times disorients and undermines the attempts to bring order to this chaos, whether in the forms of recognizable genres, clear actions with foreseeable consequences, or even personal, regional, or national identity itself. Poe's "subterranean noises" do not so much constitute and alternative line within American Studies, such as the postnational position of Melville's aesthetics and politics,[14] as much as a starkly anti-American position located below and athwart this tradition. Poe is perhaps a bit more like Gilles Deleuze's vision of Spinoza as a philosopher completely misplaced within the tradition to which he is usually assigned. Painting a vivid picture also quite suitable for a discussion of Poe, whose writings so often invoke the prematurely buried and the revenant dead, Deleuze notes that "it is easy to credit Spinoza with a place of honour in the Cartesian succession, except that he bulges out of that place in all directions; there is no living corpse who raises the lid of his coffin so powerfully, crying so loudly 'I am not one of yours.'"[15] One might make the same argument for Poe in the context of the American literary canon, except that Poe's situation is more ambiguous and anomalous than Spinoza's, or, within the American literary tradition, Melville's. Poe too has been given a place of some honor within a tradition from which he ought to be set free, but he has not frequently been championed as a representative figure of American national culture, as has Melville or Ishmael or, as far as the great American novel goes, *Moby-Dick*. While Poe is certainly among the most recognized and read writers in American literature, he remains, in the words of J. Gerald Kennedy, an "alien presence,"[16] an outsider, a nomad, and an underground man. If he lifts the lid of his symbolic coffin to shout his opposition to the eulogists and detractors alike, it is not to emerge into the open air and to correct the mistaken impression, but rather to make subterranean noises that continue to baffle those above.

The contrast between Poe and Melville is well established in American Studies. In *Call Me Ishmael*, his eccentric yet monumental study of *Moby-Dick*, Charles Olson begins with a "first fact" that in his view fundamentally determines the character of literature and culture in the United States: "I take SPACE to be the central fact to man born in America, from Folsom cave to now. I spell it large because it comes large here. Large, and without mercy." From this starting point, Olson announces the following dichotomy: "Some men ride on such space, others have to fasten themselves like a tent stake to survive. As I see it Poe dug in and Melville mounted. They are the

---

[13] Parrington, *Main Currents of American Thought*, vol. II, 58. However, for a rather different view, see also William Carlos Williams's impassioned defense of Poe's Americanness in *In the American Grain*, 216–33.

[14] For a powerful reading of Melville as a postnational figure, *avant la lettre*, see C. L. R. James, *Mariners, Renegades, and Castaways*, as well as Donald Pease's excellent introduction to this edition. See also my *Melville, Mapping and Globalization*.

[15] Deleuze and Parnet, *Dialogues*, 15.

[16] Kennedy, "Introduction," ix.

alternatives."[17] Olson does not really follow up on this assertion, but I think that one could make the case for Melville and Poe as opposing forces. However, I do not see in them two distinct approaches within American civilization so much as two visions of an alternative to those images of American culture developed during the nineteenth century and consolidated by American Studies in the twentieth. Melville wanted to "strike through the mask," as it were, to push through the Americanist ideologies of his own time, ideologies (also known as myths and symbols)[18] solidified and reinforced in the twentieth century as a kind of dogma for the secular religion of American Studies, in order to project a literary cartography of a postnational world system in its emergence. Poe also seeks to subvert these ideologies and expose the hollowness of the idols of American national culture, but Poe's critique is not really postnational or even non-national, but more pointedly anti-national, understood in terms of a rather anti-American satire, fantasy, and critique. Where Melville sought to "spread one royal mantle" over all mankind, to denounce clan and nation, and to "speak a world's language,"[19] Poe made a mockery of both humanist and national tendencies, undermining the claims of equality and universality as much as those advocating a providential American mission. Melville and Poe do not so much represent different tendencies within American civilization, as Olson had supposed, as they figure forth two approaches to a kind of post-American literature.

If American Studies operates like "state philosophy," in Deleuze's terminology, then Poe might be viewed as one of those nomad thinkers whose transgressions and movements resist the national apparatus of capture, deterritorializing and reterritorializing thought as they move. Poe's nomad thought or "thought from the outside" calls to the fore that radical alterity of fantasy, where a profoundly critical estrangement from everyday reality reveals such reality to be all the more unreal.[20] This includes the reality that is taken to be the basis of American Studies. After all, the "real" identity of its nominal subject is clothed in a buoyant rhetoric of ascent, which often masks other truths or, better, which positively generates its own mythic truths. What might be characterized as Poe's poetics of descent subjects such rhetoric to a downward pressure, submerging it below the waves or burying it beneath the soil in order that it may come face to face with "the magma of stupidity" flowing under the surface of these artificial and comforting categories of thought.[21] Poe's predominant mode of satirical fantasy is thus profoundly anti-American, in the sense of standing in opposition to that ideological or mythic substance of American literary studies, but it is also peculiarly un-American, in so far as its principal force lies in its ability to disrupt identities and continuities that go into forming that image-repertoire of American national narrative. Poe's writings tend to make that which was familiar and homely thoroughly unsettling, to weave about the reader an atmosphere of uncertainty and menace, to call into question the very possibility of knowing, to vacate one's

---

[17] Olson, *Call Me Ishmael* (San Francisco: City Lights, 1947), 11–12.
[18] See Bercovitch, *The Rites of Assent*, especially 357–8.
[19] See Melville, *Moby-Dick*, 117, and *Mardi*, 15.
[20] See, e.g. Miéville, "Editorial Introduction," 41–3.
[21] See Foucault, "Theatrum Philosophicum," 188.

own sense of self by introducing the imp of the perverse, to substitute for intelligible utterances and stable interpretive frameworks a mocking laughter from an unseen quarter, somewhere near and yet impossibly distant, right beneath our feet perhaps, but unfathomable. In this manner, Poe arranges a subversion of American literature by eroding the foundations of the national identity that is its *raison d'être*.

Notwithstanding my description of Poe's perverse literary vision as subterranean, I really view the force and function of Poe's subversion of American literature or his poetics of descent to be a matter of bringing the political and cultural rhetoric of national narrative down, not so much to the crypts and catacombs beneath us, but to the level of the mean streets themselves. That is, the most pressing aspect of Poe's fiction and criticism is his commitment to that quotidian, perhaps debased, and yet thoroughly fantastic domain in which we live and work. This may seem at odds with the prevailing image of Poe, at least in the popular image of the man, but I think the fundamentally satirical mode of his tales and the canny, businesslike approach to his compositions are best viewed in the light of his assiduously pedestrian mode of being. Olson, who establishes Poe as the alternative to Melville in forming the two poles within the characteristic experience of American civilization, mentions Poe only one other time in *Call Me Ishmael*, and even then it is only to explain an aspect of Melville's life and writings: "He [Melville] had the sea of himself in a vigorous, stricken way, as Poe the street."[22] Olson's off-hand, matter-of-fact-ness here shows the degree to which he views this proposition as uncontested, even commonplace. Poe carried the street within himself, almost as Milton's Satan carries Hell within himself, and, like Satan, the street-level Poe also attempts to drag the *faux*-heavenly nationalist rhetoric of his era down into the chaotic realities of life in the avenues and alleys of America's cities. Ironically, perhaps, Poe's fantastic tales, bitterly incisive reviews and essays, and eerie or abstract poems ground his literature in a stark reality, one that is all the more critical of the real world precisely because of its distance from a kind of strictly mimetic realism, and this allows Poe to more effectively captivate readers. Poe lays low the pretensions of the emerging American political and cultural behemoth, and he deflates the nationalist self-image of transcendent exceptionality or ever-ascendant movement. Poe's subversive literature offers the means for toppling these idols of the American secular religion, of pricking the balloon of its inflated and self-aggrandizing rhetoric, of casting some shadowy doubt upon its optative mood of sweetness and light, and of forcing the imaginations of his readers into the muck and mire of the superficial exigencies of life in the modern world. Thus, Poe is not so much an underground man as he is a man of the crowd.

The diddler's grin

Poe's attitude toward the regnant American mythos of his own time—and, by extension, toward the ideological underpinnings of twentieth-century American

[22] Olson, *Call Me Ishmael*, 13.

Studies—was fundamentally antagonistic. This antagonism found its most versatile outlet in writings striking a satirical pose, and much of Poe's work ought rightly be viewed as satire or black humor. I refer not only to the obvious burlesques and hoaxes, but also to those seemingly sincere, philosophical, and artistic tales and poems, which are classified as horror, mystery, romance, among other related genres. For instance, "The Fall of the House of Usher," for all of its Gothic beauty and grandeur, is pervaded throughout with a rather comical strain that presents an alternative narrative within the text, as when the narrator performs his absurd "experiment" with the image of the mansion in the tarn at the story's beginning (in a clear lampooning of Coleridgean aesthetic theory, incidentally) or when the fanciful exploits of the doughty Sir Ethelred are juxtaposed with the ominous rumors from the crypt at the tale's end. Benjamin Fisher has pointed out that "The Fall of the House of Usher" is really a parody of the Gothic mode or of "Germanism," in which Poe "burlesques" the cultural archetypes that both Roderick Usher, and the narrator, represent.[23] Indeed, it is not difficult to find the joking, hoaxing, and pranking Poe in even those works considered by most readers to be quite serious. Consider, for example, the absolute silliness of Poe's imaginary philosopher in the opening part of *Eureka*, the mountaineer who upon reaching the peak of Mount Ætna spins himself around on his heel in order "to comprehend the panorama of the sublimity" of the universe.[24] To begin his philosophical "prose poem" with this absurd image of the transcendental philosopher as a ludicrously whirling dervish only underscores the degree to which Poe is obviously joking.[25]

More than likely, such jokes are at our own expense. Tom Quirk, for one, argues that this is why Poe's humor is not funny, because it is "fundamentally antisocial." Referring especially to those tales written in the discernible genre of humor, but the same could be said for most of Poe's prose writing, Quirk observes that "[o]ne senses in Poe's humorous tales that the author is having a great deal of fun, but one also senses that he is laughing up his sleeve, immunized against the social contagion of general good humor and fellow feeling."[26] Sometimes Poe's own comments about the nature of satire would seem to confirm this suspicion, since Poe finds an element of malevolence to be a critical component of the form. In his review of James Russell Lowell's *A Fable for the Critics*, for example, Poe argues that sarcasm is "the principal element" of satire, but if the "*intention* to be sarcastic" is visible, then the satire fails, for the "malevolence *appears*." Malevolent sarcasm is essential to satire, but the reader cannot know it is there. For Poe, the only satire worth pursuing is that which "at least *appears* to be the genial, good humored outpouring of irrepressible merriment."[27] Poe's concern for the way in which the work appears to the reader, often a way that requires fooling the reader or even making a fool *of* the reader, is essential to his perverse literary theory.

Poe does not hesitate to use whatever literary forms or devices best suit his aim in accomplishing the task. Poe's popular notoriety as a writer of Gothic horror, complex

---

[23] Fisher, "Playful 'Germanism' in 'The Fall of the House of Usher,'" 360.
[24] Poe, *Eureka*, *Poetry and Tales*, 1261.
[25] Jennifer Rae Greeson provides an excellent reading of *Eureka* as a satire in "Poe's 1848."
[26] Quirk, *Nothing Abstract*, 57.
[27] Poe, "James Russell Lowell," *Essays and Reviews*, 816.

mystery, or Romantic poetry not only requires one to ignore over half of all of his tales, not to mention well over 80 per cent of his total corpus, but also necessitates a certain tortured reading of even those few writings that do get anthologized as tales of terror. For instance, must we keep a straight face when the narrator of "The Black Cat" offers his absurd explanation of how the mysterious cat-shaped *bas relief* appeared on his wall? (That is, some helpful neighbor wished to wake the family sleeping within the house, and did so by cutting down a dead cat from its noose and throwing it through an open window.) We might as well view Mr. Lackobreath's trials as the terrifying adventures of an epic or Byronic hero. Or we could find legitimate terror in the narrator's abuse by sailors in "The Premature Burial," where the long-feared eponymous horror amounted to merely falling asleep aboard a boat. Poe may very well have intended to write some tales of the grotesque and arabesque that induced real terror, but most often he seems to have preferred satirical fantasy, employing the formal tropes of such genres, while maintaining his critical distance. As Brett Zimmerman puts it, "*Hoax, satire, lampoon, farce, burlesque, spoof, parody, black humour, slapstick, bathos*: all these terms work well to describe Poe's *techniques*."[28] This is not to say that Poe produced nothing that was meant to be taken seriously, and many tales at least combine serious elements with the parodic ones, but Poe's satirical, fantastic, or comic mode frequently supplements and undercuts any purported gravity. The sublime beauty of his poetry is also frequently leavened with seriocomic or downright laughable content. ("The Raven," for all its *pathos*, is a story of a man talking to a bird!) At its best, Poe's work is not transcendent, but grounded. Poe does not embrace the pure concepts of the Platonic form or some Emersonian "transparent eye-ball," but operates more like a sharpened tool used to prick the balloon, revealing just what hot air such conceits comprise.

In many of his works, Poe's satirical critique takes the form of more or less subtle practical joking. It was Poe, after all, who became the great theorist of "diddling" (that is, swindling), which he was able to consider as "one of the exact sciences." In that essay, Poe humorously re-categorizes mankind, not as a social animal (Aristotle's *zoon politikon*), but as "an animal that diddles."[29] Before providing a number of fine examples of diddles, Poe delineates the "ingredients" necessary for successful diddling, which include such elements as *ingenuity*, *audacity*, and *originality*. Perhaps not surprisingly, many of the characteristics that would make someone an excellent diddler are also to be found in a successful writer of magazine articles in Poe's day. The comparison may not be particularly welcome to the reader, who is cast as the dupe in this process. Poe concludes that the final element of the diddle, its *sine qua non*, in fact, is the *grin*. "Your *true* diddler winds up all with a grin. But this nobody sees but himself. [...] This is no hypothesis. It is a matter of course. I reason à priori, and a diddle would be *no* diddle without a grin."[30] Throughout his career and extending into

[28] Zimmerman, *Edgar Allan Poe: Rhetoric and Style*, 71.
[29] Poe, "Diddling Considered as One of the Exact Sciences," *Poetry and Tales*, 607.
[30] Ibid., 609.

the afterlives of his literary legacies in the twenty-first century, the prankster-poet Poe appears to get the last laugh.

As "Diddling" suggests, but also as in the traditional view of Aristotelian poetics, Poe's comedy is low, plebian, operating at the street level, and grounded in a thorough-going disrespect for the sovereign hierarchies enshrined in social life. More ironically, perhaps, the most highly placed concept in the hierarchy of American society in the 1830s and 1840s was democracy itself, and Poe certainly enjoyed poking fun at this holiest of secular beliefs. Poe's satirical voice therefore exhibits a powerful sense of the lowly while refusing to glorify it, or, in other words, to raise it up. Again, Poe's subversive, subterranean literature has less to do with his marvelous images of premature burials, underground grottoes, descents into the vortices of whirlpools, or the like, but with undermining the established norms and mores of what Poe would probably consider a self-indulgent, self-important, and utterly wrongheaded national culture of his era. The most visible aspect of this culture is the nationalism itself, which requires American readers to disdain foreign subjects and to like "a stupid book better because (sure enough) its stupidity was of our own growth, and discussed our own affairs."[31] In this critique of the commonly held views, Poe aims to undermine and redirect them, to establish an alternative literary project, and to escape from the rhetoric of ascent that plagued cultural discourses in the United States of that era and beyond. It is not so much that Poe is an underground critic, then, but more that he is of the street, a level which is certainly deemed low by the standards of an un-self-acknowledged elite in an emerging literary culture tied to a burgeoning national identity, an identity whose adherents and proponents imagine strictly in terms of ascent, heights, and progress.[32] Theirs is another version of John Winthrop's famous shining "city on the hill" from the 1630 sermon, *A Model of Christian Charity*, an image first projected in the ephemeral moment of the New England Puritan presence and since used by propagandists throughout modern American history to justify a providential errand into the wilderness in one form or another. Poe's subterranean noises not only subvert this beatific vision, but make a mockery of it.

---

[31] Poe, "Exordium to Critical Notices," *Essays and Reviews*, 1027–8.

[32] Note that this is not the position of Douglas Anderson's *Pictures of Ascent in the Fiction of Edgar Allan Poe*, which argues that Poe's work attempts to elevate itself above the material world and the quotidian experience of mid-nineteenth-century American life. Obviously, I disagree with Anderson on this point, but I should mention, perhaps, that my thoughts on these matters were formed prior to my reading Anderson's interesting study, so I do not view my work in opposition to his. Anderson does not situate Poe within the American tradition or a national rhetoric of ascent, but argues that Poe's efforts to rise above the material reality of daily life are also attempts to escape U.S. national culture entirely.

2

A Nomad in a Land of Settlers

It seems quite trivial at first, but perhaps the most startling bit of information concerning the life and work of Edgar Allan Poe is that his first publication is credited to "a Bostonian." Has there ever been a writer less associated with a particular place than Poe? Particularly in the case of *this* writer and *that* place! Poe, who was indeed a native Bostonian, became quite possibly the literary world's fiercest critic of that city. Even those rabid fans of the Yankees, Jets, Rangers, and Knicks have less real hatred for the town Poe dubbed "Frogpondium." So it is a funny joke, a ruse of history perhaps, that one of the most famous writers in all of American literature should have launched his writing career under this sobriquet. However, such a perverse turn of events is rather typical of Poe's biography.

As is well known, Poe's life is characterized by almost constant movement. Born to parents who were traveling actors, Poe continuously traveled himself, never living in one place for more than a few years at a time, shuttling among nearly every major city in the United States during his short lifespan, and perpetually shifting about within those places when he did, for a time, alight. Poe's biography is a tale of perpetual motion, and his own movements are rather distinct from the hustle and bustle typically thought to characterize the American experience. It is true that the ideology of movement and progress, which would find its most powerful and pernicious rhetorical figure in the phrase "Manifest Destiny" during the 1840s, was already part of the national self-image in earlier years. An apt example from the emerging national literature of Poe's youth can be found near the beginning of James Fenimore Cooper's 1823 novel *The Pioneers*, in which Elizabeth Temple looks out upon the expanding settlements around Templeton, places which were changing so rapidly that "it was not difficult for the imagination of Elizabeth to conceive they were enlarging under her eye, while she was gazing, in mute wonder, at the alterations a few short years had made in the aspect of the country."[1] Such restlessness, which during Poe's lifetime and afterwards would be considered a characteristic aspect of American experience more generally, becomes the default condition for Poe's life and work, but in his case the frenzied social motion is not in furtherance of settlement. On the contrary, Poe's is an *unsettling* movement.

[1] Cooper, *The Pioneers*, 35.

Poe's movements place him at odds with the prevailing culture in the United States of the early nineteenth century, and his nomadic trajectory underscores his anomalous and ambiguous status, his apparent placelessness, in the American literary traditions established through American Studies in the twentieth century. Poe is a nomad in a land of settlers, both in the ostensibly real world of his biographical existence and in the imaginary realms in which his writings circulate even now.

The early Poe: Nomadic peripety

Except in certain crucial parts, most notably in the mysteries surrounding his final days, Poe's biography is well known.[2] But in order to highlight Poe's distinctly peripatetic life, it may be worthwhile to trace its trajectory on the map, to present a sort of geographical *curriculum vitae* that can disclose aspects of Poe's perpetual motion. Poe finds a place in nearly every major city in the early nineteenth-century United States over the span of his brief life, but he is never in any one locale for long, and it is difficult to say whether he truly belongs to any place. This fact accounts for the good natured, but sometimes bitter, rivalries among various partisans wishing to claim Poe for one city or another. Poe's place, his displacement, and his placelessness, all seem to appear (often at the same time) in the many reversals of fortune—*peripeteia*, to use the terminology of Aristotle's *Poetics*—attending Poe's life. A nomad in a country of settlers, Poe's shifting movements and fortunes form a context for his literary subversion of American literature.

Poe was born in 1809 in Boston, the city in which he would also publish his first book of poems 18 years later and whose author would be listed merely as "a Bostonian." His parents were both actors, who themselves traveled throughout the land as part of their profession, and one might that argue the perceived need to move in order to perform a part may have been characteristic of Poe's own peripeties as well.

---

[2] For this section I have drawn from a number of resources, only some of which are cited in the notes and then only when direct quotations are used. Although I have not always quoted from them, the following biographies have been invaluable. J. Gerald Kennedy's "Edgar Allan Poe, 1809–1949: A Brief Biography" is extremely useful, in part *because* it is so brief; at about 40 pages, it is ideal for students who need more than a blurb but cannot be tasked with reading a lengthy volume. G. R. Thompson's long essay, "Edgar Allan Poe," also provides a wealth of information on Poe's life and work. Peter Ackroyd's *Poe: A Life Cut Short*, though lacking the academic rigor of scholarly biographies, nevertheless offers a helpful synthesis or distillation of a number of other biographies. Hervey Allen's rather fictionalized *Israfel: The Life and Times of Edgar Allan Poe*, though sometimes ludicrous, is a telling example from an early stage of Poe Studies. Arthur Hobson Quinn's 1941 *Edgar Allan Poe: A Critical Biography* remains an important work. Jeffrey Meyers's *Edgar Allan Poe: His Life and Legacy*, James Hutchisson's *Poe*, and Kenneth Silverman's *Edgar A. Poe: A Mournful and Never-ending Remembrance* are also valuable contributions to the field. *The Poe Log* by Dwight Thomas and David K. Jackson, like Jay Leyda's earlier *A Melville Log*, is an excellent "documentary biography" in which to lose oneself for hours at a time. I have benefited as well from numerous critics and scholars who, while not technically writing biographies, have enlarged my understanding of Poe's life and works. Above all, the resources made available by The Edgar Allan Poe Society of Baltimore on their website (http://www.eapoe.org) are a nearly endless reserve of fascinating and useful information for research on Poe's life and work.

His mother, Eliza, was born in England and arrived in the United States in 1796; Poe's father, David, was from Baltimore, a city that would become a not-entirely-hospitable refuge for Edgar Allan Poe throughout his life, up to and including the moment of his death in 1849. The day after Poe was born, his father appeared on stage in Boston, and Poe's mother was performing again by February 10, just three weeks after giving birth. Roughly two weeks later, Poe was brought to Baltimore, where he joined his older brother, Henry, and was left in the care of his paternal grandparents. The actors David and Eliza Poe spent most of the following two years traveling up and down the East Coast—from Boston to Baltimore, New York, Charleston, Richmond, and Norfolk—for various performances. Such a peripatetic life for his parents could be seen as prefiguring Edgar's own wanderings in his adult years.

Sometime in mid-1811, David Poe apparently abandoned his family, and little is known of his whereabouts after this time, other than that he is thought to have died within days of his estranged wife in December of that year. On July 26, a "Floretta" writes an appeal in a Norfolk newspaper, urging citizens to support Mrs. Poe:

> And now, Sir, permit me to call the attention of the public to the Benefit of Mrs. Poe and Miss Thomas for this Evening, and their claims on the liberality of the Norfolk audience are not small. The former of those ladies, I remember (just as I was going in my teens) on her first appearance here, met with the most unbounded applause — She was said to be one of the handsomest women in America; she was certainly the handsomest I had ever seen. She never came on Stage, but a general murmur ran through the house, "What an enchanting Creature! Heavens, what a form! — What an animated and expressive countenance! — and how well she performs! Her voice too! sure never anything was half so sweet!" Year after year did she continue to extort these involuntary bursts of rapture from the Norfolk audience, and to deserve them too; for never did one of her profession, take more pains to please than she. But now "The scene is changed," — Misfortunes have pressed heavy on her. Left alone, the only support of herself and several small children — Friendless and unprotected, she no longer commands that admiration and attention she formerly did, — Shame on the world that can turn its back on the same person in distress, that it was wont to cherish in prosperity. And yet she is as assiduous to please as ever, and tho' grief may have stolen the roses from her cheeks, she still retains the same sweetness of expression, and symmetry of form and feature. She this evening hazards a Benefit, in the pleasing hope that the inhabitants of Norfolk will remember past services, And can they remember and not requite them generously? — Heaven forbid they should not.[3]

Such a reversal of fortune ("The scene is changed") offers yet another figure for Poe's later years, as his peripatetic life is characterized by any number of peripeties. To be sure, the sudden shifts from adulation and admiration to poverty and despair and back again also seem to mark Poe's own career.

Eliza Poe died on December 8, 1811, in Richmond. The cause of death was consumption, a disease that loomed large throughout Poe's life, taking his older

---

[3] Quoted in Quinn, *Edgar Allan Poe*, 41–2.

brother and eventually his beloved wife. Consumption, or tuberculosis, was the scourge of the nineteenth century, and its baleful effects offer another sad figure for Poe's own troubles. Unlike cholera, which struck hard and fast, sometimes killing its victims within hours of diagnosis, consumption operated more slowly, often allowing the sufferer temporary respite, and even hope, before the inevitable wasting away.[4] In watching his own wife succumb in later years, Poe must have recalled the others so plagued, and the metaphorical extensions of the disease, the feeling of being consumed or "used up," offer an evocative image for a person so frequently on the move.

Poe was taken in, treated as a son but pointedly not adopted, by John and Frances Allan of Richmond, where Poe spent most of his childhood. By nearly all accounts, Poe was a happy, well adjusted, and intelligent child, although perhaps a bit spoiled and given to flights of fancy. One famous but apocryphal story shows a very young Poe exhibiting terrors of the graveyard, which would certainly suit biographers looking to find Gothic elements in Poe's person, as a sort of etiology of those elements in his poetry and tales. While riding past a small cemetery, a six-year-old Poe is supposed to have "betrayed such nervous agitation" that his uncle (actually a relative of Frances Allan's) had to hold him in his arms, while "the boy kept crying out, 'They will run after us and drag me down,'" apparently in reference to graveyard ghosts.[5] One might draw a connection between this scene and a common theme in Poe's later work, the premature burial, inasmuch as several of Poe's heroes and more of his heroines find themselves unwillingly or unwittingly "dragged" down beneath the earth.

Yet Poe's own fear of being pulled down, buried, and imprisoned in one place was ungrounded, perhaps, because, even at the early age of six, his already peripatetic life was about to be marked by even more movement, this time in the form of international travels. In June 1815, John Allan took the family across the Atlantic Ocean to Scotland where he had relatives, then to England where he intended to establish a London office of his Richmond tobacco business. If Poe was fearful around graveyards, he certainly wanted it known that he was brave when it came to sea voyages. In a letter written in Scotland to his associate in Richmond, John Allan reports, "Edgar says Pa say something for me, say I was not afraid coming over the Sea."[6] The maritime terrors of *The Narrative of Arthur Gordon Pym*, among other stories, evoke the not-too-childish trepidation of overseas voyages.

Arriving in Liverpool in late July, the Allan family stayed in that city for a month or so before traveling to Scotland, and eventually settled in London where John Allan

---

[4] On the possible influences of the cholera epidemics on Poe's fiction, see Anderson's *Pictures of Ascent in the Fiction of Edgar Allan Poe*.

[5] Allen, *Israfel*, 51. This concludes an account of the influences of African Americans on persons in the South in general and on Poe in particular, as it suggests Poe's "mammy" and other servants told him "gruesome stories of cemeteries and horrible apparitions." Allen concludes, perhaps against his own will, by suggesting something that Toni Morrison has made more interesting in her own account of the cross-pollination of African-American and so-called white American literature in her *Playing in the Dark*. But as Allen puts it, referring to Poe's visits "to the servants' quarters— 'where many a tale of graveyard ghost went round' [...] To such incidents as these there can be little doubt that American Literature owes a considerable debt" (51).

[6] See Thomas and Jackson, *The Poe Log*, 26.

expected to remain for three to five years. Poe studied with the "Misses Dubourg" in Chelsea for over two years, during which he excelled in his studies—in 1818, John Allan reports that "Edgar is a fine Boy and reads Latin pretty sharply"[7]—before enrolling in Dr. Bransby's Manor House School, which would be described so luminously in the opening paragraphs of "William Wilson."[8] Over these years, young Edgar's scholarly development continues, and he takes several trips to Scotland to visit Allan's relatives. In June 1820, almost exactly five years after their departure from Richmond, the Allans set forth on the return voyage. They arrive in New York in July, and return to Richmond in August. Only 11 years old, Poe is something of a world traveler as he enters another school that autumn.

The period between Poe's return to Richmond in 1820 and his enrollment in Thomas Jefferson's newly established University of Virginia in Charlottesville in 1826 was uneventful, at least with respect to Poe's movements, but the image of Poe-the-teenager holds a great deal of material for biographers interested in his development as a writer. Not surprisingly, Poe excelled at Mr. Clarke's school, which offered an extensive curriculum.[9] Kenneth Silverman devotes only six pages to this part of Poe's life, but finds clues to Poe's considerable gifts for poetry, as well as evidence of his elitism and disdain for commerce, in the early poem "O, Tempora! O, Mores!" According to Silverman, "the poem is notable for its skill in imitation, its scorn toward the clerk as a plebian vulgarian, and its contempt for the world of merchandising."[10] This poem is also notable for its clearly satirical tone and substance. Poe's high-falutin poetic language, as in the Cato-inspired title itself, for instance, is laid low by his most earthy, quotidian subject matter. In "O Tempora! O, Mores!," a young Poe already spoofs both high Romanticism and the everyday life of middle-class America, presenting a mocking critique of both. As many biographers note, Poe's teacher was so impressed with his poetry that he discussed with John Allan the possibility of Poe's publishing a volume, but Allan thought (probably quite correctly) that being "flattered and talked about as the author of a book" would cause some harm to Poe, who certainly did not lack confidence in literary matters. Other biographical tidbits from this epoch include the following: reports of the teenaged Poe's athletic prowess (notably, a six-mile swim upstream in the James River, which presumably offers biographers a salutary contrast to the frail and sickly adult Poe would become in the minds of his later fans and detractors); his attachment to Jane Stanard (the mother of a schoolmate, who may have also represented a mixture of a maternal figure and a

---

[7] Ibid., 36.

[8] Poe, "William Wilson," *Poetry and Tales*, 338–41.

[9] In an 1820 advertisement, Joseph H. Clarke described his school as "a permanent Literary Institution,—where will be taught in the shortest possible time, not only the Learned Languages, but Writing and Arithmetic in its various departments, with Book-keeping by single and double entry; Geometry, Mensuration, Trigonometry plain and spherical; Navigation with the method of working Celestial and Lunar Observations; Land Surveying in theory and practice; Gunnery, and the doctrine of Projectiles, Gauging, Fortification and Optics with the use of the Instruments; Elementary and Physical Astronomy, Conic Sections, Algebra, Fluxions, Mechanics, &c. &c. Geography, with constant reference to Maps and Charts, and occasional illustrations from Astronomy, adapted to the student's capacity." See Thomas and Jackson, *The Poe Log*, 48.

[10] Silverman, *Edgar A. Poe: A Mournful and Never-ending Remembrance*, 24.

love-interest, whose own death adds to the roll of those beautiful and doomed women in Poe's life); his abortive engagement to Sarah Elmira Royster (then 15, while he was 16); and, in what might be Poe's most patriotic turn, his participation in the honor guard for the visit of General Lafayette, who fondly remembered Poe's grandfather, David Poe Sr., for his help in provisioning Lafayette's troops during the Revolutionary War. Another remarkable fact, although perhaps less remarkable when one factors in the not uncommon developments of a teenager's disposition, is the growing coldness between Poe and his foster father, which would soon come to such a head as to "orphan" Poe forevermore.

A young man's departure for college is not necessarily a momentous event, but in this case it actually marks the end of an era. Poe moved from Richmond to Charlottesville in early 1826, thus concluding the longest continuous period of living in one city that he would ever have. That is, his just over five years subsequent to returning from Great Britain—during which he did in fact move several times, by the way, but always within Richmond—represented the most geographically stable portion of Poe's entire life. Think of it! Poe never before and never again lived in one place for more than five years. In an era of increasing mobility in general, Poe was almost always on the move. Yet, for all the discourse of American hustle, bustle, movement, and general busy-ness, Poe stands out as remarkably unlike most Americans of his era in his failure or unwillingness to settle down anywhere for long. Given the turbulence of adolescence, one may not want to call the period from age 11 to age 17 "stable," but in Poe's case it would represent the longest epoch of staying in one place that he would ever experience.

The next few years would involve Poe in a variety of movements and peripeties, reversals of fortune that occasioned and sometimes compounded the nomadic wandering about the eastern portion of the United States. Little is definitively known about Poe's activities between leaving Allan and Richmond on or around March 20, 1827, and his enlistment in the U.S. Army, under the name "Edgar A. Perry," in Boston on May 26, but while in Boston he publishes his first book, *Tamerlane and Other Poems*, a slender (40-page), paper-bound volume written, according to its title page, "By a Bostonian." As noted above, the fact that Poe's first publication appears under this of all possible appellations is a source of never-ending delight to scholars, given Poe's later acrimony toward Ralph Waldo Emerson, Henry Wadsworth Longfellow, and other members of the Boston literati. Of course, Poe *was* "a Bostonian" by birth, and it is possible that he had hoped to find succor in the critical audiences of that city, the place "where his mother found her best, and most sympathetic friends."[11]

If Poe was looking for sympathy, he was certainly guarded in presenting these poems. In his preface, he writes that the poems included "were written in the year 1821-2, when the author had not completed his fourteenth year."[12] This admission is an act of both

---

[11] This is part of a dedication written by Eliza Poe on the back of a watercolor painting of Boston Harbor, 1808, which reads: "For my little son Edgar, who should always love Boston, the place of his birth, and where his mother found her best, and most sympathetic friends." See Thomas and Jackson, *The Poe Log*, 3–4.

[12] Poe, "Preface (Tamerlane and Other Poems—1827)," *Poetry and Tales*, 9. All other quotations in this paragraph come from this same page.

defensive distancing and youthful braggadocio, inasmuch as Poe peremptorily informs the reader that, if the poems be deemed inferior, they are merely the product of youth and not to be judged too harshly, but if they are found worthy, then the poet himself must have been a real genius to have produced such poetry at so young an age. As Poe's anonymous "Bostonian" continues, if "the smaller pieces [...] savour too much of Egotism," it is only because "they were written by one too young to have any knowledge of the world but from his own breast." Given that his dating of the poems had already identified his current age, what follows must be a kind of whimsical and Byronic joke. Speaking of the theme of "Tamerlane," Poe writes that he is conscious of "the many faults" which he could have easily corrected, but that he "has been too fond of his early productions to amend them in his *old age*." In a final *coup de grace*, Poe's preface addresses both critics and the marketplace, and one can discern in Poe already, at age 18, a querulousness and ambiguity that would characterize his relationship with the literary landscape of the nineteenth century in the years to come. As Poe concludes his preface to *Tamerlane and Other Poems*, "[h]e will not say that he is indifferent as to the success of these Poems—it might stimulate him to other attempts—but he can safely assert that failure will not at all influence him in a resolution already adopted. This is challenging criticism—let it be so. *Nos hæc novimus esse nihil.*" The Latin phrase punctuating this "challenge" to criticism reads, in English, "This we know to be nothing." At once cocky and guarded, Poe's first publication throws down the gauntlet to a world in which he will consistently move, of which he is undoubtedly a part, but which is in no way a home to him.

Lingering in Boston for a moment, we might note that Poe's publication of *Tamerlane and Other Poems* stakes out a place in the world. A "Bostonian" writing Romantic poetry, albeit while conceding in the title poem "the folly of even *risking* the best feelings of the heart at the shrine of Ambition,"[13] Poe makes his first real effort to localize himself. That is, he endeavors to establish a persona that is tied to a place, and he issues a challenge from this imaginary redoubt. In later years Poe will make similar attempts, as he becomes a representative writer of Baltimore, Richmond, Philadelphia, and New York—just see how many places in the eastern United States wish to claim him for their own today!—but the very diversity and number of these locales demonstrates conclusively that Poe does not really belong to any of them. Emerson is *of* Concord, just as Hawthorne is *of* Salem, Longfellow *of* Boston (or Cambridge), and even Washington Irving or James Fenimore Cooper *of* New York, but Poe is something else, a nomad who is *of* nowhere but always located in one place or another. In his first tentative sally into the literary marketplace of nineteenth-century American letters, Poe's feinted gesture toward establishing a distinctive place discloses all the more spectacularly his essential placelessness, or perhaps his being "out of place," within the national and regional cultures of his era. At age 18, Poe is already, as Scott Peeples has put it in referring to Poe's constant movements, a "nowhere man."[14]

Just before the publication of *Tamerlane and Other Poems* in 1827, Poe had enlisted in the U.S. Army under the name of Edgar A. Perry, and in November of that year

---

[13] Ibid.
[14] See Peeples, "Nowhere Man: The Problem of Poe and Place."

Poe's battery leaves for Fort Moultrie, on Sullivan's Island in the harbor of Charleston, South Carolina. Poe would enshrine this place in literary history by making it the setting of what was perhaps Poe's most popular tale of his lifetime, "The Gold-Bug." Poe was apparently a capable and popular soldier, and yet by December 1828 he began to feel that he had been "in the American army as long as it suits my ends or inclination, and it is now time that I should leave it," as he put it in a letter to John Allan.[15] That month, Poe's unit was transferred to Fort Monroe, in Norfolk, Virginia, where he again wrote his foster father of his desire to leave the army. This letter included an expression of Poe's "Ambition" that clearly indicates his disdain for local or even national affairs: "Richmond & the U. States were too narrow a sphere & the world shall be my theatre."[16]

On February 28, 1829, Frances Allan died, another "death of a beautiful woman" that so affected Poe's life and work.[17] Poe returned to Richmond but did not arrive in time for the funeral. However, Frances's death seems to have occasioned a brief *détente* between John Allan and Poe, and Allan agreed to help Poe gain admission to the United States Military Academy at West Point, New York. Poe returned to Norfolk, where he received his formal discharge from the army in April; from there he went back to Richmond, then traveled to Washington and Baltimore as part of his efforts to secure a place at West Point. In May, Poe was in Philadelphia, where he attempted to publish another book of poetry. The publishers Carey, Lea, and Carey expressed interest, but asked for a guarantee in case the book did not sell, so Poe sent a letter to John Allan seeking such financial insurance against possible loss. Allan, apparently infuriated with the continuing poetic ambitions of his former ward, wrote back "strongly censuring his conduct — & and refusing any aid." Meanwhile, Poe lived in Baltimore, reuniting with his brother Henry, his grandmother, his aunt Maria Clemm, and his cousin Virginia Clemm. At the end of this year in limbo, as he continued to await word on whether he would be able to enter West Point, Poe managed to publish his second book of poetry, *Al Aaraaf, Tamerlane, and Minor Poems*, through the Baltimore publishers Hatch and Dunning, now with his own name *Edgar A. Poe* on the by-line. Poe did not write a preface for this volume, but he did include three brief epigraphs, one of which (from an unnamed Spanish play) translates: "Fabio, do you understand what I am saying to you? / Yes, Thomas, I understand. / Fabio, you lie." This line playfully introduces a theme Poe also continuously sounds throughout his career, and which will be discussed further in the chapters that follow, to wit, the inscrutability of the text. Mixed reviews, some admiring the potential and genius of certain poems while also noting the boyishness or immaturity of others, indicate that the understanding of the poems, whether sought or shunned by their author, was not always available.

After several more months of finagling letters of recommendation from military and political connections, Poe finally enrolled as a cadet at West Point in the summer

---

[15] Poe, "To John Allan" (December 1, 1828), *The Letters of Edgar Allan Poe*, 10.
[16] Poe, "To John Allan" (December 22, 1828), ibid., 12.
[17] In "The Philosophy of Composition," Poe maintains that "the death [...] of a beautiful woman is, unquestionably, the most poetical topic in the world"; see *Essays and Reviews*, 19.

of 1830. One fellow cadet recalled that Poe was "an accomplished French scholar, and had a wonderful aptitude for mathematics"; Poe was "a devourer of books, but his great fault was his neglect of and apparent contempt for military duties." The same cadet, in noting how Poe would write "most forceful and vicious doggerel" aimed at certain disliked professors, wrote that "I have never seen a man whose hatred was so intense at that of Poe."[18] Such nastily sardonic poems were probably what his fellow cadets hoped to get when they collected money in order to help Poe publish a book of poems, but any of those students would be sorely disappointed if they dipped into Poe's 1831 book, titled simply *Poems, by Edgar A. Poe*, which mostly reprinted slightly revised versions of earlier work. Certain facts regarding Poe's brief tenure as a West Point cadet indicate his growing personal distance from the emerging national self-image, and he may have secretly delighted in the (false) rumor that he was the grandson of Benedict Arnold, a fiction that would have coded the young Poe both aristocratic and patently anti-American. Considering that the name "Benedict Arnold" was, by the early nineteenth century in the United States, synonymous with treason, Poe may have enjoyed the pleasures of minor subversion in allowing this myth to flourish. Also, for a bright young student wishing to tweak the noses of his imperious and straight-laced professors, the fact that Arnold's great treasonous act involved his part in a conspiracy to hand this very West Point over to the hated British forces must have added a bit of spice to the youthful rebelliousness.

In any case, Poe successfully managed to have himself expelled from the military academy in February 1931, having deliberately neglected his duties and disobeyed orders, one of which was simply to attend a church service. At this time, Poe also makes a nearly definitive break with John Allan, who had recently remarried. Poe's anguished letters to Allan in 1831 themselves display a pathetic mix of emotions, from petulant and wounded indignation ("*Your* love I never valued") to supplicatory cajoling or begging ("Please send me a little money — quickly — and forget what I said about you" and "for the sake of the love you bore me when I sat upon your knee and called you father do not forsake me this only time"). Allan's responses, whether noted only to himself or sent to Poe, also betray some emotional wavering on his part; Allan's initial reaction is angry incredulity ("I do not think the Boy has one good quality [...] since I cannot believe a word he writes"), but later that year he apparently does send some money to Poe in Baltimore.[19] However, by the end of 1831, Allan would cease to have anything to do with his former foster son, and Poe is not mentioned at all in Allan's revised will.[20] Some years later, Poe tries one last time to gain succor from Allan, in an April 12, 1833, letter in which he pleads, "For God's sake pity me, and save me from destruction." Allan does not answer, but writes on the back of Poe's earlier letter (from February 21, 1831): "Apl 12, 1833 it is now upwards of 2 years since I received the above precious relict of the Blackest Heart & deepest ingratitude alike destitute

---

18 Thomas and Jackson, *The Poe Log*, 107–8.
19 Ibid., 112–13, 115, 124.
20 A subject for a speculative fiction or alternative history, perhaps, but Allan dies a very wealthy man in 1834, and if Poe had inherited, his life and American literature would have taken very different trajectories.

of honour & principle every day of his life has only served to confirm his debased nature — Suffice it to say my only regret is in Pity for his failings — his Talents are of an order that can never prove a comfort to their possessor."[21] Thus, the final falling out between Poe and Allan in 1831 ensured that Poe would never have the opportunity to settle down in the life of a quasi-aristocratic Southern planter-merchant, and that his peripatetic existence thus far would continue on its shifting, wayward course, keeping Poe steadily on the move in the years to come.

Leaving West Point in the spring of 1831, Poe is "at sea," with no particular place to go and no one particularly eager to see him, it seems. In New York City, he expresses interest in going to Paris, perhaps petitioning the Marquis de Lafayette to secure "an appointment (if possible) in the Polish Army."[22] In April, Poe publishes his third book, *Poems, by Edgar A. Poe*, perversely listed as the "second edition," which again reprints a number of the early poems, including "Tamerlane" and "Al Aaraaf," and certainly contains no jaunty verses lampooning the U.S. Military Academy's instructors. In lieu of a preface, Poe inserts a "Letter to Mr. — —," addressing a "B—," who is presumably Elam Bliss, the publisher of *Poems*. In this letter, Poe delineates a somewhat playful, partially plagiarized (from Samuel Taylor Coleridge's *Biographia Literaria*), and impassioned defense of poetry. Poe is here especially interested in shielding poetry against those who would bend its power to didactic and nationalistic ends. Enunciating a theory of poetry that he maintained and refined throughout his career, Poe writes that poems are not means to truth, and that to the extent that poetry provides pleasure, it is only an indefinite pleasure, quite unlike the pleasures associated with fiction or romance. As Poe puts it,

> A poem, in my opinion, is opposed to a work of science by having, for its *immediate* object, pleasure, not truth; to romance, by having for its object an *indefinite* instead of a *definite* pleasure, being a poem only so far as this object is attained; romance presenting perceptible images with definite, poetry with indefinite sensations, to which end music is an *essential*, since the comprehension of sweet sound is our most indefinite conception. Music, when combined with a pleasurable idea, is poetry; music without the idea is simply music; the idea without the music is prose from its very definitiveness.[23]

I will return to Poe's literary theory later, but for now it may be worth noting that the 22-year-old poet, college dropout, and former soldier already positions his "art" outside of the world that can be ascertained as definite or true, "out of place, out of time," yet somehow operating in such a way as to provide an almost ecstatic experience of the thing itself: here, *indefinite pleasure*. Impossible to pin down, such experience is nevertheless necessary and unavoidable. At the same time, however, Poe's defense of poetry is profoundly pragmatic, in so far as it rescues poems from tasks not suited to their power. Poe does not, as is popularly believed, merely subscribe to an "art for

---

[21] Thomas and Jackson, *The Poe Log*, 128–9.
[22] Poe, "To Colonel Sylvanus Thayer" (March 10, 1831), *The Letters of Edgar Allan Poe*, 44.
[23] Poe, "Letter to Mr. — —," *Poetry and Tales*, 27.

art's sake" philosophy, even though he does wish to free art from specifically didactic or scientific purposes. Poe's art is constrained by its own laws, limited to a legitimate domain, and then given free rein within its proper sphere. In other words, by releasing poetry, as well as other forms of art, from an indentured servitude to this or that utilitarian end, Poe makes poetry all the more worldly—and, perhaps ironically, otherworldly as well—in allowing art to create and operate within its own alternate reality, a reality that nevertheless speaks to, but is not imprisoned by, the "real world" in which it is encountered.

By the end of 1831, Poe had made his way from New York to Baltimore, where he lived in abject poverty with his family. His brother Henry died of consumption in August, and the entire city was engulfed in a terrifying cholera epidemic at the time. Over the summer, he had entered a literary contest sponsored by the Philadelphia newspaper *The Saturday Courier*. The notice explained the aim of the competition as the "promotion of the cause of Literature" and named the prize: "a premium of One Hundred Dollars will be awarded for the best American Tale." The winner was announced on December 31, 1831. Poe submitted five tales, none of which won the prize, but on January 14, 1832, the *Saturday Courier* published his first short story, "Metzengerstein," thus launching Poe's career as a writer of tales as well as poems. The *Courier* published four other tales by Poe in 1832, and, although it is not clear that he ever received any pay for these pieces, Poe undoubtedly discovered that what he would later call "the magazine prison-house" was a potential way to make a living. Now 23 years old, a published author of both poetry and short fiction, Poe was just about to begin a writing career, the fruits of which are the basis for his worldwide fame, for his multitude of admirers and detractors, and for the myths and histories surrounding the man.

As is well known, Poe's new career as a magazinist—serving in multiple roles as editor, promoter, poet, fiction writer, book reviewer, and critic, often performing several of these offices at the same time—will not afford him much of an opportunity to settle down. Between 1833 and his death in 1849, Poe traces a wildly circuitous path through every major city on the eastern seaboard of the United States. Occasionally just visiting and sometimes dwelling there, but only for a few years at most each time, Poe lives in Baltimore, Richmond, Philadelphia, and New York, but also finds himself at times in Boston, Washington, D.C., and Providence, Rhode Island, as well as numerous points in between. In concluding my itinerary with what is really the pre-history of Poe's career, his childhood and young adulthood before he becomes the Poe we know, or the Poe we think we know, I merely want to register the bizarrely nomadic life he had already led. To recapitulate: Poe was born in Boston, spent an infancy in Baltimore and his early childhood in Richmond, moved to Scotland and London, returned to Richmond, lived briefly in Charlottesville, then traveled north, eventually arriving in Boston, before shipping off to Charleston then Norfolk, and from there back to Richmond, Baltimore, and eventually New York, where he enrolled in and then was expelled from the academy at West Point, only to travel back to New York City and Baltimore, all before his 23rd birthday. Poe thus led a rather nomadic life up to this point, and his writings thereafter would typify a kind of nomadology that placed an even greater figurative distance between Poe and the settled modes of thought coming to characterize the national culture of the time.

The mature Poe: Unsettling movement

Poe's peripatetic life, a life frequently characterized by peripety, marks him as a bit of an outsider in the emerging American national culture of the early to mid-nineteenth century. Many other writers from this era who have become enshrined in literary and cultural history are generally associated with a particular place, from which they are then able to transcend their locality on the way to becoming representative national or international literary figures, sometimes both at once, as has happened to Hawthorne, Melville, and, in a later generation, Mark Twain. Hawthorne's tales would appear peculiar to New England, for instance, but twentieth-century American Studies has made it possible to see in the eccentric places and characters the embodiments of a discernibly national character, such that Young Goodman Brown or Hester Prynne come to be seen as representative American characters. Twain's Huckleberry Finn, more or less intended to represent a backwoods culture on a remote fringe of the United States, has become through the efforts of many twentieth-century critics the hypercanonical figure of the representative national subject. In the discourse of American Studies, Huck is no longer an outsider (an Irish one, at that!) to be chuckled over, but an everyman with whom all readers are supposed to identify.[24] To the extent that his corpus contains similarly memorable individuals, Poe's most famous characters are either explicitly non-American, like the Frenchman C. Auguste Duplin, or not identified with or located in a particular geographical setting at all, whether they are named, like Roderick Usher, or unnamed, like so many of Poe's anonymous narrators. Even when certain characters are clearly identified as American and placed in an identifiable locale—for example, William Legrand of "The Gold-Bug"—they are in no way the sort of American Adams associated with the "image repertoire" of American national narrative.[25] Indeed, when Poe does introduce someone who might be viewed as distinctively American, more than likely the person appears in an unfavorable light, as an object of satire like the buffoonish Peter Proffit in "The Business Man" or the sadly preposterous General John A. B. C. Smith in "The Man

---

[24] On the term hypercanonization, and on "the nationalization of literary narrative" more generally, see Arac, *Huckleberry Finn as Idol and Target*, especially 133–53. In a letter to his publisher, Twain complained that early illustrations to be included in *The Adventures of Huckleberry Finn* by E. W. Kimball had made Huck look "too Irishy."

[25] As Pease explains, "The image repertoire productive of the U.S. national community can be ascertained through a recitation of the key terms in the national meta-narrative commonly understood to be descriptive of that community. Those images interconnect an exceptional national subject (American Adam) with a representative national scene (Virgin Land) and an exemplary national motive (errand into the wilderness)"; see Pease, "National Identities, Postmodern Artifacts, and Postnational Narratives," 4.

That Was Used Up."[26] Poe's most famous literary characters and settings do not seem to "fit" in the landscape of American literature.

As early as 1876, George Parsons Lathrop remarked upon Poe's inherent non-nationality or un-Americanness. Contrasting his writings to those of Hawthorne and Irving, in particular, and to writers of "American" literature more generally, Lathrop notes that Poe "exhibits nothing" of the American national character in his works. Lathrop attributes this partly to "the ingrained rebellion in him," and points out that Poe "revolted against the moneyed mediocrity of this country," and this antagonism "underlies his want of deep literary identification with the national character in general."[27] But Lathrop goes on to conclude that "more probably his genius was a detonating agent which could have been convulsed into its meet activity anywhere, and had nothing to do with a soil."[28] Hence, in Lathrop's view, Poe's fundamentally anti-American attitude in the end is less noteworthy than the inherently non-national character of his "detonating" genius.

Poe's eccentricity in the geographical and literary milieu of his era is perhaps also responsible for some of confusion over where to place his work in the American literary history of which he is obviously a part, but in which he does not neatly fit. For instance, in his innovative and informative contribution to the *Cambridge History of American Literature*, Arac uses a generic approach to narrative forms emerging in the period between 1820 and 1860, and divides such forms into four more or less broad categories: *national*, *local*, *personal*, and *literary*. Arac takes as his point of departure the fact that "literary narrative," embodied in works still valued for their artistic merit rather than their mere historical curiosity, emerges at mid-century in such works as *The Scarlet Letter* (1850) or *Moby-Dick* (1851), but flourishes only briefly, before largely disappearing until after the Civil War and Reconstruction. After the Civil War, literary narrative returns and becomes the dominant cultural form with the advent of modernism, and, above all, the formal or academic study of literature, in the twentieth century. The dominant narrative form of the early to mid-nineteenth century was national narrative, which "was part of the process by which the nation was forming itself and not merely the reflection of an accomplished fact."[29] Against these two competing forms were local and personal narratives. The former were generally regional in character and setting, and in practice they functioned as a way to demonstrate the differences between discrete locales and the larger national culture. As such, local narratives implicitly or explicitly offered a critique of that culture, as the eccentric little "nooks of still water" (as Washington Irving called them in "The Legend of Sleepy Hollow") were undisturbed by the torrent of the mainstream national civilization.[30] Personal narratives, which by and large presented reports from

---

[26] Poe's Peter Proffit was named Peter Pendulum when the story first appeared as "Peter Pendulum, The Business Man" in 1840; see Mabbott, ed., *Tales and Sketches*, 480–1.

[27] Lathrop, *A Study of Hawthorne*, 313.

[28] Ibid.

[29] Arac, *The Emergence of American Literary Narrative*, 3; Arac's study first appeared in 1995 as "Narrative Forms" in *The Cambridge History of American Literature, Volume 2: 1820–1860*, edited by Sacvan Bercovitch.

[30] See Irving, "The Legend of Sleepy Hollow," 340.

the fringe of that civilization—whether coming from unfamiliar places overseas, from the wilderness, or from a little-known quarter of one's own society, as with slave narratives—also revealed opposing visions, but these narratives tended to operate as a means of colonizing those exotic experiences, domesticating them by making the unfamiliar familiar to mainstream readers in the metropolitan or national centers. In this manner a number of personal narratives, including Melville's *Typee*, Douglass's *Narrative of the Life of Frederick Douglass*, or even Thoreau's *Walden*, integrated the exotic experiences of a typical American individual into a national narrative. But Poe's work does not fit very well into Arac's four divisions of prose narratives written in the United States during this period, as it exhibits few of the generic aspects of any of these narrative forms.

Arac might have wished to omit references to Poe entirely, but some rather obvious historical and institutional factors would have made such an exclusion impossible. Interestingly enough, Arac envisions Poe as contributing material to three of the four genres, although his writing is not clearly representative of any one. (No other author's work is considered representative of more than two genres, with Hawthorne listed as a key figure of local and literary narrative, and Melville connected to personal and literary narrative.) Not surprisingly, Arac sees no place for Poe in his discussion of national narrative, and Poe certainly does not produce any works that promote the unity and stability of an American national identity, although he does occasionally lampoon such narratives. But Arac makes the case for Poe's short fiction as examples of local narrative, for *The Narrative of Arthur Gordon Pym* as a personal narrative, and other writings, especially Poe's theory and criticism, as laying the foundation for literary narrative. What one notices right away is that Poe is the only author treated at any length by Arac who participates equally in three categories, and yet he does not really seem to fit any of them. For example, aside from Poe, the producers of local narratives are all examined as primarily regional writers, with Irving's Dutch New York distinct from Hawthorne's New England, which is itself a world away from the backwoods of Georgia, Tennessee, and Arkansas in the writings of Southwestern Humorists. Arac argues that Poe's "local" narratives involve the urban atmosphere rather than any particular locale, but this already makes Poe an anomaly within the genre as Arac attempts to define it. Furthermore, the personal narratives discussed by Arac are all very much autobiographical, again with the exception of Poe's *Pym*, a narrative in the personal narrative form "written" by an entirely fictional character and depicting fantastic or otherworldly experiences. Contrasted with Richard Henry Dana's *Two Years Before the Mast*, Douglass's 1845 *Narrative*, Melville's *Typee*, Francis Parkman's *The Oregon Trail*, or Thoreau's *A Week on the Concord and Merrimack Rivers*, Poe's "personal narrative" is a wildly imaginative piece of satirical and Gothic fiction, whereas these others are almost strictly autobiographical accounts, albeit ones that were heavily embellished in places. (Even the timing of *Pym* sets Poe at slight odds with Arac's argument, which notes that the personal narrative form dominated the literary scene of the 1840s, but *Pym* appeared in 1837 and 1838.) Similarly, although Arac gives Poe a great deal of credit for helping to establish the terms that would define literary narrative, Arac cannot identify Poe's narratives as themselves literary.

And, tellingly, Arac finds that part of Poe's lack of fit in the national culture was also related to his eccentricity within the literary culture of the age: "Split between his five cities, Poe shared neither in a national culture nor in the Republic of Letters; he was an engineer of sensations, his craft neither the 'purest art' to which it aspired not the 'literature' against which modern readers judge it."[31] Poe's peripatetic movements find a counterpart in the literary nomadism that allows him, or condemns him, to move between and among genres while never quite settling into any one of them.

Poe was a nomad in a land of settlers, and his life of nearly constant movement contrasts with the rather different sort of mobility that typified the American national culture of the day, a movement geared toward pioneering, homesteading, and then, well, staying put. Poe's more dynamic and unsettling movements are also visible in his poetry and fiction, which also do not have a set place in literary history and are themselves frequently unsettling. From Boston to Sullivan's Island and all stops in between, not excluding the transatlantic interlude, Poe's youth was marked by constant displacement. As a professional writer and editor, Poe spent his adult life wandering back and forth, between and among the "great cities" of the United States at that time: Baltimore, Boston, Richmond, Philadelphia, New York. As Charles Olson has put it, what the sea was to Melville, the street was to Poe, and Poe's movements along the thoroughfares and avenues of early American civilization define his seemingly unique place within it. He witnessed the growth of urbanization at first hand. He would have been jostled plenty and kept on the move, like the man of the crowd, even if he had remained amid the hurly-burly of only one city, but Poe continued to wander. As the United States grew both geographically and culturally, a persistent ideology of movement—especially embodied in such non-urban notions as "the pioneers," "the frontier," "Virgin Land," "Manifest Destiny," or even "upward mobility"—grew with it, but this kind of movement is really nothing like Poe's. The celebrated "movement" of early America is actually a process of *settling down*, of going to a place and staking a claim, of cordoning off private property, of homesteading, or of finding a place called "home." But this is not movement; this is stopping. Poe's actual physical or geographical movements are anomalous, and so are his more figural and metaphysical ones. Poe is not "at home" anywhere in America. In the words of J. Gerald Kennedy, Poe is "an alien presence" in early American literature.[32]

Poe's peripatetic career aptly registers a corresponding element of his poetics and his work. A nomadic movement characterizes and animates much of his writings, whether in specific "travel" narratives (such as those of Arthur Gordon Pym, Hans Pfaall, Julius Rodman, or any number of unnamed narrators), in the movements of characters (like the man of the crowd or his curious pursuer, the author of a manuscript found in a bottle, or the narrators of tales like "Ligeia" or "The Fall of the House of Usher"), or in the pervasive nomadism of Poe's own thought (as in his theory of "the perverse" itself). To borrow terminology made famous in Gilles Deleuze's philosophy, Poe's nomad thought opposes the state philosophy of American

---

[31] Arac, *The Emergence of American Literary Narrative*, 75.
[32] J. Gerald Kennedy, "Introduction," ix.

literature. Deleuze initially makes the distinction between nomad thought and state philosophy in *Difference and Repetition* in describing different approaches to ontology in Spinoza versus those of Descartes, but Deleuze developed the metaphor further in *A Thousand Plateaus* to indicate opposing social orders or organizations of life itself.[33] For Deleuze, the nomad is "the Deterritorialized par excellence," because he is never reterritorialized, and the nomad exists in a middle ground between various points which are not themselves destinations. Unlike the migrant, who moves only to get to a point at which to stop, the nomad moves from point to point as "relays in a trajectory," not destinations or ends. Never strictly at a beginning or an end, the nomad is always in the middle; or, as Deleuze puts it, "The life of the nomad is the intermezzo."[34] Like the man of the crowd and like the nomad, Poe too is always moving and always "in the middest," *in mediis rebus* ... in the middle of things.

In Poe's own time, another thinker mused over the nomad-versus-state distinction. In his 1841 essay on "History," Emerson draws the distinction out from its ancient context and makes it part of his theory of the present. "In the early history of Asia and Africa, Nomadism and Agriculture are the two antagonistic facts. The geography [...] necessitated a nomadic life. But the nomads were the terror of all those whom the soil or advantages of a market had induced to build towns. Agriculture was therefore a religious injunction, because of the perils of the state from nomadism. And in these late and civil countries of England and America these propensities still fight out the old battle, in the nation and in the individual."[35] Emerson goes on to assert that this distinction applies to minds as well as bodies, arguing in favor of the intellectual homebodies and against those minds that take to the roads. As Emerson views it, "this intellectual nomadism, in its excess, bankrupts the mind through the dissipation of power on a *miscellany of objects*. The home-keeping wit, on the other hand, is that continence [...] which finds all the elements of life in its own soil."[36]

It would be hard to argue that the relatively sedentary Sage of Concord had Poe in mind when he conceived of this "intellectual nomadism," but the label could easily be applied to Poe. Poe's peregrinations were as frequent and unsettled as the miscellany of his poetry and prose. Perhaps it is that "miscellany of objects" that one finds in Poe, the results of so many travels—flights of fancy, maybe, along with the endless steamboats, sloops, carriages, and trains that carried him up and down the East Coast—that has led some scholars to doubt Poe's power, while others embrace him with such warmth. While Poe is famously a great outsider in American literature, I maintain that his lack of fit is not based on any misunderstanding, but on his fundamental differences with those values that would become consecrated *as* those of American literature. Indeed, Poe's nomad thought discloses a subterranean and countervailing force, and his works constitute a collection of notes from the underground of American civilization.

Poe's peripatetic peripety discloses another rift between himself and the increasingly dominant national identity being forged by other writers during the nineteenth

---

[33] See Deleuze, *Difference and Repetition*, 36–7; see also Deleuze's "Nomad Thought."
[34] Deleuze and Guattari, *A Thousand Plateaus*, 380–1.
[35] Emerson, "History," *Selected Essays*, 161.
[36] Ibid., 161–2.

century. Perhaps America's state philosopher *par excellence*, Emerson enunciated yet another version of the nomad-versus-state distinction in "Self-Reliance," in which he criticizes those who value movement, and especially foreign travel, over and against those, whom Emerson favors, who have elected to stay put. "It is for want of self-culture that the superstition of Travelling, whose idols are Italy, England, Egypt, retains its fascination for all educated Americans. They who made England, Italy, or Greece venerable in the imagination, did so by sticking fast where they were, like an axis of the earth. In manly hours, we feel that duty is our place. The soul is no traveller; the wise man stays at home."[37] Of course, a clear objection to Emerson's sentiment is the fact that England, Italy, and Greece have become such landmarks and centers of Western Civilization precisely because of the extensive travels made by the English, Italians, and Greeks about and away from those countries. These places are indeed centers, but centers of a world system organized around transnational and transcultural movements. Furthermore, it cannot be merely coincidental that these places are also associated with large, terraqueous empires, and cities like London, Rome, and Athens owe much of their grandeur to the influence—and, in some cases, the direct acquisition, appropriation, or imitation—of foreign cultures. In fact, the majesty of these places reflects a mingling of civilizations made possible only through the travels of their respective citizens, visitors, and exiles, along with the influx of "exotic" travelers into their precincts. It is not for nothing that the great "national" narratives of these nations tend to be travelers' tales, from the wanderings of Odysseus and Aeneas to the shipwrecks and discoveries of Robinson Crusoe and Lemuel Gulliver.

Emerson did travel, of course, and widely, both throughout the United States and around Europe. However, his adherence to his own place, the place he felt he carried within himself as he ventured forth to other locales, meant that his travels were not so much an unsettling experience of the foreign or the strange, but an imperial incursion into domains he wished to subject to his own, more powerful sense of domesticity. That is, to continue the sentence truncated above, "[t]he soul is no traveller; the wise man stays at home, and when his necessities, his duties, on any occasion call him from his house, or into foreign lands, he is at home still and shall make men sensible by the expression of his countenance that he goes, the missionary of wisdom and virtue, and visits cities and men like a sovereign, and not like an interloper or a valet."[38] It is revealing that Emerson imagines travel as irrelevant, even antagonistic, toward thought. The notion that an American should not travel at all, or should only leave his own house when "his necessities, his duties" call him away, suggests the degree to which his own sense of nationalism and of place is grounded in an utterly sedentary and settled condition. The nearly total lack of interest in most foreign affairs is a national characteristic that Alexis de Tocqueville had also noted with surprise, and it continues to disclose itself in all sorts of unfortunate ways in the twenty-first century. For Emerson, the state philosopher of the U.S. national culture *par excellence*, the one who moves is not true to himself or to his country. Emerson finds domestication or

---

[37] Emerson, "Self-Reliance," ibid., 197.
[38] Ibid.

staying at home to be the highest virtue, not only for oneself as a philosopher or intellectual, but for the nation as a whole.

The late Poe: Extravagant trajectories

The pun, or perhaps better the terminological slippage, that I have used throughout this chapter does seem apt in the case of Poe's life and works. Poe combines the *peripatetic* with *peripeteia* (or, in English, *peripety*). Both terms are most closely associated with Aristotle, leader of the peripatetic school of thought, so named for the physical wanderings of its adherents, in addition, perhaps, to their metaphysical ones. In the *Poetics*, Aristotle designates *peripeteia* or "the reversal of the situation" as the component essential to a complex plot.[39] The example he gives is that moment of the messenger's arrival in *Oedipus the King* of Sophocles; the messenger was to have brought tidings that would have alleviated Oedipus' doubts and put to rest his worst fears but which actually end up confirming them. With their own dashed hopes and surprising turnabouts, Poe's life and work themselves supply many examples. As a peripatetic or a wanderer, Poe experiences his share of peripeties or dramatic reversals of fortune. Indeed, I think his own theory of the perverse may be another figure for Poe's nomadology, and the vexing ideas on display in Poe's writings are partly responsible for his eccentric and ambivalent place in literary history. Poe's subversion of American literature involves his perplexing disruption of both common sense and rationality. Frequently, what we think *ought* to be the case is shown to be false, as with Dupin's revelation in "The Purloined Letter" that the openly visible surfaces make for better hiding places than the obscure depths or veiled recesses. Just as Poe himself moves away from the comforts of settlement toward the unsettling and un-American nomadism, his theory is "unsettling." The perverse, which literally or etymologically suggests a "turning away" (for example, the Latin *perversus* referred to a "misguided person"), turns one away from what is thought to be right and good. And yet, Poe identifies the "impulse of the perverse" to be an irresistible force.

Poe's tales of terror, grotesque, and arabesque, frequently posit something like the "spirit of perversity" as the underlying motive in human endeavors, and the result is an inscrutability, an utter inability to understand. Like the "man of the crowd," the texts do not permit themselves to be read. Poe goes a step further in his analysis of "the spirit of perversity," what the narrator of "The Black Cat" calls "this unfathomable longing of the soul to *vex itself*."[40] Here, it is not only the text, but the reader, that cannot be read. The spirit of perverseness disrupts the Cartesian certitude of and in the ego. Dismissing the certainty with which such thought presumes to proceed, Poe notes in "The Imp of the Perverse" that the only reason science has overlooked this *primum mobile* of the human soul is "the pure arrogance of the reason."[41] The phrase

---

[39] Aristotle, *Poetics*, XI.i.
[40] Poe, "The Black Cat," *Poetry and Tales,* 599.
[41] Poe, "The Imp of the Perverse," *Poetry and Tales,* 826.

invites mention of Immanuel Kant, whose *Critique of Pure Reason* also imagined another nomad-versus-state antagonism. In the Preface to the first edition, Kant depicts metaphysics as "the Queen of the sciences" whose empire is frequently under siege by skeptics: "a species of nomads, despising all settled modes of life, [who] broke up from time to time all civil society."[42] Like skepticism, but worse since it undermines not only the dogmatic view of others but also the best interests of oneself, Poe's "spirit of the perverse" introduces an element that casts uncertainty upon the agent and the author, as well as upon the subject and the text. Even Poe's critical theory thus opposes itself to the hopeful, progressive views of the science and literature of the American Renaissance. Poe's nomadology counteracts the emerging state philosophy of what would come to be foundational to the myths and symbols of American Studies as a disciplinary field.

Here again Poe reveals himself to be an alien in his own country. Poe's fictional travels would seem to comport well with those popular and enduring works of his contemporaries, whose own voyages aimed at producing truth, which could then be used as groundwork for further settlement. The obvious example is the personal narrative form, in which a traveler relates his or her own exotic experiences but, in narrating, domesticates them, literally "bringing them home" to the readers. Intentionally or otherwise, personal narratives of this sort functioned to colonize such places, making them less exotic and thus clearing the way for future settlement. As I will discuss at greater length in the next chapter, Poe's personal narratives, if they can be thought of as "personal narratives" at all, do nothing of the sort. Poe's voyages lead less to knowledge and conquest than to greater mysteries and insecurity. One need only think of *The Narrative of Arthur Gordon Pym*, with its baffling ending and odd note appended by the "editor" (Poe himself). Far from domesticating foreign experiences, from making them more like home, Poe makes even the domestic sphere seem very "un-homely," *unheimlich* or uncanny. What could be more un-homely than the facts in the case of "The Black Cat," that "most homely narrative," which is after all just "a series of mere household events," for example?[43]

Poe's writings undermine not only the hopeful and ascendant spirit of the American Renaissance, but also the image of nation itself and the uses of literature. Poe's perverse "turning away" expresses the nomadic rejection of the norm while also exploring territories of the unthought and unrepresented. In this, Poe's nomad thought reveals itself as a powerful counter-philosophy to the prevailing nationalist thinking of his epoch. This thoroughgoing nomadism marks him as fundamentally anti-American, and not just because he was hostile to democracy and skeptical about the providential promise of the nation. It goes deeper and further.

Peeples has pointed out that the various scholars who wish to claim a place for Poe in this or that city overlook the degree to which Poe's very urbanism places him in a different kind of world altogether, what the sociologist Lyn H. Lofland called "the world of strangers," in which "the people to be found within its boundaries at a given

---

[42] Kant, *Critique of Pure Reason*, A.ix.
[43] Poe, "The Black Cat," *Poetry and Tales*, 597.

moment know nothing personally about the vast *majority* of others with whom they share this space."[44] Reflecting on the various tendencies to place Poe geographically and culturally within the imaginary space of American culture over the past century, Peeples writes:

> One tradition of Poe scholarship sees him as a writer unconcerned with real places or even reality itself, a writer who mentally inhabited his own "Dream-land," "Fairyland," "Al Aaraaf," "The City in the Sea," and "The Valley of Unrest." On the other hand, recent scholarship has placed much greater emphasis on Poe's place and time—his engagement with the antebellum publishing world, with contemporary cultural controversies and politics. I don't think we should go back to seeing Poe as an isolated dreamer unconcerned with his environment—far from it. If we must characterize him in terms of place, though, I think what needs to be stressed is neither placelessness nor an identification with a single place, but rather a relationship to place that I see as strikingly modern and American: rootless, down-at-the-heels, opportunistic, and cosmopolitan.[45]

However, by identifying the "American" as rootless and cosmopolitan, Peeples also posits a kind of subterranean or nomad thought, in which the imaginary community of the nation-state becomes unmoored from the specific geography and "homeland" that is the putative subject of American Studies. Poe's nomadism, his persistent occupation of space without settling down in a place, characterizes that poetics of descent undergirding his satirical, fantastic, and subversively critical literature.

Poe remains a nomad in a land of settlers. In his own time, his perpetual motion within the social body of the United States marked him as a stranger or outsider wherever he went. In the American literary tradition, Poe remains an "alien presence," one that the tradition never ceases to try to domesticate. As Deleuze has written of Nietzsche, but it seems equally applicable to Poe, "[i]t is common knowledge that nomads fare miserably under our kinds of regime: we will go to any lengths in order to settle them, and they barely have enough to subsist on. Nietzsche lived like such a nomad, reduced to a shadow, moving from furnished room to furnished room."[46] Poe's eccentricity, perversity, and alterity do much to prevent his total assimilation within the national narrative of American Studies. He is at least spared the fate of becoming a representative national writer whose literary creations are made into avatars of a distinctly American national identity, a fate that has befallen such nineteenth-century iconoclasts as Melville and Twain. But the "regime" of American literature, in the realms of both academic scholarship and popular culture, still tries to "settle" Poe, to fix him in place. Despite such efforts, Poe's nomadism still emerges as if from the underground, with subterranean noises troubling the (only apparent) clarity of the discourse above. Poe is like the planet earth in that apocryphal line often, if

---

[44] Lofland, *A World of Strangers: Order and Action in Urban Public Space*, 3.
[45] Peeples, "Nowhere Man: The Problem of Poe and Place," 90. See also Peeples, "'To Reproduce a City': New York Letters and the Urban American Renaissance."
[46] Deleuze, "Nomad Thought," 149.

erroneously, attributed to Galileo when faced with the Inquisition's wrath: "And yet, it moves."

Against the optative mood of the American Renaissance, Poe posits a terrifying perversity. Against the manifest destiny of movement directed toward settlement, Poe insists upon perpetual, unsettled movements. Against the narrative aims of knowledge and understanding, Poe offers inscrutability. Poe is an anti-American literary figure, ironically but not surprisingly right in the middle of the American tradition. Poe is the nomad who disrupts "all settled modes of life," even those of the life of the mind. Poe remains an unsettled and unsettling force in American literature today, where he continues to be on the move. Poe's nomadology glides beneath and athwart the state philosophy of both American national narrative in the nineteenth century and American Studies in the twentieth. His journeys into parts unknown rarely bring the comforts of the familiar or the reassuring back home. The nomadic movements of Poe's thought remain, in the end, nomadic.

3

Points of No Return

Poe's subversion of American literature may be illustrated, in part, by examining a characteristic piece in the contexts of contemporary narratives and of the cultural work to which such narratives have be put in twentieth-century American Literary Studies. In this chapter I focus especially on Poe's 1833 tale, "MS. Found in a Bottle," which helped to launch his career as a magazinist and professional writer and which, I think, contains many of the elements that render so many of Poe's tales "Poe-esque" in the minds of scholarly critics and casual fans. However, given the variety of forms, tones, and effects in Poe's tales, not to mention the great pride he took in his own versatility as a writer,[1] it is probably not altogether suitable to identify any one tale as "characteristic" of Poe's style. "MS. Found in a Bottle" is, by my reading, at least partly a satire upon the popular personal narratives of the nineteenth century. The tale is a send-up of the scientific discourse of voyages of discovery, and Poe employs a fantastic mode in leveling his critique of the pretensions of knowledge and progress in this period. Moreover, Poe's blend of horror and satire makes possible a subtle critique of the foundational myths and symbols of a national narrative, thus undermining in advance the story that American Studies would attempt to fabulate. In structure and form, at least, the personal narrative of a seemingly representative individual, who makes a groundbreaking discovery in parts hitherto unknown, and who, by reporting this discovery, advances the frontiers of knowledge while domesticating the foreign experience, fits well within the framework of American national narrative. In Poe's perverse version, however, these familiar elements are made strange and perplexing, and the progressive march of knowledge becomes a descent into greater obscurity.

The return of the personal narrative

As Jonathan Arac's study of nineteenth-century narrative forms makes clear, many of the most popular and still valued tales in nineteenth-century American literature were

---

[1] See, e.g. Poe, "To Charles Anthon" (*ante* November 2, 1844), in *The Letters of Edgar Allan Poe*, 271.

personal narratives.[2] These included such nonfictional accounts as Richard Henry Dana's *Two Years Before the Mast*, Herman Melville's *Typee* and *Omoo*, Frederick Douglass's 1845 *Narrative*, Francis Parkman's *The Oregon Trail*, or even Henry David Thoreau's *Walden*, as well as more fantastic voyages such as Poe's *The Narrative of Arthur Gordon Pym*. For the most part, the plots of these personal narratives followed a recognizable descent-and-return trajectory: the protagonist, who is almost always also the narrator, ventures away from home and into some unfamiliar if not wholly exotic locale or situation, only to return home safely, usually wiser or otherwise better for having made the trip. The narrator's formula might look like this: first, "here I am, readers, one of you"; then, "I ventured into this exotic or mysterious or terrifying place"; and finally, "I have returned now to tell the tale," the telling of which is the substance of the narrative itself.[3] This formula is equally effective in fictional or nonfictional accounts, allowing the reader to marvel at the foreign experience while taking comfort in the return to more familiar environs. Operating like Freudian *Nachträglichkeit*, the return registers the significance of the voyage, imbuing the story with authenticity as well as authority.

The allegorical significance of this descent-and-return formula is manifest in religious literature going back at least to Dante and his precursors, and Dante's re-emergence from the Inferno might be considered the *Ur*-text of these later spiritual voyages. This rhetorical model is also employed in such early colonial American writings as Mary Rowlandson's captivity narrative (1682) and Jonathan Edwards's personal narrative (1743). These texts recall and reconstitute that American Jeremiad in which the errant pilgrim descends into the wilderness, literally or figuratively, often as divine retribution for his or her worldly sins. At this point, the pilgrim repents and, by the grace of God, is released, returning to the mainstream or dominant culture, now with a tale to tell.[4] Sacvan Bercovitch and others have noted that this "American Jeremiad" becomes the basis for a national cultural rhetoric, even where the religious component, seemingly essential to the Puritan jeremiads, has disappeared.[5] In the

---

[2]　See Jonathan Arac, *The Emergence of American Literary Narrative*; the book-length study originally appeared as "Narrative Forms," in Sacvan Bercovitch, ed., *The Cambridge History of American Literature, Volume 2: 1820–1860*.

[3]　The slave narrative appears to be the exception to this formula. As Arac points out, in slave narratives the movement is one of ascent, from slavery to freedom (see Arac, *The Emergence of American Literary Narrative*, 77). That said, one could argue that even slave narratives partook of the compelling descent-and-return formula, since there is usually a "hitting-bottom" within the narrative that leads to the ultimate push for freedom. To take a very famous example, Frederick Douglass's encounter with Mr. Covey was clearly the "low" point in his life, especially compared to his earlier time as a "city slave" in Baltimore; "A city slave is almost a freeman, compared with a slave on the plantation" (Douglass, *Narrative of the Life of Frederick Douglass*, 21). "Mr. Covey had succeeded in breaking me. I was broken in body, soul, and spirit. [...] the dark night of slavery closed in upon me, and behold a man transformed into a brute!" (38). From that nadir, Douglass makes his emergence to freedom.

[4]　In these religious personal narratives, the instructive and theological value of the tale makes its telling a pilgrim's duty. For example, Rowlandson's narrative originally bore the title, *The Soveraignty & Goodness of God, Together with the Faithfulness of His Promises Displayed; Being a Narrative of the Captivity and Restauration of Mrs. Mary Rowlandson, Commended by her to all that Desire to Know the Lord's Doings to, and Dealings with Her. Especially to her Dear Children and Relations*.

[5]　In addition to his influential *American Jeremiad*, see Bercovitch, *The Puritan Origins of the American Self*.

nineteenth-century United States, such narratives also had the effect of establishing and reinforcing a vision of the national narrative, with a distinctly national or representative subject (an American Adam), an exemplary scene (the Virgin Land), and particular national mission or project (the errand into the wilderness).[6] Ideologically, at least, such a "narrative of return" functioned as a means of exploring, revealing, and ultimately homogenizing foreign places and experiences, incorporating them into a national metanarrative in which the return could also be figured forth as a rebirth, a second flowering of some idealized past moment ... in other words, an American Renaissance.[7]

The personal narrative of the individual traveler, who descends into some lower social or natural milieu, such as a subordinate social class or a primitive culture, only to return to his or her rightful place a better person, does not necessarily have to form the basis for a national narrative. It could just as easily be used to highlight a distinctively non-representative and literally outlandish example of experiences quite foreign to, and inassimilable within, the national narrative. However, in the context of the early to mid-nineteenth-century United States, representative movement of personal narratives, figured as a descent-and-return formula, did fit well within the framework of the emerging American national narrative. This national narrative was not necessarily fixed and unchanging, for, as Arac has observed, nineteenth-century national narrative "was part of the process by which the nation was forming itself and not merely a reflection of an accomplished fact."[8] Personal narratives, in Arac's view, are quite distinct from national narratives, but in practice they often served the purposes of the nation's ideological self-fashioning. Although the authority of the personal narrative lies in the individual narrator, he or she may nevertheless be representative of the nation as a whole, either by being a typical representative or by appealing to an idealized national character. In this manner, the seemingly personal account easily shifts from the unique or esoteric experience presented from an individual perspective to a typical, representative, or even allegorical narrative that speaks to a potentially national community. The exemplary and perhaps national or proto-national individual makes some journey into a domain that is situated apart from the national heartland,

---

[6] See Donald E. Pease, "National Identities, Postmodern Artifacts, and Postnational Narratives," 3–4.

[7] In using the term, I do not mean to suggest that this is F. O. Matthiessen's argument in *American Renaissance*; rather, I mean the concept that emerged in the aftermath of Matthiessen's and others' work in the disciplinary fields of American literature and American Studies more broadly. "American Renaissance" in this sense provides an ideological underpinning for a certain characterization of the American national identity, which in turn dominated the political discourse and foreign-policy rhetoric of the United States from roughly the post-war period to the present. The notion of renascence, with its almost uniformly positive connotations, still operates in ways that mask deep-seated and often intractable cultural and material problems facing communities within the United States and abroad. The ideology of the American Renaissance fosters a quasi-religious belief in a providential overcoming of such social problems, thus undermining the potential support for secular and humane projects that might actually solve them. This is surely one of the ways that the post-war literary or cultural analysis of mid-nineteenth-century texts has affected the national discourse in the twentieth, and now twenty-first, centuries. On Matthiessen's unintended influence on this aspect of American Studies, see Arac, "F.O. Matthiessen: Authorizing the American Renaissance."

[8] Arac, *The Emergence of American Literary Narrative*, 3.

be it an adventure abroad or within the geographical boundaries of the nation-state, where he or she encounters persons, events, and circumstances quite distinct from the mainstream or predominant culture back home. But then the narrator returns to tell the tale, domesticating these strange experiences and incorporating them into the broader national narrative. As noted above, in the United States such a formal structure becomes almost a rubric for a popular vision of the national narrative, as a "rugged individual" or an "American Adam" on an "errand into the wilderness" across a "Virgin Land" may eventually form a "city on the hill" that stands as a "beacon" to the rest of the world. It is relatively easy to see how the personal narrative form would supplement and reinforce the ideological effects and the cultural program of national narrative.

Furthermore, by colonizing places and kinds of experience, the personal narrator in this genre domesticates them within a sphere of knowledge, bringing the exotic "home" to the readers. This becomes a model of knowledge production or scientific discovery, where the unknown becomes known through the narrative. As Arac points out, the very word *narrative* has its etymological roots in *knowing* (from the Latin *gnarus*, from which the word *ignorance* also derives), and personal narratives tended to involve quasi-scientific reports from the periphery. The authority of the narrator/observer rested in the eyewitness account, and the narrative form itself thus operated as an instrument of knowledge production. In this form, the metropolitan narrator, returning from the wilderness, assumes control over the narrative and, in some cases, over events depicted within that narrative. The personal narrative form allows the central narrative voice to present and represent the exotic content, homogenizing the experiences and situating them within a familiar framework.[9] Hence the knowledge of the otherworldly or outlandish, of the exotic or peripheral experience, is produced and disseminated within the structure of the dominant culture vis-à-vis the narrative form. In returning to tell the tale of the periphery, the narrator drags these foreign experiences back into the national center.

But what happens when the narrator does not come back, when there is no return? What if, as in Poe's "MS. Found in a Bottle," the story is just that, *found*, floating in a bottle? The narrative in its peculiar form exists, apparently, only because the narrator does not. That is, presumably, the story would be quite different had the narrator returned to tell the tale. Here, the comfortable and comforting images of return and rebirth founder. From the reader's point of view, the manuscript is a curiosity, an accidental voyage by an unwitting participant to uncharted domains from which there can be no return. The adventure is itself an accident, the observations are fleeting, the mysteries observed remain unexplained, and the end admits of no possible redemption or resurrection. The irreversible narrative of "MS. Found in a Bottle" exhibits certain characteristics that place it squarely at odds with personal and national narratives that dominated popular writing in the United States during Poe's career. The irreversibility of the tale marks a moment in Poe's poetics of descent, an aesthetic based largely on

---

[9] See Mary Louise Pratt, *Imperial Eyes: Travel Writing and Transculturation*.

fleeting, ineffable, and ineluctable experience, and manifested in the satirical, fantastic, and critical modes of his literary work.

"MS. Found in a Bottle" presents a detailed depiction of a real descent, a fall into an otherworldly maelstrom from which there is no return, unlike a similar experience vividly described in Poe's "Descent into the Maelstrom." But even beyond the plot of "MS. Found in a Bottle," which certainly has a downward trajectory and entirely lacks a buoyant "return," the irreversibility of that narrative marks it as one of inevitable descent. The narrator's inability to bring his ineffable experience into the discursive register or archive of knowledge production offers another way in which this story differs from, or perhaps subtly satirizes, the personal narratives of the era. Overall, in its content and its form, the tale does not allow for one to attach any clear meaning to the fantastic voyage. Unlike the popular personal narratives of the mid-nineteenth century, it does not offer an occasion to domesticate the foreign experience, to know it, or to render it familiar. The narrator's "discovery" does not illuminate the subject, but casts the mystery into an even more mysterious gloom. Without the possibility of return, the tale has a unidirectional and irreversible movement that heaps discomfort onto uncertainty. The messianic possibilities of personal narrative, especially when allied with the providential mission of national narrative, founder on the rocks—or, perhaps, are submerged in the undertow—of Poe's fantastic, irreversible descent.

"Of my country and of my family I have little to say"

Although he had previously published three books of poetry, as well as several individual poems and tales, one might argue that "MS. Found in a Bottle," first published in 1833, is in some ways Poe's first short story, although it was the sixth he had been able to see into print.[10] As the winning entry the *Baltimore Saturday Visiter* [*sic*] contest, it launched his career as a professional writer, as well as providing some recognition of Poe's talent as a fiction writer. Moreover, "MS. Found in a Bottle" appears to be the first tale for which Poe was certainly paid—he was awarded a prize of $50—and hence "MS. Found in a Bottle" marked the beginning of Poe's career as what Charles Baudelaire called, rather derisively, a "making-money author." Written in the first person and recounting bizarre happenings from unknown regions of the globe, the story might seem to be a kind of personal narrative, though not exactly in Arac's sense of the term. "MS. Found in a Bottle" does follow that form's conventions, even as it undermines a reader's expectations. The title alone indicates that the narrator is not available, and the expectation that the unknown will become known is therefore frustrated in advance. When the reader has completed the story, very little new knowledge has actually been revealed, apart from the dubious Antarctic polar hole in the earth's surface. But with no return of the narrator, there is also no authority to translate this utterly ineffable experience into the language proper to a sort of

---

[10] Another tale, "Epimanes (Four Beasts in One)," was composed by 1833, but remained unpublished until Poe placed it in *The Southern Literary Messenger* in 1836.

scientific discovery. Although there are numerous elements in common between this irreversible narrative and the personal narratives of the era, in Poe's story these elements are modified, twisted, or distorted in such a way that the very knowledge the narrative sets out to display descends into an all-consuming unknown. Poe's subterranean noises contrast sharply with that optative mood and redemptive spirit visible in much of the work of Poe's celebrated contemporaries. And, like the narrator of "MS. Found in a Bottle," who begins that narrative with the line, "[o]f my country and family I have little to say,"[11] Poe does not really feel a sense of belonging to the imagined community of the United States or its national literature.

Of course, it is not surprising to hear that Poe is at odds with his contemporaries, or that he does not fit neatly within this or that version of an American national culture. Poe has almost always been considered the great anomaly in American literature. One thinks of F. O. Matthiessen's snub in leaving Poe out of his field-establishing *American Renaissance: Art and Expression in the Age of Emerson and Whitman*, for example.[12] That has not stopped Poe from being popularly and critically acclaimed, of course, and Poe certainly is and has been a canonical figure within American literature ever since such a canon began to crystallize in the early twentieth century. But even those who have heaped praise upon Poe acknowledge the fundamental eccentricity of Poe's status within the American literary traditions. For one thing, there's the problem of genre. It is not always clear what kind of texts Poe has produced.[13] Where does Poe "fit" within American literature?

Poe does not easily find a spot in Arac's examination of nineteenth-century narrative forms. As I noted in the last chapter, Poe figures prominently in three of Arac's four categories, but within each genre Poe is also an anomaly. For instance, whereas the other writers of *local* narrative discussed by Arac are clearly also *regional* writers—e.g. Washington Irving's Dutch New York in *The Sketch Book of Geoffrey Crayon*, Hawthorne's New England, and the bucolic backwoods of the Southwestern Humorists—Poe's tales are not localized in any particular region.[14] And unlike the

---

[11] Poe, "MS. Found in a Bottle," *Poetry and Tales*, 189.

[12] Although the principle reason Poe was left out was strictly historical—i.e. the book focused on works produced between 1850 and 1855, and Poe died in 1849—Matthiessen gives other reasons for excluding him. Unlike the other figures (Hawthorne, Emerson, Thoreau, Melville, and Whitman), "Poe was bitterly hostile to democracy," and "his value, even more than Emerson's, is now seen to consist in his influence rather than in the body of his own work." Matthiessen concludes that Poe's "stories, less harrowing upon the nerves as they were, seem relatively factitious when contrasted with the moral depth of Hawthorne and Melville" (Matthiessen, *American Renaissance*, xii, note 3). That is, Poe was both un-American and artificial; he lacked both political and artistic authenticity. However, it should also be noted that Matthiessen did contribute a largely positive essay on Poe to Robert Spillers's 1948 *Literary History of the United States*, in which he concludes that Poe "took his place in international culture as an original creative force in contrast to the more superficial international vogue of Cooper and Irving" (342); in other words, Poe's true internationality may also have set him apart from any *American* renaissance, however popular overseas some other more "national" writers may have been.

[13] See, for example, Joseph Ridgely, "Tragical-Mythical-Satirical-Hoaxical: Problems of Genre in *Pym*," *American Transcendental Quarterly* 24 (Fall 1974): 4–9.

[14] Poe "did not have a well-established regional residence, nor do his writings draw upon local history, lore, and customs" (62), but Arac suggests that Poe's work represented local narrative by representing a distinctive type of locale: that is, the city. For Arac, Poe is really America's first *urban*

personal narratives of Dana, Parkman, Thoreau, and even Melville, Poe's one personal narrative discussed by Arac, *The Narrative of Arthur Gordon Pym of Nantucket*, is not even loosely based on autobiographical experience.[15] It is a work of pure fantasy, and the text's stated ambiguities of authorship, as well as the unstated publication history, only deepen the impression that Poe is slyly operating outside, or underneath, the genre of personal narrative.[16] Finally, although Poe's critical theory and his ambiguous embrace of German and English Romanticism pave the way for *literary* narrative, it is the romances of Hawthorne and Melville that exemplify that form, in Arac's estimation. Even where Poe is closely involved in the making of an American literary tradition, he remains somewhat apart from it.

Poe's alterity may be figured as well in another aspect of "MS. Found in a Bottle," among other tales: its apparent fatalism. Fate, with its attendant problem of individual agency, looms large in literary narratives, especially in Romantic literature.[17] Fatalism might be viewed as almost archetypically un-American, since a founding ideological component of the nation's *mentalité* is individualism. Alexis de Tocqueville actually coined the term *individualism* in *Democracy in America*, and he observed that economically self-reliant individuals "owe nothing to any man, they expect nothing from any man; they acquire the habit of always considering themselves as standing alone, and they are apt to imagine that their whole destiny lies in their hands."[18] It is but a short step from this latter phrase to John O'Sullivan's term, *manifest destiny*. If the characteristic denizens of the United States do believe in fate, it seems, it is only a fate created by themselves. This self-determination lies at the heart of the American national narrative. Yet, throughout Poe's works, individual agency is constantly questioned, undermined, or flatly denied.[19] Fate, which so neatly yet problematically combines necessity and chance, is the underlying principle of Poe's irreversible narrative. Unlike those stories that might champion the individual agent, "MS. Found in a Bottle" emphasizes the degree to which the principal character, who is also the first-person narrator, has little or no control over the events befalling him. Not only

---

writer, bringing the image of the city to bear on both his urban sketches (like "The Man of the Crowd") and his gloomy, though more rustically set, tales, such as "The Fall of the House of Usher." This circumscription of space and the urban atmosphere of his tales make Poe a writer of local narrative, in Arac's view.

[15] This did not stop the publishers, Harper and Brothers, from advertising *The Narrative of Arthur Gordon Pym* as a work of travel; see Arac, *The Emergence of American Literary Narrative*, 100.

[16] For example, in the "Preface," the narrator (Pym himself) has to explain why the first parts of the narrative were already published under the name of "Edgar A. Poe" in *The Southern Literary Messenger*; the ruse becomes even more bizarre in the concluding "Note" by the editor (Poe), and is confounded further by the open secret that Poe is the author and Pym is a fictional character. Indeed, even though Harper and Brothers continued to list *The Narrative of Arthur Gordon Pym* among its works of nonfiction travel, the title page of *The Prose Romances of Edgar A. Poe* names Poe as the author of "Arthur Gordon Pym."

[17] On Romanticism and the problem of agency, see Arac, *The Emergence of American Literary Narrative*, 171–80.

[18] Tocqueville, *Democracy in America*, vol. II, 99.

[19] This is, of course, not unique to Poe. Romantic thought often called action and agency into question. Indeed, such problematization of agency is one of the hallmarks of literary narrative. One need only think of the references to fate that pervade *Moby-Dick*. See Arac, "'A Romantic Book': *Moby-Dick* and Novel Agency."

does the individual lack the agency to control his environment, but the events are themselves ineluctable; they are the necessary results of causes set in motion without the narrator's input or knowledge. Thus, in the irreversible narrative, there is no time for retrospective reflection, no backward-looking or second-guessing, no sense that, if only things had been done differently, this would not have happened. The narrator is, quite literally and quite figuratively, at sea.

In "MS. Found in a Bottle," this fatality is also re-inscribed in the form that the narrative takes. Often Poe's narrators, the very ones who should be controlling the presentation of the events in the narrative, appear to be caught up in the narrative and the narration, such that they seem to be either out of control or controlled by some other force, like fate or chance. Obviously, in "MS. Found in a Bottle," the form is conditioned by the headlong rush of the plot as well as the *ad hoc* and mobile quality of the narrative voice itself. The "author" of the narrative is dead or irretrievably lost. The titular conceit, that the narrative is found, indicates that the text itself is merely the trace left behind. The structure of the narrative is similar to that used by Poe in later tales, in which an introductory section tells us a bit about the narrator, a middle section describes the strange events befalling him, and a quick final section marks the hurried and irreversible end. This irreversibility is emphasized in the pace of the narrative; Poe's principal temporal technique is acceleration. From the slow, patient description of the opening paragraphs to a fast, frenetic conclusion, Poe guides the reader by using relatively lengthy and discursive introductions in which little but background is offered, then offering a gentle acceleration through the curious middle sections that philosophically attempt to make sense of the inexplicable, and finally rushing on to an end designed to leave one breathless and without hope for further resolution. There is no clear denouement or coda following the terrific climax. The end is inevitable, and when it comes, it comes swiftly.

All of this operates in such a way as to subvert or, at least, render problematic that optative mood, with its messianic promise, that held sway over so much popular rhetoric in mid-nineteenth-century American letters. Poe's irreversible narrative points to a different way of thinking, not only about the individual in relation to the cosmos, but about the nation's role and position in history. The image is not of return, rebirth, or rising, but of descent, ineluctable and irreversible, into the unknown. As noted above, the very word *narrative* is etymologically related to *knowing*, and, in its more restrictive traditional definition, *narrative* suggests a straightforward setting forth of facts. In its formal aspect, the author of "MS. Found in a Bottle" appears to do just that, calmly laying out the facts before the reader, only to pull the rug out, shocking the reader, and offering an unexpected (and, perhaps, not altogether pleasant) experience of the unknown. This unknown may be the scariest aspect of Poe's tales of terror, inasmuch as it undermines the guiding principles of personal and national narrative. Whereas personal narratives tended to shine a light on the dark places of the world and of society, illuminating unknown experiences that could then become part of the dominant national culture, a national culture that, itself, was to be a beacon for enlightening the rest of the world, Poe's perverse, anomalous narrative presented an initially shadowy and gray picture, only to plunge the reader into a deeper darkness below.

Irreversible descent

Let us examine this process in "MS. Found in a Bottle."[20] We are told at the outset that the unnamed narrator is himself an outsider: "Of my country and family I have little to say. Ill usage and length of years have driven me from the one, and estranged me from the other" (189). It is a beginning completely unlike either "Call me Ishmael" or "My name is Arthur Gordon Pym," although this opening line might be said to foreshadow both. The irony of these others is the way in which the ostensible naming, whether the poetic and ambiguous exordium of an "Ishmael" or the more straightforward deadpanning of Pym,[21] actually veils the anonymity or pseudonymity of the narrators. Whereas "Ishmael" is clearly a figurative label and mask, Arthur Gordon Pym's name becomes little more than a placeholder for an unnamed narrator, whose personal biography and psychology have little bearing on the plot itself, as becomes clear to the reader rather quickly. In "MS. Found in a Bottle," as in so many of Poe's other tales, the narrator offers no proper name in the first place, and he goes on more or less to disavow the role that personal history or character might have in the narrative as a whole. Lacking nation and family, the narrator does reveal that "[h]ereditary wealth afforded me an education of no common order." This disclosure serves at least two functions: it emphasizes his orphan status (i.e., he is a legatee of dead ancestors), and it serves to explain why such literate prose writing might be found floating in a bottle (e.g. he is no common sailor, but a well-educated traveler). The narrator then informs us that his education has led him to be scrupulously scientific and rational, even to a fault. "I have often been reproached for the aridity of my genius; a deficiency of imagination has been imputed to me as a crime." In other words, he is skeptical and truthful, and in no way is he susceptible to flights of fancy. This self-characterization is crucial to establishing the truth of what follows. "I have thought it proper to premise thus much, lest the incredible tale I have to tell should be considered rather the raving of a crude imagination, than the positive experience of a mind to which the reveries of fancy have been a dead letter and a nullity" (189). The first paragraph, then, sets forth what the narrator is—a man without family or country, committed to scientific principles, skeptical, truthful—if not *who* he is. The narrator's namelessness further complicates the personal narrative form, since the reader is given no sign to attach to the narrative. We are assured that the narrator maintains this or that characteristic, but we still do not know him. The personal aspect of this first-person narrative is not explored.

The commitment to truth-telling, to narrative in the narrow, etymological sense of the word, is a common ruse in Poe's fiction.[22] Poe's later tales frequently begin

---

[20] Poe, "MS. Found in a Bottle," *Poetry and Tales*, 189–99. Hereinafter page numbers cited in the text.

[21] For example, in order to get across the plain style of this opening sentence, Charles Baudelaire used what in French would be the very awkward and somewhat grating "Mon nom est ..." formulation, rather than the more common "Je m'appelle ..." phrasing.

[22] See, for instance, "The Facts in the Case of M. Valdemar," *Poetry and Tales*, 833–42. Poe's commitment to verisimilitude is most artfully on display in his hoaxes, but it is clear from his own literary theory and his "reading" of the literary marketplace that Poe understands successful fiction to be wholly dependent on seeming earnest, on a "power of simulation," as he terms it in a review of his own *Tales*; see "Edgar Allan Poe," *Essays and Reviews*, 873.

with a narrator attesting to his truthfulness and sanity, thus peremptorily demanding credibility from a potentially incredulous audience. "MS. Found in a Bottle" includes an epigraph attesting to the truthfulness of the account, in addition to the narrator's plea for credibility:

Qui n'a plus qu'un moment à vivre
N'a plus rien à dissimuler. — Quinault - Atys.

In English, the quotation reads, "he who has but a moment to live has nothing more to dissimulate." While it might actually strain the credulity of the reader to imagine this unnamed narrator inscribing a quote from Quinault—*en français*, no less—just before plunging into the abyss, the epigraph serves to add that extra assurance that the tale must be true. Not only will the narrator assure us that he does not subscribe to fanciful thoughts, that he has no talent for imaginative fiction, but he has no reason to lie even if he were so inclined. This entire truth-telling apparatus, constructed by Poe at the start of the tale, emphasizes the knowledge-production to come. In effect, these assurances tell the reader, "Get ready, something important is about to be revealed." Of course, Poe is really just setting his readers up; although many curious things will be described, the revelation will not happen. Instead, the giddy anticipation of new-found knowledge will give way to the horrifying descent into a further unknown.

Preliminaries out of the way in the first paragraph, the narrator gets on with the story. After many years of foreign travel, he had set sail again as a passenger from Java on a large cargo ship. Later in the voyage, caught in the Doldrums and becalmed for some time, the ship was suddenly "blasted" by a "Simoon," which managed to kill everyone aboard except the narrator and an "old Swede" (191). Dismasted, the hulk of the ship is at the mercy of the storm, and the wind blew it steadily southeast by south for five straight days, until the sun appeared sickly and pale, "a dull and sullen glow" (192). The sixth day did not come, as they were "enshrouded" in "eternal night." Here the swells on the ocean were mountainous: "At times we gasped for breath at an elevation beyond the albatross—at times became dizzy with the velocity of our descent into some watery hell" of the trough (193). At the bottom of one of these "abysses," the narrator and the Swede descry high above them a gigantic ship, under full sail, riding the crest of the wave, "pausing on the giddy pinnacle" ... and coming down (194). The narrator stumbled aft, just in time to be flung into the rigging of the spectral ship as it crushed the narrator's poor bark (and with it, the Swede) underneath. The narrator, fearful of its eerie crew, then hid aboard his strange new craft. The one crewmember he did see, an ancient mariner whose aspect mixed the "peevishness of a second childhood" with the "solemn dignity of a God" (194), murmured in some unknown language. Here the narrative pauses.[23]

The pause serves several purposes. For one, it reminds the reader that this is supposed to be a "found manuscript." Heretofore, the narrative has been one

---

[23] This pause is indicated typographically on the page by a series of asterisks, which also appeared in the original publication in *Baltimore Saturday Visiter* in 1833, and not merely by the change in narrative tone that is clearly audible in the paragraph that follows.

continuous short story, providing background, and then describing events as they had occurred. The format was consistent with a personal narrative, of the type that would seem to follow a familiar descent-and-return formula. Now the narrative form changes, along with the style of narration. Broken up by a series of asterisks, which suggests that what follows is a new "entry," the next paragraph also marks its difference by changes in both tone and tense.

> A feeling, for which I have no name, has taken possession of my soul—a sensation which will admit of no analysis, to which the lessons of by-gone times are inadequate, and for which I fear futurity itself will offer me no key. To a mind constituted like my own, the latter consideration is an evil. I shall never—I know that I shall never—be satisfied with regard to the nature of my conceptions. Yet it is not wonderful that these conceptions are indefinite, since they have their origin in sources so utterly novel. A new sense—a new entity is added to my soul. (195)

The transition to the present tense registers a divergence from the assumed genre of personal narrative and the entry into some other form. Suddenly, the story is no longer an account of past experiences as much as a hasty recording of present or near-present perceptions. The change in tense is awkward here. It jars the reader out of the accustomed suspension of disbelief, reminding him or her that the narrative is an *ad hoc* or contingent tale, not a carefully crafted story—which, of course, is precisely what it is: that is the great hoax implied by the title and the tale, a hoax whose ostensible victims freely participate.

This all-too-visible transition also, implicitly, calls into question the narrator's authority, even as it insists on his character's continuing integrity as a person who abhors the mysterious and inexplicable. The authoritative personal narrator, whose authority lies principally in his faithful representation of events personally experienced, gives way to a sort of baffled onlooker. This does not in itself discredit the narrator, but it does invite the reader to question the calm, authoritative tone of what came before. Surely, the narrator's previously established reliability is compromised when the narrative disintegrates midway through. The stolid, straightforward narration of the first several pages is interrupted by this new kind of narrating, one that specifically questions its own ability to deliver the truth of the matters at hand. The narrator introduces "a new entity," an inscrutable and inexplicable novelty, which changes the nature of the game. Up to this point, the story follows the familiar pattern of personal narrative, inasmuch as it details an odd voyage into the unknown, registering its oddness even as it brings the tale back into a familiar vernacular and quasi-scientific framework, thereby becoming a ripping yarn to be recounted by the fireside. Now, it is something else, something disturbing and ominous. The narrator's "evil" consideration—that he will be unable to analyze, explain, or in the future *know* what has happened to him—is perhaps a metonymic figure of the ineffable narrative itself.

Following this awkward break, "MS. Found in a Bottle" presents a paragraph of pseudo-explanation, offering further perplexities for the close reader. The narrator describes the mysterious crew ("Incomprehensible men!"), and notes that he no longer needs to hide from them. "Concealment is utter folly on my part, for the people *will not* see" (195). As fantastic as this revelation might be, more incredible are the next few lines, in which the narrator provides the information required to explain the physical existence of the text itself, at least so far as the "text" exists in the form of a manuscript found in a bottle. After disclosing that he snatched the writing materials "with which I write, and have written" from the captain's cabin, the narrator promises to continue his journal "from time to time," and he vows to transmit it to the public somehow. "At the last moment I will enclose the MS. in a bottle, and cast it into the sea" (195).

Although this paragraph serves to answer some pesky questions troubling the narrative thus far, it raises others that are, perhaps, more troubling still. First of all, would an attentive reader not be shocked to see that this paragraph, not to mention the final one, was actually written after the straightforward narration of the previous pages? If the narrator can calmly describe himself, his history and temperament, his voyage and its calamity, and the mysterious situation in which he now finds himself for so many pages, then why the rude interruption, with its present tense and metaphysical tone? Why change the narrative from the reflective, personal narrative of the past to a diary of current events and impressions? And, most distressingly, if he is now speaking in the present tense, how does the narrator know (apart from some dim foreboding) that the end is coming in precisely such a manner that he may have to throw a manuscript in a bottle overboard? Does this not suggest a breakdown between the author (Poe) and the narrative voice of the "MS."? Is it the case that Poe, as I suggest is frequently if not always the case, is laughing at us, making a mockery of our own interest in these phantasy-pieces he writes?

A short, but ultimately unsatisfying, answer to these questions may be that Poe simply erred, much as he did in allowing the many inconsistencies in *The Narrative of Arthur Gordon Pym* to stand.[24] A better explanation, one might argue, is that Poe decided to ratchet up the urgency of the narrative by introducing the break at the midway point. I mentioned above the matter of pacing, and acceleration of the plot seems to be a salient feature of many of Poe's tales. The measured setting forth of the facts of the case ultimately yields to the hurried, even frenzied, scribbling down of events almost *as they are happening* (and Poe's own use of italics in such instances underscores the urgency even further), thus making the narrator and the reader breathless in the effort to capture the meaning of the event before it evanesces. Poe's awkward little paragraphs, placed squarely in the center of "MS. Found in a Bottle," mark this transition directly, and warn readers that they are on the brink of the great cataract and that they might want to adjust the level of apprehension accordingly. The narrative rupture in "MS. Found in a Bottle" thus functions as a meticulously constructed device employed to elicit a particular sensation.

It also marks the narrative as irreversible, since clearly even the narrator realizes that he has passed a point of no return. In other words, the story will ineluctably descend into its conclusion, without potential for a return to normalcy. The tale's

---

[24] For example, one thinks of Pym's suggestion that he and his comrade, who actually dies during the course of the narrative, discussed matters of the narrative later.

next paragraph, in what might be considered the concluding scene of this middle or transitional act, emphasizes this abnormality with a strange depiction of an uncanny event, as the skeptical and scientific narrator is forced to wonder, "[a]re such things the operation of ungoverned Chance?" While pondering his remarkable fate, the narrator had "unwittingly daubed with a tar brush the edges of a neatly-folded studding-sail." Later, when the sail is raised, "the thoughtless touches of the brush are spread out in the word DISCOVERY" (195). Here the entry ends, leaving the reader to wonder what significance, if any, the remarkable coincidence carries.

This "discovery" paragraph directly announces the theme of new knowledge, but does so by explicitly invoking "the operation of ungoverned Chance." The knowledge to be gained, the discovery, does not necessarily follow from the personal journey into the unknown and the narrative about it. Rather, the discovery is itself bound by the uncertainty and contingency of chance. Fate, the absolute inevitability of circumstances, combines necessity and chance in a problematic way. In some respects, chance, involving as it does the random, the chaotic, the accidental or contingent, seems the opposite of necessity, which connotes certainty, design, purpose or intention. Necessity is not supposed to be the same as rolling the dice. Yet, as Gilles Deleuze has shown in his analysis of Nietzsche's thoughts on these matters, the dice throw actually combines necessity and chance. "The dice which are thrown once are the affirmation of *chance*, the combination which they form on falling is the affirmation of *necessity*. [...] What Nietzsche calls *necessity* (destiny) is thus never the abolition but rather the combination of chance itself."[25] Thus the affirmation of the aleatory is also an affirmation of fate. Nietzsche's *amor fati* thus becomes the love of both necessity and chance. Returning to "MS. Found in a Bottle," then, the aleatory principle relates to the fatalism in Poe that subsumes the positive effects of personal narrative, including the production of new knowledge or of new data to be incorporated into an existing system of knowledge. The supra-individual forces of chance or fate, which shock the narrator and inspire in him awe at the seemingly inscrutable designs of the cosmos (or chaosmos, perhaps), further frustrate the expectation of the reader. We are alerted to the possibility of "discovery," only to find no cognizable thing dis-covered. This little paragraph presents a wonder taken for a sign; the thing itself remains unreadable. Thus "the operation of ungoverned Chance" undermines our ability to attain the knowledge that the discovery was supposed to have revealed. However, it is a nice example of "the singular wrought out into the strange and mystical," one of the aspects of successful magazine fiction that Poe identified in an 1835 letter.[26]

The several paragraphs that follow the description of this bizarre event delineate the narrator's observations and surmises about the strange ship. Although the enormous ship is outfitted for battle, it is not a warship. Its features, like those of its crew, are altogether ancient, evoking in the narrator "an unaccountable memory of old foreign chronicles and ages long ago." The ship's material is unknown, though it resembles some otherworldly version of Spanish oak, grown beyond all realistic size,

---

[25] Deleuze, *Nietzsche and Philosophy*, 26.
[26] Poe, "Letter to Thomas W. White" (April 30, 1835), in *The Letters of Edgar Allan Poe*, 58.

as if sea itself has caused the ship to "grow in bulk like the living body of a seaman" (196). The crew members, like the one seen earlier, are ancient, marked by "hoary old age." About them lay scattered "mathematical instruments of the most quaint and obsolete construction" (196). The captain, likewise marked by "evidence of old age, so utter, so extreme," is surrounded by "strange, iron-clasped folios, and mouldering instruments of science, and obsolete long-forgotten charts." Muttering in that same unknown foreign language used by the ancient sailor earlier, the captain is bent over "a paper which I took to be a commission, and which, at all events, bore the signature of a monarch" (197–8). All the while, the ship races southward at incredible speed, as if "under the influence of some strong current, or impetuous under-tow."

The final paragraphs of "MS. Found in a Bottle," as expected, emphasize the dizzying speed of the ship and the headlong rush toward … what? The narrator registers his horror by mentioning that he should be ashamed of his earlier fear, considering how much more frightening the elements have become: "shall I not stand aghast at a warring of wind and ocean, to convey any idea of which the words tornado and simoom are trivial and ineffective?" (198). But this terror is also mixed with excitement, the thrill of discovery hinted at in the tar-brush incident. "It is evident that we are hurrying onwards to some exciting knowledge—some never-to-be-imparted secret, whose attainment is destruction" (198). The internal exhilaration at approaching the brink of a new knowledge and the external horror of wind and water and ice come together in the last lines, as the ship and its accidental stowaway plunge "madly within the grasp of the whirlpool." Breathlessly, and presumably scribbling furiously just before cramming the pages into an appropriately buoyant receptacle, the narrator tells us that, "amid a roaring, and bellowing, and thundering of ocean and of tempest, the ship is quivering, oh God! and—going down" (199).

This ending is abrupt, final, and inconclusive. The narrator's putative discovery, apart from the polar whirlpool itself, must remain unknown. A "secret" knowledge, "never-to-be-imparted," the discovery lacks the structure to edify or enlighten. Unlike many of the personal narratives of the mid-nineteenth century, the experiences here described cannot be incorporated into a national narrative or mission. Discovering that a vast whirlpool lies at the South Pole would indeed be a significant scientific discovery, but—unlike "The Balloon-Hoax," a deliberate attempt to fool the public with a "true" report of a transatlantic balloon journey—"MS. Found in a Bottle" does not really pretend to be a scientific account, notwithstanding its narrator's protestations. The presumptive voyage of exploration leads to a dead end.

In "Doodling America," Harold Beaver has suggested that the spectral ship and its eerie crew are none other than those of Christopher Columbus.[27] The references to the unknown language (an old form of Spanish, perhaps?), the otherworldly *Spanish* oak, the obsolete instruments (technology of the fifteenth century?), and the royal signature (King Ferdinand's or Queen Isabella's?) would lend support to this reading. But if Poe wished to invoke Columbus, the discoverer of the New World and thus, in

---

[27] See Beaver, "Doodling America," 20. Beaver acknowledges that Burton Pollin first noted this resemblance in 1971; see Pollin, "Poe's Use of Material from Bernardin de Saint-Pierre's Études," 336.

a sense, the founding father or grandfather of "America," the politico-mythic national entity if not the geographical place, he does not offer a Columbus that would serve national narrative very well. Perhaps like Tennyson's Ulysses this former adventurer longs for the open sea again; or even better, like Dante's Ulysses, this Columbus seeks ever new discoveries until, just as the *terra nova*—in Dante's vision of it, Mount Purgatory, also located at the South Pole, in fact—comes into sight, a great whirlpool pulls him and his crew down beneath the surface of the world. Or perhaps this weary voyage *is* his purgatory, in which Columbus is doomed to sail the oceans searching for some hitherto undreamed of knowledge. Poe's narrator sees no signs of joy or wonder in the leader of this voyage of discovery, and the eerie, spectral captain does not have the wild characteristics of a Romantic hero. In any event, if Poe did intend there to be a reference to Columbus in "MS. Found in a Bottle," this one does not evoke any celebratory idea of nation formation. The discovery is not of a new world, a promised or "virgin" land where a new people can take root. And there is no triumphant return, with an explorer's reports of newfound knowledges and territories to dazzle the readers in the metropolitan center in tales of exotic locales. The ghostly craft, whether it be the *Flying Dutchman* or the *Santa Maria*, does not trace the shorelines of any *terra incognita*. Again, the main discovery, if it can be called such, is that of an abyss.

Irreversible, this tale plunges the reader into an unknown without allowing a return to the normal or the familiar. Without the element of return, the eccentric, the exotic, or the unknown must remain that way. That is, it cannot be reclaimed by or incorporated into the culture of which the tale's readers are presumably a part. The irreversibility of this narrative is opposed to the return of other narratives, the latter assuming an ability to represent (or re-present) the exotic material, now made familiar by the operations of the narrative form itself. The narrator's return assures at least the possibility of knowing. In Poe's irreversible narrative, however, the unknown remains hauntingly and tantalizingly unknowable.

Uncharted territories

A curious note is appended to the "MS." The note did not appear in the original, but was added only in the 1850 version included in the posthumous *Works of the Late Edgar Allan Poe*. Presumably Poe had added this note after 1845, since it did not appear in the version published that year in the *Broadway Journal*, and perhaps Poe intended it to become part of the final version, which was included among the papers turned over to his literary executor, Rufus Griswold. The little end-note would appear, but only appear, to explain something crucial about the text. In the voice of Poe, not of the narrator (of course), the note reads: "The 'MS. Found in a Bottle,' was originally published in 1831, and it was not until many years afterwards that I became acquainted with the maps of Mercator, in which the ocean is represented as rushing, by four mouths, into the (northern) Polar Gulf, to be absorbed into the bowels of the earth; the Pole itself being represented by a black rock, towering to a prodigious height" (199). Whether it is merely an oversight by Poe or a final ruse designed to lampoon the pretensions of scientific exactitude once more, we can see that his date is incorrect; the tale was first published in 1833. But the note also seems to suggest that, once again, the knowledge imparted in the tale is to be doubted, and the authority of the manuscript's narrator and now of Poe himself, apparently, is undermined. In fact, however, the note itself does not really explain anything at all. The reader's first response to learning that Poe later looked at Mercator's maps might well be, "So what?" Does this note attempt to re-establish the scientific quality of the narrative? Is it a *mea culpa*, Poe's admission that he erred by sending his narrator to the wrong Pole or down the wrong hole? Does the note change the way one now reads or rereads the tale? Certainly the reader does not care that Mercator's map differs from Poe's, particularly since both would be rather fanciful "maps." Perhaps Poe returns to his early tale once again in order to make a point about the nature of narrative itself.

In a sense, the narrative of return is necessarily a cartographic enterprise. That is, like the explorers of Mercator's sixteenth century, personal narratives brought back the raw data, including geographic information, and re-presented it in an organized or systematic form. The travel narratives were themselves maps, filling in the hitherto blank spaces with newly discovered details, thus making sense of the unknown by representing it within a familiar structure of knowledge. With irreversible narrative, the mapping project unravels. Rather than assuming the ability to represent the uncanny and the unknown, Poe's irreversible narrative calls into question the means and the processes of representation. Lacking a return, the tale also lacks a clear representation. The skeptical and rational narrator, to his own horror, turns out to be unable to comprehend what is happening. The personal narrative form, which takes as its fundamental project the discovery or representation of that which had been previously unknown, loses its ability to enlighten. The voyage of discovery cannot disclose that which is discovered. The effect of all of this is deeply alienating. That alienation may be figured as an inability to represent one's position within the world, or, in other words, the inability to map.[28] The collapse of personal narrative in Poe's tale allegorizes that alienation. Unable to accurately map, one is irretrievably lost. Something similar happens with the abrupt, incomplete ending of *The Narrative of Arthur Gordon Pym*, as the appended "editor's note" only appears to offer some explanation, but leaves the reader more bewildered than ever. The personal narrative form, like an individual's itinerary through a crowded city, cannot offer the clarifying overview of a map, even if the narrative arrogates to itself all the scientific pretensions of knowledge production.[29] This fundamental unknowability seems to be a crucial aspect of Poe's own perverse theory and practice of literature. His subterranean noises, his notes from the underground, or, here, his messages from the deep, found floating at sea, disrupt the familiar discourses in the centers of American culture above ground or on dry land.

"MS. Found in a Bottle" might be viewed as a challenge to the established personal narrative form so prevalent and popular in mid-nineteenth-century American letters.

[28] See Fredric Jameson's conception of cognitive mapping, especially in his *Postmodernism, or, The Cultural Logic of Late Capitalism*, 51–4, 399–418.

[29] On this distinction between itinerary and map, see Michel de Certeau, *The Practice of Everyday Life*, 115–30.

Whether explicitly incorporating national narrative elements or merely serving national narrative through its form of knowledge production, personal narratives employed the figure of return to re-inscribe a national ideology within a national culture that is still in formation. By questioning the authority of the narrator, by openly acknowledging the operation of fate or chance, and by disallowing any rehabilitation through return to normalcy, Poe's narrative perverts the governing ethos of nineteenth-century American culture, as represented in many of its most popular fictional and nonfictional narratives. In "MS. Found in a Bottle," the inability to map, the failure of narrative to disclose the truth, the ineluctable downward trajectory into the unknown, all haunt the project of personal and national narrative, so persistently undertaken by the writers of this era. The poetics of descent discloses Poe's anomalous power in American literature, a power more suited to seeing things from below, from a perspective located at sea-level or on the street rather than from some lofty vista, such as the vantage of the ludicrously twirling transcendentalist philosopher atop Mount Ætna in the opening passage of *Eureka*. The false knowledge that the transcendental reader only seems to gain from some imaginary perch in the heavens must yield, in Poe, to the earthly observer's recognition of the ultimate inscrutability of the text.

4

The Nightmare of the Unknowable

Poe begins and ends his enigmatic story "The Man of the Crowd" with the phrase, *er lässt sich nicht lesen*, "it does not permit itself to be read."[1] This curious tale or sketch emphasizes the point as the narrator follows his fascinating but illegible subject through the streets of London all night and throughout the following day; at the end of these wild perambulations, he knows no more about the man than he did at first, and he is unable to bring his reader any closer to understanding—to really *knowing*—this "man of the crowd." The narrator had prided himself on his ability to "read, even in that brief interval of a glance, the history of long years" in the visages of each passerby,[2] and he acts as a kind of social scientist in identifying, classifying, ranking, and judging the multifarious crowds of pedestrians streaming past his coffeehouse window. However, this story only pretends to offer a kind of fictional anthropology or psychology, a pseudo-science that will grant us a view into the unknown in order to solve a riddle posed by it, only to pull the rug out from under us. At the end of the tale, the mysterious figure remains a mystery; the hieroglyphic remains indecipherable. The narrator's conclusion, that this man of the crowd is "the type and genius of true crime," does not so much offer any understanding of the old man's character as it proffers the notion of inscrutability itself as a terrifying prospect. Like his counterpart, the author of a manuscript found in a bottle, this narrator had seemed so self-assured and knowledgeable but now finds himself "at sea" in the city, in a world of strangers, with an ominous and pervasive uncertainty coloring his interactions. As a dramatization of the futility of reading, "The Man of the Crowd" is itself a tale that does not allow itself to be read. The same observation might apply to much of Poe's work, in which inscrutability is itself a basis for terror. This is the nightmare of the unknowable.

The legitimate sources of terror

If Poe is perhaps best known today for his tales of terror, it is worth noting that the inscrutable, or that which will not let itself be read, seems to lie at the heart of

---

[1] Poe, "The Man of the Crowd," *Poetry and Tales*, 388, 396.
[2] Ibid., 392.

many of them. To some extent, Poe's engagement with the inscrutable follows from his powerful conceptual affiliations with transatlantic Romanticism, whose practitioners frequently sought to represent the unrepresentable by giving form to mystic, ecstatic, or ineffable experience. Whatever it is that invokes real terror, for Poe, cannot be adequately understood. Famously, Poe defended his work from charges of "Germanism" by situating terror in an altogether different locus. "If in many of my productions terror has been the thesis, I maintain that terror is not of Germany, but of the soul." According to Poe, as he continues in the preface to his *Tales of the Grotesque and Arabesque*, he "deduced this terror only from its legitimate sources, and urged it only to its legitimate results."[3] Terror is "of the soul," the *ego* or *res cogitans* of Descartes, the very seat of knowledge and knowability, and in locating this terror at its source and extrapolating it to its foreseeable ends through his perverse narratives, Poe establishes inscrutability itself as the most terrifying phenomenon.

This terror is rightly associated with both the *grotesque* and the *arabesque*, terms Poe almost certainly adopted from Sir Walter Scott's famous 1827 essay on E. T. A. Hoffmann, entitled "On the Supernatural in Fictitious Composition." In Scott, the terms appear to be nearly synonymous, and both seem to mean little more than *Gothic* or even just *bizarre* or *baroque*.[4] Notwithstanding his nearly compulsive propensity for classification or categorization elsewhere, as with his distinction between originality and peculiarity or between the analytical and the merely attentive,[5] Poe does not really make much of a distinction between the grotesque and the arabesque either. However, when one considers that Scott had employed these terms in a rather disparaging way to suggest that Hoffmann had exceeded the bounds of good taste, the fact that Poe elected to name his first published collection of short stories *Tales of the Grotesque and Arabesque* demonstrates that he found the terms less objectionable, or even, more positively, that he embraced the terms outright. Or perhaps he felt that the title would better attract readers and book-purchasers. Poe would have undoubtedly taken the latter consideration to be as significant as the former.

Even if Scott or Poe did not make a clear distinction, others have, and one way that readers have drawn the line between the two is by designating as *grotesque* the horrifically unfamiliar or weird, while using the label *arabesque* to refer to the bizarre and complicated. In this distinction, one can still see that both genres would operate in such a way as to undermine clear and distinct knowledge.[6] Eerie tales of the inexplicable would plunge the reader deeper into the unknown, and their narrators are able to, and rarely attempt to, lead the reader back out of the labyrinth, but more often offer up the unknown and the unknowable as the final horror. Take, for example, the

---

[3] Poe, "Preface (*Tales of the Grotesque and Arabesque*—1840)," ibid., 129.
[4] It should be remembered that, before the term was re-evaluated in the wake of Heinrich Wölfflin's art history and then its embrace by modernist critics such as Walter Benjamin, the word "baroque" was almost always used in a strictly derogatory sense to refer to unnecessarily or excessively ornate architecture; it was often used as a synonym of the word "bizarre."
[5] See Poe, "Nathaniel Hawthorne," *Essays and Reviews*, 580–2; and "The Murders in the Rue Morgue," *Poetry and Tales*, 397–9.
[6] For a rather different view of this distinction, see Daniel Hoffman's *Poe Poe Poe Poe Poe Poe Poe*, 201–27.

house of Usher's unaccountably catastrophic collapse into the "black and lurid tarn" while the narrator, who never fully understood or reported the underlying causes of the structural instability of the edifice or of the family, flees in horror. Similarly, in the complexity of an arabesque tale, the reader is lost and becomes uncertain. The Byzantine intricacy and detail enhance the confusion and thwart the reader's and narrator's best efforts at comprehension, as in the perplexities of the narrator's studies with the Lady Ligeia with "the goal of wisdom too divinely precious not to be forbidden!"[7] In both cases, the specter of unknowability is at the root of the experience of terror. Such terror clearly interacts with the strange or exotic, and it typically manifests itself as the form of a fear of the unknown. Much more fearsome still is the unknowable, the dim and gloomy sense that what is at first merely unfamiliar and perplexing is actually inscrutable, something that we do not and cannot ever really understand. As Poe maintains, the soul is both the source of terror and the ground upon which it unfolds, and yet the soul is also the seat of knowledge, the foundation upon which all other knowledge was to be built. The Cartesian *res cogitans* or "thinking thing," which was supposed to safeguard our understanding of ourselves and the world, stamping rational meaning upon the chaos of unmeaning out there, is now implicated in the very fears it was to have dispelled. The whole Enlightenment project of demystification takes its point of departure from this Copernican revolution in thought, which enables the human mind or soul to gain the upper hand over the phenomenal and bewildering world "out there," allowing the mind to obliterate the terrors of the unknowable through rational understanding. In a number of Poe's tales of the grotesque and arabesque, this selfsame soul turns out to be the very source of such terrors. Without this trustworthy foundation upon which to stand and interpret, this terror "of the soul" reasserts itself emphatically as a terrifying inscrutability.

Poe's work frequently renders problematic the relation between storytelling and knowing. In tales such as "MS. Found in a Bottle," or "The Man of the Crowd," Poe makes the seemingly knowledgeable narrator a kind of dupe, one who prides himself on his knowledge and perspicacity only to discover that he cannot really figure out what is happening. In some cases, the reader is the one who is duped, as in "The Balloon-Hoax," whereby Poe obviously delighted in his ability to gull readers into believing a story that is utterly fantastic. Elsewhere, for example in "The Facts in the Case of M. Valdemar," Poe presents a quasi-scientific case study that some readers did accept as true; although there is some question as to whether it was Poe's intent to fool the reader, Poe was apparently delighted that he had been able to do so. Poe first published the tale under his own name as "Facts of M. Valdemar's Case" in early December 1845 in the *American Review*. It apparently elicited such interest that Poe almost immediately reprinted it in the *Broadway Journal* on December 20, 1845, adding an editorial note (signed "*Ed. B. J.*") clearly designed to fuel speculation: "An article of ours, thus entitled, was published in the last number of Mr. Colton's 'American Review,' and has given rise to some discussion—especially in regard to the truth or falsity of the statements made. It does not become *us*, of course, to offer one

---

[7] Poe, "Ligeia," *Poetry and Tales*, 266.

word on the point at issue. We have been requested to reprint the article, and do so with pleasure. We leave it to speak for itself. We may observe, however, that there are a certain class of people who pride themselves upon Doubt, as a profession." Unlike "The Balloon-Hoax," therefore, in which Poe colluded with the editor of *The New York Sun* to produce an *Extra* morning edition and went to great lengths to provide the relevant context in which the narrative could more readily be believed as factual, here Poe seems to have been pleasantly surprised by the tale's reception among the more credulous readers. That such a fantastic tale could be accepted by some as true demonstrated Poe's talent for verisimilitude. For example, in April 1846, Elizabeth Barrett (not yet married to Robert Browning) wrote a letter to Poe, reporting that "[t]here is a tale of yours [...] which is going the round of the newspapers, about mesmerism, throwing us all into 'most admired disorder,' and dreadful doubts as to whether 'it can be true,' as the children say of ghost stories. The certain thing in the tale in question is the power of the writer, and the faculty he has of making horrible improbabilities seem near and familiar."[8] Later, in response to one curious reader, Poe stated that " 'Hoax' *is* precisely the word suited to M. Valdemar's case. [...] Some few persons believe it—but *I* do not—and don't you."[9]

If Poe's "hoaxes" place the reader in an uncomfortable position,[10] it is one not much more awkward than that in which the reader is situated by his apparent non-hoaxes. In a number of stories, the reader is forced to question the reality of the events and sentiments presented, to question whether to take seriously the narrative unfolding before the reader's eyes, and to wonder what, if any, knowledge is really to be gained. Even taking these narratives as sheer entertainments, Poe's readers must be perplexed, forever asking just what the hell is going on. Poe shapes his stories in such a way that the narratives themselves thwart the aim of clear understanding, deconstructing their meanings on their very pages.[11] An underlying project in many tales seems to be the critique of knowledge itself. Indeed, the principal characteristic of Poe's tales of terror, if not his writings more generally, is inscrutability, or the inability to read clearly and to know with even remote certainty. This, in the final analysis, is the true horror of Poe's writings: it is less the fear of the unknown, which at least suggests the possibility of knowing and hence of dispelling the fear, than the terror of unknowability.

As discussed in the previous chapter, in "MS. Found in a Bottle," the unnamed narrator's thrill of "discovery" literally descends into the unknown and the unknowable. The very narrative style serves to highlight the inscrutability of the experience, as the first-person narration shifts its forms, tenses, and emotional intensity during the tale. While the conceit manifested in the title assures the reader that the tale is authentic,

---

[8] See Thomas and Jackson, *The Poe Log*, 632.

[9] Poe, "To Arch Ramsey" (December 30, 1846), *The Letters of Edgar Allan Poe*, 337.

[10] On Poe's satirical hoaxing more generally, see Dennis Eddings's edited collection, *The Naiad Voice*.

[11] Perhaps such a facet of Poe's narratives helps to explain the powerful effect they have had upon a number of poststructuralist thinkers, famously including Lacan and Derrida. See, e.g. Jacques Lacan, "Seminar on 'The Purloined Letter' "; Jacques Derrida, "The Purveyor of Truth," as well as the other essays in John P. Muller and William J. Richardson, eds, *The Purloined Poe: Lacan, Derrida, and Psychoanalytic Reading*. See also Patrick Quinn, *The French Face of Poe* (Carbondale: Southern Illinois University Press, 1971).

the narration belies it, as it begins in a calm, dry, reflective autobiographical style (including the past or perfect tense), then moves to a more fragmentary style of diary entries, then breathlessly scrawls its final message as the mysterious ship plunges into the vortex. A quite similar pattern occurs on a larger scale in *The Narrative of Arthur Gordon Pym*, but "MS. Found in a Bottle" already offers a useful dramatization of this nightmare of the unknowable.

This inscrutability is registered in "MS. Found in a Bottle" with respect to the narrator's failed attempts at reading the scene before him and to his frustrated attempts to understand himself. Both the "impossible" men he sees on the ghostly ship and his own self are unreadable, as the narration oscillates among various narrative voices and modes. These shifts may be registered by comparing a few lines from the text. The opening words of the narrative lay out the *faux* autobiographical foundation, while also omitting or withholding the sort of information that most readers of personal narratives would desire. "Of my country and my family I have little to say. Ill usage and length of years have driven me from the one, and estranged me from the other."[12] In other words, an "I" is firmly established as the narrator, but very little about the narrator will be known. Indeed, the remainder of the first paragraph is devoted to establishing the narrator's credibility. By underscoring how rational and how unimaginative he is, the narrator insists that he is the least likely type of person to create fictions or to be taken in by "the *ignes fatui* of superstition." Yet, aside from being the sort of person who thinks in a certain way, the narrator's personality and history are completely unknown. In some respects, this comports with the generic conventions of nineteenth-century personal narrative, which tended to present extroverted accounts of unfamiliar or exotic experiences, rather than introspective narratives of spiritual or personal development, as, for example, in eighteenth-century narratives of religious experience like Jonathan Edwards's "Personal Narrative" or twentieth-century autobiographies that likely include some type of psychological auto-analysis. However, Poe's perversion of the conventions of personal narrative undermines the authority of such narratives, an authority that rests in personal narratives' purported ability to know or to understand the exotic or foreign experiences they contain. Again, *narrative* by definition was supposed to be in the business of "knowing,"[13] but in Poe's narratives, the aesthetic force comes from the subversion of narrative's truth-telling conventions.

The first half of "MS. Found in a Bottle" recounts events in the somewhat dispassionate past tense, explaining the odd things that have happened, but maintaining a relatively sober tone of one merely describing one's experiences and encounters. As I discussed in Chapter 3, a curious break midway through the text—emphasized by a literal interruption in the textual layout of the page, with a single paragraph separated from the foregoing and subsequent text by a series of asterisks—offers a change in the narration ... and in the narrator. "A feeling, for which I have no name, has taken possession of my soul—a sensation which will admit of no analysis, to which the lessons of by-gone times are inadequate, and for which I fear futurity itself will offer

---

[12] Poe, "MS. Found in a Bottle," *Poetry and Tales*, 189.
[13] Arac, *The Emergence of American Literary Narrative*, 76–7.

me no key. To a mind constituted like my own, the latter consideration is an evil. I shall never—I know that I shall never—be satisfied with regard to the nature of my conceptions."[14] This presents the romantic transformation from rational man of science into sensitive, and notably passive, subject of mystical or inexplicable experience. Not only is the ineffable experience something that "will admit of no analysis," but apparently it cannot even be articulated. He who would *know* has become a narrator who only knows that he *cannot* know. The sensation that admits of no analysis is a text that does not allow itself to be read. So, too, is the reader now placed in the untenable position of not being able to read, or at least to interpret with confidence, this text either, since the source of its authority is now wholly compromised. Moreover, Poe is introducing the text's inscrutability at the very moment at which a kind of knowledge, or at least, a new sensibility or a new conception, has presumably been discovered by the narrator, exacerbating the frustration of anyone who desires to know.

Following from this pivotal and bizarre little paragraph, the tense changes again. "It is long since I first trod the deck of this terrible ship, and the rays of my destiny are, I think, gathering into focus." The "is" and the "are" indicate that the narration has shifted from a personal narrative of interesting past experiences to a running commentary of almost immediately occurring events. Indeed, it is in this paragraph that the narrator announces his plan to write down his experiences (including, obviously, the foregoing text) and predicts that he will not survive to see it published, vowing instead to enclose his manuscript in a bottle and, "at the last moment," throw it into the sea.[15] Previously the reader had been allowed to follow without regard to its self-conscious textuality, apart from the guiding conceit of the title. Now, the inevitable consequence of this shift in tense and of the decision to foreground the *writtenness* of the tale is that the narrative ceases to venture into the unknown-but-still-knowable, and becomes a kind of perceptual barrage of stimuli that in themselves seem inscrutable. That is, the narrator is no longer the scientist collecting data and analyzing it at his leisure; from this point on, he moves to the unreflective present tense, as if to say, "I cannot make sense of this, but here it is! Do with it what you will." The experiences are, in the narrator's own estimation, "so utterly novel" as to admit of no analysis, which also seems to mean that it cannot really be understood, by himself or by the reader.

The final lines of "MS. Found in a Bottle" accelerate this process and amplify the inscrutability of the text by leaping into the future tense, and thus peremptorily foreclosing on any hope of understanding these experiences at some future time. The narrator himself indicates this by notifying the reader that he will be unable to consider the matter further. "But little time will be left me to ponder upon my destiny—the circles rapidly grow small—we are plunging madly within the grasp of the whirlpool—and amid a roaring, and bellowing, and thundering of ocean and of tempest, the ship is quivering, oh God! And—going down."[16] This ending serves to

---

[14]   Poe, "MS. Found in a Bottle," 195.
[15]   Ibid.
[16]   Ibid., 199.

consummate the title's foundational ruse and allows the manuscript to be transmitted by bottle, but it also invokes a fake scientific "discovery": that is, the discovery of the whirlpool at the South Pole.[17] Poe's bizarre footnote added to the final edition published after Poe's own death (and according to the note, it is Poe's not the narrator's) seems to "correct" the false impression left by the manuscript and cites no less an authority than the cartographer Gerardus Mercator to vouch for the "truth" that such a whirlpool must be located at "the (northern) Polar Gulf."[18] But this only confounds matters further. The pseudo-scientific explanation further undermines the sense of clear legibility by suggesting an alternative, false knowledge, typical of Poe's more direct hoaxes.

I have suggested that Poe uses this narration to undermine the personal narrative form, the appeal of which lay, in large part, in its ability to present scientific or quasi-scientific knowledge concerning those exotic regions its first-person narrators had explored. Indeed, a sign of both the popularity of personal narratives and the injunction that they be accurate or "true" may be seen in the fact that the publisher of *The Narrative of Arthur Gordon Pym*, Harper and Brothers, declined to publish Herman Melville's *Typee* in 1846 on the grounds that "it was impossible that it could be true and *therefore* was without real value."[19] Whereas the personal narrative form aimed at making the unfamiliar familiar, domesticating the exotic, or making the unknown known, Poe's perversion of the form strikingly asserts the inscrutability and unknowability of these uncanny experiences or events. With Poe, these cannot be "brought home" in the sense of being made knowable, and the anxiety or terror is therefore enhanced. At the risk of invoking another sort of "Germanism," Poe's treatment of the ineffable experiences might well be considered *unheimlich*, after Freud and Heidegger, who emphasize the very not-at-home-ness of the uncanny (or un-homely). "In anxiety one feels '*uncanny*' [*unheimlich*] […] but here 'uncanniness' also means 'not being at home.'"[20] As I will discuss later, this aspect of Poe's inscrutable tales of the grotesque and arabesque will distinguish it from the tradition of Gothic horror, as well as from other nineteenth-century narrative forms.

Terror as anti-epistemic

In what are generally regarded as tales of terror, such as "The Fall of the House of Usher" or "Ligeia," Poe deliberately puzzles his readers, leading them to imagine a stable meaning that then will not hold. In such stories, the lure of new knowledge is tantalizingly dangled before the reader's eyes, and often the narrator's as well, only to evanesce or, more frequently, to be violently dashed away. The prospect of scientific discovery forms a desire from which arises the pleasure of the text. What exactly this

17 For an interesting account of the ways in which the prospect of Antarctic exploration affected national self-fashioning in the United States, see Lenz, *The Poetics of the Antarctic*.
18 Poe, "MS. Found in a Bottle," *Poetry and Tales*, 199.
19 See Leyda, *A Melville Log*, 196, my emphasis.
20 Heidegger, *Being and Time*, 233.

knowledge is or is in relation to, is not always important; at times it appears to be arcane or forbidden knowledge, perhaps, while at others it may be the mere satisfaction of one's curiosity about some odd happenstance. But the terror that excites the reader often derives from the failure of knowledge, the persistence of the inscrutable. In such tales, Poe's famous single effect is enveloped in this terrifically unknowable phenomenon. If the pleasures of certain narratives may be found in the essentially epistemological project of figuring things out, solving mysteries, or simply learning something new, the terrors of others are fundamentally anti-epistemic.

In "The Fall of the House of Usher," for instance, we are presented with another unnamed and largely unknown narrator, who elaborates the wondrous events of the tale in a relatively straightforward, patient manner, thus inviting us to make sense of them. However, true to a form frequently employed in Poe's writings, this presentation is a ruse, and by the story's end the elements of the narrative render themselves inscrutable once more. An interesting illustration of the process can be found in the story's opening pages. The narrator's "childish experiment," in which he tries to look at the reflection of the mansion on the murky surface of a dark lake in an effort to alter the gloomy effect that the house has upon his spirits, turns out only to increase the "gloom" engendered by that scene.[21] This experiment is itself a spoof, a comical attempt to implement the romantic (and more specifically a Coleridgean) theory of the sublime for practical effect by rearranging the elements of the scene in order to disarm their power to affect the viewer. Of course, no one should be surprised to learn that the gloomy mansion would appear even gloomier by being distorted, not to mention upside-down, in the water's reflection. In attempting to fix things, to assign them stable meanings, and to understand them in their own being, the narrator, like Poe himself, demonstrates just how such methods are not only ineffective, but they also have the opposite of the intended effect: the act of reading the text seems to render the text all the more unreadable. Here Poe seems to be mocking the romantic view that the poet's use of the imagination can transform nature into the sublime, a theory express in Coleridge's *Biographia Literaria* and also adopted by Emerson in his belief that poets are "liberating gods" (as I discuss later in this chapter). The narrator experiences "an iciness, a sinking, a sickening of the heart—an unredeemed dreariness of thought which no goading of the imagination could torture into aught of the sublime."[22] In attempting to ascertain the cause of this sensation, he performs the experiment that offers him no enlightenment whatsoever, but only strengthens and deepens his original impression. Later in the same tale, Poe includes a scene of reading in order to introduce and frame the story's climax. In what amounts to an absurd blend of horror and humor, Poe's narrator reads the grotesque chivalric romance of a doughty knight, Ethelred, the "Mad Trist" of Launcelot Canning (a preposterous-sounding romance invented by Poe for this tale). The point of reading "The Mad Trist," humorous as it seems, is to calm Roderick Usher's nerves, but the effect is just the opposite, of course, and the ghastly end to the tale leaves us no more knowledgeable about the goings-on

[21] Poe, "The Fall of the House of Usher," *Poetry and Tales*, 317–19.
[22] Ibid., 317.

at the house of Usher than the narrator had been when receiving his first impression of the mansion in the opening paragraph. The narrator can encounter and witness the phenomenon of the fall of the house of Usher, but neither he nor the reader has any greater certainties about it. It is another text that does not let itself be read.

In "Ligeia," knowledge, or rather, unknowability, might be considered the actual subject of the tale, embodied in the figure of the mysterious woman herself. The narrator, just like those in "MS. Found in a Bottle" or "The Fall of the House of Usher," is not merely one who tells what he knows but, like the reader, one who *seeks to know*. He appears to perpetually withhold his knowledge even as he reveals it, or perhaps one could argue that his ignorance and his expertise are completely at odds throughout his narration. More to the point, his disclosure of what has happened is invariably mediated by the fact that he does not really understand what has happened. In the very first line, he bizarrely concedes that he cannot recall how he "became acquainted with" the woman who is the object of such intense passion and love. He suggests that her most powerful and distinguishing characteristics—"her rare learning, her singular yet placid cast of beauty, and the thrilling and enthralling eloquence of her low musical language"—entered his soul "unnoticed and unknown"; this "entity" entering his soul is also reminiscent of the narrator of the "MS. Found in a Bottle."[23] Yet, surprisingly, he admits that he has "*never known*" (emphasis in the original) Ligeia's family name. Hence, both the narrator and the subject of the study remain unknown. Many of the characteristics of Ligeia that *are* known, the reader discovers, turn out to be mental and physical attributes, especially the shape and luster of her eyes, to which lengthy descriptions are devoted. Ligeia's intellectual prowess is also known, and the narrator lovingly describes her supernatural intelligence, on display in her voluminous learning in the moral and physical sciences, mathematics, and the seemingly arcane, "forbidden" knowledge. The narrator's explanation of Ligeia's erudition builds to an ecstatic, and extremely erotic, climax in disclosing his sensations at being educated by her. "With how vast a triumph—with how vivid a delight—with how much of all that is ethereal in hope—did I *feel*, as she bent over me in studies but little sought—but less known—that delicious vista by slow degrees expanding before me, down whose long, gorgeous, and all untrodden path, I might at length pass onward to the goal of wisdom too divinely precious not to be forbidden."[24] The phantasmagoria that follows from Ligeia's death and the narrator's second marriage makes visible the grotesque and arabesque features of the "divinely precious" wisdom, but the narrator's delirium, as well as his confessed opium haze, renders any prospect of acquirable knowledge a dubious proposition. In the apocalyptic end, the avatar of knowledge is a hallucinatory vision, not a triumphant revelation.[25]

The horror of tales such as these lies not in a particular fright, but in a general mood of uncertainty. Again and again, Poe presents the arcane, the exotic, the

---

[23] Poe, "Ligeia," ibid., 262.

[24] Ibid., 266.

[25] Etymologically, *apocalypse* relates to disclosure or uncovering (from the Greek), but in Poe's tales the apocalyptic endings frequently leave matters veiled. In "Ligeia," the mystery of the story's end only compounds the mysteries unfolding at the story's beginning.

otherworldly, or unique, but he refuses to explicate in detail the foreign material and to bring it into a safe and familiar intellectual archive. On the contrary, Poe's work frequently undermines the scientific or pseudo-scientific practices of a more straight-forwardly empirical exposition, and he casts doubt on the possibility of reading the meaning of events from either their surfaces or their hidden depths. Poe injects greater uncertainty into such proceedings. Even in the detailed science fiction of a work like "The Facts in the Case of M. Valdemar," which is written almost in the form of a sort of medical case study, the horror of the inexplicable and unknowable undermines the scientific knowledge it purports to present. The last word there, as always, involves the arrogance of imagining that this knowledge is actually attainable. Poe's work actively defies interpretation, at times subtly and at others overtly undermining the reader's assumptions that the story's "meaning" will reveal itself. In some pieces, like the "tales of ratiocination" or "Descent into the Maelstrom" or "The Gold-Bug," Poe is willing to offer some explanation of the puzzles presented, but, more often than not, Poe's texts frustrate the desire for comprehension. Even in those tales in which an explanation to the mystery is provided, as, for instance, in "The Man That Was Used Up," where the searching narrator finally learns the grotesque truth behind the rumors about Brigadier General John A. B. C. Smith, Poe is as likely to confound as to confirm the reader's surmises. Unlike modern detective fiction, to name a familiar genre, the readers are not given clues. They are never really invited to solve the mysteries themselves, but are asked only to marvel at the ingenuity of the author who has so entertained them with his insoluble puzzles. Perhaps this is another variation on the theme of a text that does not allow itself to be read.

Unfathomability

The narrator in "MS. Found in a Bottle" marvels at the strange sailors who inhabit the spectral ship: "Incomprehensible men!" Poe makes incomprehensibility a hallmark of the tales of mystery, suspense, and terror. As a young man, he seems to have found the nightmare of the unknowable within his own breast. As a contemporary put it, "[h]e said often that there was a mystery hanging over him he could never fathom."[26] Poe's tales also present mysteries that cannot be fathomed, texts that do not let themselves be read.

Poe's Dupin trilogy, the "tales of ratiocination," would seem to offer a notable counter-example, but even in these mysteries Poe does not really give the reader the satisfaction of interpreting clues and gaining knowledge. Rather than offering a puzzle, like a crossword or a Sudoku, where the pleasure is derived precisely from figuring it out, Poe insists on insoluble puzzling. Although the genre of detective fiction would seem to offer the very model for enjoyable puzzle-solving, Poe's Dupin stories continue to emphasize the inscrutability of his subject. Unlike later examples in the detective genre, Poe's tales do not really invite the readers to "play" the detective,

---

[26] Mary Devereaux, quoted in Ackroyd, *Poe: A Life Cut Short*, 58.

to solve the mystery themselves. Rather, Poe places the reader in the position of the perplexed observer who will stand in awe of the ingenious person who actually *can* figure things out. As the unnamed narrator of the three Dupin mysteries indicates in his own often astonished *reportage* of the particulars of each case, C. Auguste Dupin's analytical prowess is itself a marvel. Dupin's powers lie in his own uncanny ability to read, whether he is reading clues (as in "The Murders in the Rue Morgue") or reading people (as in "The Purloined Letter"). But we, the readers of the tales themselves, cannot read such clues or persons in the same way.

Poe's famous amateur detective is introduced in "The Murders in the Rue Morgue" only after the fine distinction is made between the chess-player, who merely pays close attention to pieces and moves on the chessboard, and the draughts- or whist-player, who must also be able to analyze his or her opponent. Poe introduces this story by noting that "[t]he mental features discoursed of as analytical are, in themselves, but little susceptible of analysis."[27] Hence, even the faculty for which Dupin (like Poe?) is best known is itself tantalizingly unknowable. Further, Dupin represents a reader that Poe's work does not, in the end, permit any of us to be. Poe acknowledged this aspect of the tales of ratiocination, and joked about how some readers confused the ingenuity of the detective with that of the author. In response to his friend Phillip Pendleton Cooke's observation that Dupin is "fine in his deductions from over-laid & unnoticed small facts, but sometimes too minute & hair-splitting," Poe writes:

> You are right about the hair-splitting of my French friend: —that is all done for effect. These tales of ratiocination owe most of their popularity to being something in a new key. I do not mean to say that they are not ingenious—but people think them more ingenious than they are—on account of their method and *air* of method. In the "Murders in the Rue Morgue," for instance, where is the ingenuity of unravelling a web which you yourself (the author) have woven for the express purpose of unravelling? The reader is made to confound the ingenuity of the supposititious Dupin with that of the writer of the story.[28]

Hence, the real mystery might be Dupin himself, whose enigmatic background makes him another Ligeia or Roderick Usher, but one whose fantastic intelligence or madness lies in ratiocination rather than phantasm.[29] These detective stories, like the tales of terror, present knowledge not so much as a problem, something to be gleaned or solved, but as a wonder, something to be marveled at. Dupin's apparent ability to read the inscrutable text makes our own inability to read, and the text's inscrutability, all the more striking.

In his quarter-deck speech explaining why he must pursue Moby Dick, Ahab tells Starbuck and the crew, "[h]e tasks me; he heaps me; I see in him outrageous strength, with an inscrutable malice sinewing it. That *inscrutable* thing is what I chiefly hate; and be the white whale agent, or be the white whale principal, I will wreak that hate upon

---

[27] Poe, "The Murders in the Rue Morgue," *Poetry and Tales*, 397.

[28] Poe, "To Phillip P. Cooke" (August 9, 1846), *The Letters of Edgar Allan Poe*, 328.

[29] This is a point also made by Silverman; see his *Edgar A. Poe: A Mournful and Never-ending Remembrance*, 172.

him."[30] In Melville's novel, it seems that it is really inscrutability itself, rather than the inscrutability of the underlying "malice," that is most hated. The inability to read and know is a concern throughout the novel, as Ishmael's cetological system must remain "a draught of a draught," and the Leviathan "must remain unpainted to the last," and "the mystic-marked whale remains undecipherable." Melville actually concludes his chapter on the "face" of the whale with a brazen taunt: "Read it if you can." Poe and Melville, so different in so many respects, both recognized the horror of inscrutability in the context of the nineteenth-century United States. In a society self-consciously fashioning itself as a model for future successes, such inscrutability appears as a real terror, a repressed but urgent, unconscious tainting of that "optative mood" and "progressive" vision of mid-nineteenth-century American thought.

This is what Harry Levin discussed years ago in *The Power of Blackness*, in which he says "our [i.e., the United States'] most perceptive minds have distinguished themselves from our popular spokesmen by concentrating on the dark half of the situation."[31] Tocqueville had recognized that American ideology was thoroughly imbued with dreams of scientific and social progress, progress based in part on the firm belief that knowledge will helpfully expand horizons and that the world and everything in it are indeed legible. Is not the very label, "American Renaissance,"[32] an acknowledgement of this hope? But Levin argued that that other part of America, the subterranean or dark vision of a mysterious, inscrutable world, was typical of a powerful counter-cultural strain in American literature. Melville and Hawthorne picked up on it, but Poe appeared to make such perverse terror his stock-in-trade.[33]

Poe is more anomalous still. Much of what I have been discussing as Poe's exploration of the unknowable and his inscrutability would seem to place him firmly within a Romantic or Gothic tradition, a tradition in which, by reputation at least, he has long been at home. It is certainly true that Poe is strongly influenced by Romanticism and that many of his tales deploy conventions of the Gothic genre to great effect. But, as Ecaterina Hanțiu has noted in "Humor and Satire in Edgar Allan Poe's Absurd Stories,"

> The Gothic revival in America had to do not so much with monsters, vampires or apparitions, but with people and their inner phantasms. Romantic irony and baroque elements, poetry and cruelty are intermingled with laughter and horror in the works of the American writers attracted by such issues. Poe created a whole by uniting opposites and his work always makes his readers aware of man's

---

[30] Melville, *Moby-Dick, or, the Whale*, 164, my emphasis. The other quotations in this paragraph are from pages 145, 264, 306, and 347, respectively.

[31] Levin, *The Power of Blackness*, 7.

[32] As Levin explains, he—rather than his mentor, F. O. Matthiessen—is actually responsible for this term. "Matthiessen had wanted to call his book, after an apt phrase from Whitman, *Man in the Open Air*. The publisher had wanted something more descriptively categorical. My groping formulation must have caught Matthiessen's liberal idealism, his warm feeling for the creative potentialities of American life. But it left out that 'vision of evil' which clouds the hopeful picture from time to time" (vii–viii).

[33] On Poe as a force opposing, or rather *perverting*, Matthiessen's vision of an American renaissance, see Betsy Erkkila, "Perverting the American Renaissance: Poe, Democracy, Critical Theory," in Kennedy and McGann, *Poe and the Remapping of Antebellum Print Culture*, 65–100.

mysterious position in the universe. He seems to suggest that there are impenetrable areas that surround things we can never understand, things that bring forth anxiety and a sense of loss.[34]

Poe's inscrutability cannot really be ascribed to his Romantic or Gothic affiliations, and I am tempted to add that this disposition in Poe actually distinguishes his work from what is traditionally understood as the Gothic. In other words, Poe's terror, the nightmare of the unknowable, is not actually compatible with the terror commonly associated with Gothic literature.[35]

Although the Gothic is a genre well known, indeed perhaps paradigmatically known, for its presentation of the mysterious, the fantastic, and the terrifying, Gothic novels in practice tend to domesticate these terrors, in so far as they offer up a comforting narrative in which to contain the inscrutable elements. Gothic novels frequently introduce the exotic only to integrate it by mapping its strangeness onto a more familiar terrain. In *The Gothic Text*, Marshall Brown proposes a surprising reassessment of Gothic literature in the era of Romanticism. Contrary to expectation, Brown's first thesis concerning the genre is that "[r]omantic gothic fiction is not exciting." Although some students today find Gothic tales boring, we generally think of the Gothic as a genre which offers a great deal of excitement. But, as Brown explains, "[f]ascination rather than excitement is the hypnotic core of the great gothic novels."[36] Because Gothic novels tend to be devoted to a kind of epistemological project—that is, they are interested precisely in *knowing*—the fascination is largely intellectual and not visceral. Indeed, Brown maintains that lack of excitement, rather than the inability to maintain a "unity of effect," may have been the real reason Poe was so opposed to the length of the novel form. "But if there is a comprehensible reason why Poe dismissed long fiction as an impossibility, it is perhaps because the novels in his gothic mode do in fact constitutively lack the excitement he sought."[37] Noting the lengthy descriptive passages in Horace Walpole or Ann Radcliffe devoted to landscapes or architecture, Brown understands Gothic novels as participating in a project similar to that of many philosophical texts, notably Immanuel Kant's *Critique of Pure Reason*. In other words, the Gothic text is fundamentally epistemological, and the function of the novels in the genre is to bring the unfamiliar data of sensual experience into the structural framework of a knowable system. Scrutability, therefore, lies at their heart.

Poe's appreciation for excitement[38] might already disqualify his work from Brown's definitions of the Gothic, but another factor would seem to be Poe's commitment to inscrutability, for in most of his ostensibly Gothic writings, mysteries remain stubbornly mysterious and the unexplained somehow persists in being inexplicable.

---

[34] Hanţiu, "Humor and Satire in Edgar Allan Poe's Absurd Stories," 34.
[35] I am not, of course, arguing that Poe's writings are in no way Gothic, although I do think that, as with so many of the genres Poe employed, Poe often uses Gothic tropes in a satirical way.
[36] Brown, *The Gothic Text*, 3, 4.
[37] Ibid., 4.
[38] In his 1847 essay on Hawthorne, Poe writes: "A poem must intensely excite. Excitement is its province, its essentiality. Its value is in the ratio of its (elevating) excitement." See Poe, "Nathaniel Hawthorne," *Essays and Reviews*, 584.

In a sense, Poe's work is opposed to the Gothic, inasmuch as the Gothic as understood by Brown presents mysteries only in order to explain them away. "As their chaotic events unfold, the novels return insistently to problems of orientation in time and place, to coherence of experience in a world of magic or mystery, to participation in a community under threat of isolation—in short, to the various continuities of meaning that stabilize a world at risk."[39] Thus, the Kantian acknowledgement of the limits of reason nevertheless functions as another way of establishing the comfortable knowability of the world. In constructing an epistemological framework, the Kantian critique of "pure reason" becomes a homely or familiar system for understanding precisely those ineffable phenomena that first struck the individual as irremediably strange. But Poe will not allow space for this comforting domestication. Poe insists on insoluble puzzling, where the principal investigator does not actually gain knowledge so much as he or she recognizes the ineffability and uncertainty of knowledge. Poe's terror, which, we recall, is not of Germany but of the soul, comes down to a nameless fear of the text that cannot be read.

It is for this reason that I respectfully disagree with the otherwise engaging argument of Jeremey Cagle, who argues that Poe's dramatization of illegibility in "The Man of the Crowd" makes Poe an apt figure, not only of Romanticism, but also of an American Transcendentalism embodied by Emerson and Thoreau. Although he acknowledges Poe's critique of Emerson's transcendentalism, Cagle concludes that Poe actually imagines that the transcendentalist ideal will win the day. "Poe's interest in exploring the irrational or unreadable—certainly a prominent theme in 'The Man of the Crowd'—is both a marked divergence from the *zeitgeist* of the mid-nineteenth century and also one of the hallmark tenets of romanticism which connects Poe to American Transcendentalists like Emerson and Thoreau."[40] Cagle argues that Poe resisted the rationalistic "Common Sense" philosophy of his day and embraced a "new philosophy" that incorporated the irrational or the perverse by virtue of a "Higher Reason" based on intuition or imagination, not on rationality itself. Drawing on Emerson's view of the Poet as a "liberating god" who "unlocks our chains, and admits us to a new scene,"[41] Cagle then argues that Poe endorses the image of the poet as the gifted and ideal *reader*, the one who can read well. In other words, rather than presenting us with a text that does not let itself be read, Poe (in Cagle's view) offers a critique of traditional scientific or rational reading techniques and promulgates a view of a poetic reading that somehow can read the unreadable texts.

This strikes me as a surprising misreading in its own right, all the more striking since Cagle does acknowledge, albeit *en passant*, Poe's active critique of Emerson's position. Citing Lawrence Buell's assessment of Emerson as a poet-priest of a fixed universal order—but, notably, not citing Emerson's view that the "religions of the world are the ejaculations of a few imaginative men,"[42] thus rendering poetry and religious thought

---

[39] Brown, *The Gothic Text*, xiv.
[40] Cagle, "Reading Well: Transcendental Hermeneutics in Poe's 'The Man of the Crowd,'" 29.
[41] Emerson, "The Poet," 277–8.
[42] Ibid., 279.

identical—Cagle observes that Poe "presents a riposte to Transcendentalists"[43] and that Poe utterly denies the Emersonian view that the poet has access to more liberated knowledge of the world. Poe's is not merely a kind of watered-down Romanticism, in which scientific method must take a back seat to poetic impulse; in fact, as his critical writings make perfectly clear, Poe does not view the poetic and scientific as a binary opposition, so much as he reserves for each certain proper terrain upon which to exert their characteristic powers. Poe makes a much more forceful argument about the actual legibility of phenomena. Emerson, the former Unitarian minister, must maintain that a transcendental Truth can not only be found but can be understood, whereas Poe is much more skeptical. When Poe notes, in "The Poetic Principle" (as elsewhere), that "[i]n the contemplation of Beauty we alone find it possible to attain that pleasurable elevation, or excitement, *of the soul,* which we recognize as the Poetic Sentiment, and which is so easily distinguished from Truth, which is the satisfaction of the Reason, or from Passion, which is the excitement of the heart,"[44] he is not saying that poetry provides a mere alternative form of truth-finding or knowledge, one epistemological form among such others as the rational treatise or the romantic story. That is, he does not believe that poetry is another, better way to read an otherwise illegible text. Rather, he is saying that the poetic principle operates differently and within a different sphere altogether: to wit, the *soul,* as distinct from the intellect. Just as the narrator of the "MS. Found in a Bottle" discovered "a new entity is added to my soul," describing it, but—and this is essential—*unable to interpret it,* as "a sensation that will admit of no analysis," so too does Poe allow ineffable experience to permeate his tales without allowing them "to be read." The terror, which is rightfully deep-seated in the soul itself, is one of inscrutability. The reader does not experience terror by reading tales of terrifying events, but rather encounters a vague, unspecified fear of not being able to make sense of these experiences. It has been suggested that Poe's humor is not really funny.[45] Whether that is true is a matter for further debate, I think, but in that spirit we might suggest that Poe's tales of terror are not actually scary. Instead, they are puzzling, perplexing, and unsettling.

Poe, as he apparently suspected in his youth, is unfathomable in this respect. Although he clearly maintains affiliations with various modes and schools of thought, Poe certainly cannot be captured by labels like Romantic, Gothic, Transcendentalist, Platonist, irrationalist, and so on. Just as his writings do not lend themselves easily to casual categorization according to genre, his subterranean literature thwarts our understanding of the sites it is frequently supposed to occupy. Like Poe himself, it is as if the works are in constant motion, and cannot be pinned down, or, at least, not for long. (Republished treatises on the nature and origin of subterranean noises still offer no clues.) Poe remains a savage anomaly in nineteenth-century American literature, and a part of that anomalous status is this unwavering presentation of the inscrutability of the texts his readers must encounter. Incomprehensible man! Much like his own man of the crowd, Poe is a text that does not permit itself to be read.

[43] Cagle, "Reading Well," 29.
[44] Poe, "The Poetic Principle," *Essays and Reviews,* 78.
[45] See, e.g. Quirk, *Nothing Abstract: Investigating in the American Literary Imagination,* 53–63.

5

Captivating the Reader

If Poe's tales of terror ultimately disclose the nightmare of the unknowable, his writings in other genres might offer even less comforting certitude. Despite the prevailing popular view of Poe as an author of spooky tales, complete with the image of Poe himself as a sort of "Goth," eldritch and melancholy and wreathed in darkness, Poe's success as a professional writer and artist often depended on his mastery of multiple forms. In a famous letter in which he complains that he has been "essentially a Magazinist," Poe laments that the reading public, that only reads "a paper here or there," will fail to give the author "his due on the score of *versatility*."[1] Poe clearly took pride in his own versatility, and endeavored to produce almost every recognized type of literature, as well as inventing new types if need be, in order to capture the imaginations and emotions of his readers. To use a phrase he employs in an essay on Catherine Maria Sedgwick, Poe hoped to achieve a species of tenure over the audience well suited to "literature proper." In accomplishing this goal, Poe would appear to have been a strong advocate of Voltaire's guiding literary principle: *tout les genres sont bons, hors le genre ennuyeux* ("all genres are good, except the boring genre").[2]

Perverse designs

Poe's literary theory and practice also summoned a demon that he would name the *imp of the perverse*. Poe's perversity is certainly visible in the psychological phenomenon he identifies as perverseness, in which one sometimes consciously and deliberately acts against one's own interest and better judgment so as to vex oneself, to thwart one's own desires, or to amplify one's own pain.[3] But one may also find the spirit of the perverse operating in Poe's peculiar approach to his craft, an approach that often prevents the author from making that communicative bond with the reader that would engender understanding and empathy.

---

[1] Poe, "To Charles Anthon" (*ante* November 2, 1844), *The Letters of Edgar Allan Poe*, 270–1.
[2] Voltaire, *L'Enfant Prodigue*, Preface.
[3] See "The Imp of the Perverse," *Poetry and Tales*, 827.

Poe's writing is itself perverse. In many of his short works, not only is the audience left baffled or uncertain about the events, experiences, and narrative voice of the tale, but the reader is also occasionally subjected to a sort of mockery and abuse. At times the reader may share in the joke, as when Poe invites his audience to recognize the satire of others, as in "The Man That Was Used Up," for instance, which pokes fun at both the celebration of war heroes and absurdities of the gossip mongers. At other times, readers themselves appear to be the butt of the joke, most obviously apparent in "The Balloon-Hoax," an elaborate practical joke involving a complicit newspaper publisher and an author's healthy disdain for the reading public. Even in those tales that were not designed to be hoaxes, like "The Facts in the Case of M. Valdemar" or "The Murders in the Rue Morgue," Poe delighted in "putting one over" on gullible readers.[4] Of course, part of Poe's delight arises from the implicit or explicit praise for his own talent, for only an extremely talented literary artist could produce a believable narrative of such patently fantastic events. Poe's skill at creating this *vraisemblance* indicated how great a writer he was. But this also suggests a more general skill, in which Poe also took some measure of pride. In elaborating his theory of what makes a work of fiction or poetry successful, Poe reveals the degree to which readers themselves must be carefully and thoroughly manipulated by the author. In Poe's view, the reader must be held captive, while the author generates sensations and engineers effects according to the author's own designs. There is something perverse about this entire process. Notwithstanding the sheer pleasure of reading experienced by so many of Poe's legions of fans, the readers of his tales are frequently his victims.

Poe's literary theory, broadly conceived, is supplemented by his view of what constitutes "literature proper." According to this view, the truly literary text must be the result of a special form of writing that maintains its hold on the minds of the readers through the talent or genius of a skilled artist, rather than by adventitious or inessential means. Although the highly aestheticized vision of the literary might seem at odds with the supposedly sub-literary genre fiction craved by an emerging mass market, Poe found no contradiction whatsoever between the high art valued by sensitive, critical readers and the mass appeal to be found by engaging in what might be denigrated as mere sensationalism or unwieldy extravagance. From Poe's perspective, the ability to captivate an audience is demonstrated precisely through one's skill in generating sensational and original combinations of images and plots, and the successful negotiation of these circumstances was the mark of literary genius. Poe sums it up neatly in an 1835 letter to Thomas W. White, the editor of *The Southern*

---

[4] Poe appears to have been a bit surprised, but then pleased, to learn that some readers had treated "The Facts in the Case of M. Valdemar" as nonfiction, and the tale was actually reprinted in a nonfiction work on the subject of Mesmerism. However, he also referred to the tale as a "hoax," warning one friend not to believe it. With "The Murders in the Rue Morgue" or "The Purloined Letter," many readers found Dupin's genius amazing, and Poe found their awe hilarious, since, after all, Poe had written both the mystery *and* the solution, so he had only fashioned puzzles the solution to which he also formed in advance, rather than solving unknown puzzles presented to him by others (a talent on which Poe also prided himself, of course). See Poe, "To Phillip P. Cooke" (August 9, 1846), *The Letters of Edgar Allan Poe*, 328.

Literary Messenger: "To be appreciated, you must be *read*."[5] As an artist who craved the good opinion of literary intellectuals as well as a wide readership among the magazine-buying public, Poe was certainly prepared to explore the various species of tenure over the minds of his readers if that would ensure both critical recognition and a substantial audience.

Even today, Poe remains best known to the public at large for Gothic tales of horror or suspense. In addition, he is often credited with inventing the genre of detective fiction with his Dupin trilogy or even with helping to launch science fiction with such *outré* stories as "The Unparalleled Adventure of One Hans Pfaall" and "The Facts in the Case of M. Valdemar," among other works. However, as scholars and enthusiasts well know, Poe wrote far more pieces that could be considered humor or satire, and he did so throughout his career, from some of his earliest fiction to his last. If his first published tale ("Metzengerstein," which some have viewed as a burlesque) was not meant to be comical, then certainly his second ("The Duc De L'Omelette") was, and one of the last tales published during Poe's lifetime, "X-ing a Paragrab," was a silly little piece lampooning the newspaper or magazine industry itself. As David Galloway has pointed out, "comedies, satires, and hoaxes account for over half of his output of short stories."[6] Thus, one could make the case that Poe was primarily a humorist, if sometimes a black humorist, and that his tales of terror or mystery were secondary to the main body of his collected works. It also seems to me that many of those tales that are viewed as "serious" or, at least, not intended as humor nevertheless contain elements of satire and critique which make them sometimes difficult to take seriously. Such aesthetically well wrought and philosophically or psychologically profound tales as "Ligeia," "The Fall of the House of Usher," or "The Oval Portrait" are still imbued with that perverse spirit of prankishness that permeates Poe's literary career. In "The Oval Portrait," for instance, the brief narrative of the portrait's production enables a grand build-up for what is essentially a bad joke: in the artist's otherworldly talent for verisimilitude, the model was literally painted to death! For the ungenerous critic, this could be a fable representing Poe's own method, in which the detailed representation of seemingly unrepresentable experiences and effects ultimately rob them of whatever life they had seemed to have. But this may be Poe's design, after all. One wonders, perhaps with good reason, whether Poe is laughing at us. Poe's laughter is itself rather unsettling, whether it is the maniacal cackling of a Roderick Usher or the mirthless giggles of Montresor and Fortunato in the catacombs or the triumphant harlequin's chortle of a Hop-Frog. Perhaps it is more like the laugh of Michel Foucault, fugitive and mocking, which Michel de Certeau has described, in suitably Poe-esque language, as "a live voice that still eludes the tomb of the text."[7]

As we have seen, Poe's tales of terror, of the grotesque and arabesque, frequently posit the unknown or unknowable as the truly horrifying phenomenon. The absence of fixed, stable, and wholly ascertainable meanings is dramatized in such works as

---

[5] Poe, "To Thomas W. White" (April 30, 1835), ibid., 58.
[6] Galloway, "Introduction," *The Other Poe*, 8.
[7] Certeau, "The Laugh of Michel Foucault," 193–4.

"The Man of the Crowd" in the inherent inscrutability of the narrator's putative subject, a text that does not permit itself to be read. Poe's meditation on the inscrutable goes a step further in his analysis of "the spirit of perversity," which the narrator of "The Black Cat" calls "this unfathomable longing of the soul to *vex itself*."[8] Here, it is not only the text that is illegible, but the reader as well. The spirit of perverseness disrupts the Cartesian certitude and integrity of the ego, and Poe's narrator notes, in "The Imp of the Perverse," that the only reason science has overlooked this *primum mobile* of the human soul is "the pure arrogance of the reason."[9] Poe's critique of rational inquiry, of the system of classification in psychology and philosophy that renders the text—here, the individual human subject itself—unknowable, might be compared to the Foucauldian exposition of unreason and the Deleuzian analysis of the encounter with stupidity.[10] With perverseness, Poe introduces an element that confounds the sense-making project, imposing an uncertainty principle on the agent and the author, as well as on the subject and the text. Poe's critical theory thus opposes itself to the more hopeful and progressive ideologies of the science and literature of the American Renaissance.[11]

Poe's perverse literary theory is further developed in his well-known conception of the "single effect," which requires a skilled but also dominant author to captivate the reader, at least for the limited duration of the poem or tale. In Poe's assessment, the effectiveness of a work can be gauged only in its ability to produce in the reader a desired effect. The poem or short story thus operates upon the reader, who is held captive by an author who seeks to exert such control through literary talent or genius. Like the narrators of "The Black Cat" and "The Raven," the reader is here swept up in a process of vexing oneself by continuing to read.

The effective power of the imagination, as Poe conceives it, is tied to the author's apparatus of capture. The literary work is a trap, in which the reader or critic is ensnared. In some respects, we can see that this is an alternative vision of genre itself, in which the generic boundaries designate various modes of surrounding and hemming in the reader's own imagination. Rather than seeing genre as a sort of implied contract by which the author and reader agree to limit the excessive interpretations a reader could extract from a given work, Poe attempts to isolate the reader within a careful circumscribed hermeneutic domain in which the reader, by almost passively experiencing a sort of visceral effect, is not aware that interpretation is available or welcome. As we will see, this is accomplished by a bit of trickery, as Poe will explain in his rather eccentric theory of the "true originality," which gulls the reader into believing that he or she is a co-author of the intended effects, while all the while positioning the readers as a unwitting object of the author's meticulous machinations. The intended effect of the story or poem, "the excitement of the soul," is perversely accomplished through the very spirit of the perverse that Poe both elaborates and dramatizes in his

---

[8] Poe, "The Black Cat," *Poetry and Tales*, 599.
[9] Poe, "The Imp of the Perverse," ibid., 826.
[10] See, e.g. Deleuze, *Difference and Repetition*, 150–3; see also Foucault, "Theatrum Philosophicum,"187–92.
[11] See Errikila, "Perverting the American Renaissance."

work. As such, Poe's critical theory and his practice splice together, forming a single force through which he exerts his tremendous artistic power. With his peripatetic, zigzagging explorations of the territories encompassing lofty poetic aesthetics and the prosaic literary marketplace of his era, Poe imagines all those species of tenure over the minds of his readers and enfolds them into a new unity, whose final tone is one of mockery and whose final word may just be a last laugh.

"To be appreciated, you must be *read*"

Still on the brink of his career as a writer and magazinist in 1835, Poe hoped to make a living as a writer for Thomas W. White's newly established publication, *The Southern Literary Messenger*, on which he would later secure a position as assistant editor. Poe submitted a number of pieces for White's consideration, but, not surprisingly, the one that stood out was "Berenice," the first of Poe's tales to appear in the *Messenger* (in March 1835) and truly one of Poe's most disturbing short stories. Egæus, the narrator of "Berenice," is an ardent lover who develops a strange, monomaniacal obsession. In the tale, not only does he prematurely bury his beloved Berenice but, in a frenzy, he disinters her and removes all of the teeth from her still-living, hideously shrieking mouth, a horrifying image brought home to the reader only in the tale's final line. White's letter to Poe does not survive, but we can easily infer its contents from Poe's response, in which he acknowledges that White's "opinion of it is very just" and the "subject is by far too horrible." However, Poe then defends his choice by saying that the story offers "a specimen of my capabilities," for it "originated in a bet that I could produce nothing effective on a subject so singular, provided I treated it seriously." In other words, even in acknowledging that the tale "approaches the very verge of bad taste," Poe insists that his skill as a writer trumps the distastefulness of the subject. That is, he must have won his bet, inasmuch as White for one *was* affected by "Berenice."

Poe further argues that "Berenice" is precisely the sort of article that will captivate a paying audience of readers. In this letter, Poe elegantly and emphatically lays out the criteria for commercially and aesthetically successful magazine writing:

> The history of all Magazines shows plainly that those which have attained celebrity were indebted for it to articles *similar in nature—to Berenice*—although, I grant you, far superior in style and execution. I say similar in *nature*. You ask me in what does this nature consist? In the ludicrous heightened into the grotesque: the fearful coloured into the horrible: the witty exaggerated into the burlesque: the singular wrought out into the strange and mystical. You may say all this is bad taste. I have my doubts about it. Nobody is more aware than I am that simplicity is the cant of the day—but take my word for it no one cares any thing about simplicity in their hearts. Believe me also, in spite of what people say to the contrary, that there is nothing easier in the world than to be extremely simple. But whether the articles of which I speak are, or are not in bad taste is little to the purpose. To be appreciated you must be *read*, and these things are invariably sought after with

avidity. They are, if you will take notice, the articles which find their way into other periodicals, and into the papers, and in this manner, taking hold upon the public mind they augment the reputation of the source where they originated.

Poe goes on to note that, once White receives more tales from him, "[i]t is unnecessary for you to pay much attention to the many who will no doubt favour you with their critiques. [...] The effect—if any—will be estimated better by the circulation of the Magazine than by any comments upon its contents."[12] In the tumultuous year or so that Poe contributed tales, poems, and essays to the *Messenger*, in addition to acting as its assistant editor or editor, Poe's savvy reading of the literary marketplace proved entirely accurate, as the circulation of the magazine increased from 700 to 3,500 subscribers.[13]

This one letter alone reveals the canny, or perhaps uncanny, commingling of the resources of both the poetic artist and the worldly professional that were embodied in Poe. Especially given the context of Poe's life in 1835—his personal ambitions, his crushing poverty, the understandably ambiguous emotions he would have felt about returning to Richmond, and so forth—Poe's argument is clearly calculated to press all the right buttons, to appeal to White's own ambitions without debasing them by referring to money, for example, and to couch "success" in this emergent and struggling industry in terms of reputation and appreciation. Even Poe's somewhat pedantic tone is carefully mitigated in advance by his (some would say disingenuous, obsequious, or manipulative) appeal to White's inherent knowledge and good judgment of such matters: "I beg you to believe that I have no intention of giving you *advice*, being fully confident that, upon consideration, you will agree with me."[14] Poe insists that only fantastically extravagant pieces, those that escape from the comfortable confines of the simple and straightforward ("the cant of the day"), can achieve a lasting effect upon the intended audience. *Extravagance* literally or etymologically suggests transgression, as it is a sign of "wandering out of bounds." Thus *fantasy*, a mode in which one ventures "beyond the flaming walls of the world," may be the genre best suited to Poe's critical and artistic project.

Poe's gift for the sensational, the extravagant, or the fantastic would yield results both in the literary marketplace of the day and in literary history more broadly, as the interplay of realistic and fantastic writing becomes a key aspect of the modern or postmodern engagement with the world. In this, Poe is perhaps prototypical of a tendency seen later in Franz Kafka, Jorge Luis Borges, Italo Calvino, and others who would solidify the claims to the aesthetic power of the fantastic mode in the twentieth century. Furthermore, by denying the value of what was considered a virtue ("there is nothing easier in the world than to be extremely simple"), Poe makes the case for extravagant complexity or an *outré* sensibility as characteristic of a kind of writing

---

[12] Poe, "To Thomas W. White" (April 30, 1835), *The Letters of Edgar Allan Poe*, 57–8.
[13] See Ackroyd, *Poe: A Life Cut Short*, 74. As Ackroyd notes, Poe would have similar success in managing *Graham's Magazine*, whose circulation "climbed from five thousand to twenty-five thousand" and "would soon become the largest selling monthly magazine in America" (89–90).
[14] Poe, "To Thomas W. White" (April 30, 1835), *The Letters of Edgar Allan Poe*, 57.

better suited to high literary art. That is, Poe argues, these sensational articles do not just help to increase magazine sales, but they also exhibit artistic originality and genius. To the lines quoted above, Poe provides additional examples of successful British magazines and their typical content, and concludes that "the first men in [England] have not thought writings of this nature unworthy of their talents, and I have good reason to believe that some very high names valued themselves *principally* upon this species of literature."[15] Poe avers that, far from offending and turning away either the masses of the popular audience or the tastefully refined critical readers by publishing literature in this fantastic and bizarre vein, tales such as "Berenice" can captivate the minds of all.

The apparatus of capture

In establishing exaggeration or extravagance as the "nature" of successful magazine writing, Poe indicates that both the art and the business of literature call for some attention to genres. The question of genre is inextricably related to Poe's general poetics and his theories about the literary marketplace. In the somewhat crude sense that the term "genre fiction" is used today, that is, as designating a non-literary or sub-literary form of writing that occupies this or that marketing niche and relies on strictly formulaic plots or settings, genre is sometimes distinguished from "literature" itself. A visit to any large bookstore seems to bear this out, where one finds the "literature" section housing such diverse titles as *Bleak House*, *The Sound and the Fury*, *Gravity's Rainbow*, or *Beloved*, whereas the thousands of volumes crowd the shelves of fantasy, science fiction, mystery, and so on, are presumed to be something other than "literature" proper. This is not to say the generic boundaries are immutable or impermeable, since clearly a given author, text, or genre will shift or shake things up from time to time. One merely has to look at the different covers between the early and late editions of the works of some writers to see how this operates in practice.[16] But strangely enough, *literature* has come to mean something like a genre-less genre: some kind of imaginative or creative writing, usually fiction, which does not really fit into any identifiable genre.[17] It may be for this reason that some scholars and critics have had difficulty taking Poe seriously as a writer of "serious" literature, since

---

[15] Ibid., 58.

[16] To take one amusing example, consider Kurt Vonnegut's 1959 novel *The Sirens of Titan*, whose early covers feature luridly underdressed and buxom women amid planets and satellites, imagery typical of the science fiction marketing at that time; however, since Vonnegut's mainstream success after the 1969 publication of *Slaughterhouse-Five*, *Sirens of Titan* has appeared with a much more tasteful cover of simple geometric shapes or, most recently, with Vonnegut's own sketch drawing, albeit one unrelated to that particular novel, used as a cover illustration. This change in marketing, based on book-cover design, may be representative of the perceived distinction between a sub-literary science fiction and a work of literature.

[17] See Arac, *The Emergence of American Literary Narrative*, 2. Prior to 1800, the word *literature* generally referred to any culturally valued writing. Arac has also noted that, as soon as "literature" came to take its modern significance, that is, as being limited to creative or imaginative writing, *literature* quickly came to refer almost exclusively to the novel. See Arac, *Impure Worlds*, 3.

so many of his works can and do fit into various marketing categories, like horror, science fiction, detective stories, fantasy, humor, although it should be added that none of Poe's tales are, strictly speaking, limited to these marketing categories. Poe's discussion of "Berenice" suggests that he was well aware of the use and disadvantages of genre for literary life, but he boldly stakes a claim for the overall effectiveness of "the ludicrous heightened into the grotesque: the fearful coloured into the horrible: the witty exaggerated into the burlesque: the singular wrought out into the strange and mystical."[18]

That Poe deliberately produced specific types of writing that he thought would pique the interest of readers is not surprising. However, through his approach to genre Poe also exerted greater control as an author over his reader and his own work. Genre in this way functions as an apparatus of capture, limiting or attempting to limit the reader's response, and stamping the author's individuality on the work itself. As Fredric Jameson has observed, "[g]enres are essentially literary institutions, or social contracts between a writer and a specific public, whose function is to specify the proper use of a cultural artifact."[19] That is, lacking the multiple and subtle contextual cues that render meaningful communication between a live speaker and auditors so effortless (most of the time, at least), the written text requires additional, often extra-textual apparatuses to ensure that the author's intended meaning—or, in Poe's more pointedly calculated, mechanical term, *effect*—is carried across to the reader. Obviously, genre is not the only way this is accomplished. For example, the medium in which the message is presented might do much of this work, as most of us are less willing to suspend our disbelief in reading a newspaper article than we would be in reading a tale in a journal devoted to fiction. The tremendous, if short-lived, success of "The Balloon-Hoax" lay in Poe's presentation of it as an "Extra" in the *New York Sun*, complete with an advertisement from the early morning's edition, with the requisite elements of typography (bold headlines, large font), breathless language (including multiple exclamation points!!!), realistic illustrations, and even using the names of real, well known balloonists (Mr. Monck Mason) and writers (Mr. Harrison Ainsworth).[20] Yet within various forms of literature, genre does present both writer and reader with a figurative road map to meaning.

Perhaps genre might be better likened to a kind of template, by which to arrange the elements presented in the text and to have them appear in an already-meaningful ensemble, which can then be "read" as if unmediated by the genre that, once asserted as the ever-present substratum of the narrative, can now safely be forgotten. Once the reader and the text are fully subsumed within the generic framework, the artificiality of the genre fades into the background. At its most successfully deployed, genre becomes invisible, and the world in which events unfold is a totality supported by its own internal regulations that no longer pay homage to an extrinsic world that the reader may inhabit once the reading is complete. To use an overly simplistic example,

---

[18] Not everyone agreed, of course. In a letter dated February 9, 1836, Poe's friend and early champion, John P. Kennedy, warned Poe that his "love of the extravagant" was his primary flaw.

[19] Jameson, *The Political Unconscious*, 106.

[20] See, e.g. Kevin J. Hayes, *Poe and the Printed Word*, xii.

we can see that, once it is established that we are operating within the genre of Tolkien-like fantasy, it is no longer necessary to explain whether dragons are possible or probable inhabitants of the world. Dragons are *of* that world just as trees and birds are, and we do not need to think of the genre while immersed in the fictional world.[21] However, as I will discuss in the next chapter, in Poe's case it was not always clear what type of work he was writing. This could lead to amusing confusions, such as whether "The Facts in the Case of M. Valdemar" were "true" or not. But it could also invite the charge of inauthenticity, calculation, and a lack of empathy, as when James Russell Lowell famously quipped, in his *A Fable for Critics*, that in Poe's work "the heart somehow seems all squeezed out by the mind."

Poe's meticulous, rational methodology probably lends some credence to Lowell's jibe, and in his own literary theory Poe certainly depicts the poem or short story as a device carefully crafted to produce an intended effect upon the reader. While not essential to this program, genre undoubtedly affects it. From the author's perspective, genre can be a tool for guiding the reader to the appropriate impressions or conclusions. Although it is not completely possible to avoid all confusion or to wield such total control over the reader's interpretation that alternative meanings are impossible, the skilled writer can produce the intended effect, to use Poe's terminology, in the reader's mind, heart, or soul. Public "performances" of literary works, such as lectures or poetry readings, offer the additional opportunity to make clear the meaning of one's own work. In reciting "The Raven" publicly, for instance, Poe could make sure that his pronunciations, intonations, and rhythms were all directed toward his goal. "The Philosophy of Composition," which in my view also contains elements of satire, forms a continuation of this authorial guidance, since it explains not only how "The Raven" was constructed by the poet, but how the poem should be interpreted. "The Philosophy of Composition" appears to explain how the poem was meticulously crafted, element by element; the essay emphatically offers a reading of the poem that might alter the initial perceptions of the reader and provide additional meanings. For a reader who is not properly trained (and "The Philosophy of Composition" certainly has a didactic quality to it), the potential meanings of "The Raven" might fly off in all directions, arriving at significances unintended, and perhaps unforeseen, by Poe. As Jameson puts it, "as texts free themselves more and more from an immediate performance situation, it becomes more difficult to enforce a given generic rule on their readers. No small part of the art of writing, indeed, is absorbed by this (impossible) attempt to devise a foolproof mechanism for the automatic exclusion of undesirable responses to a given literary utterance."[22] Poe's more general philosophy of composition involves a theory of how such a "foolproof mechanism" can be devised.

Above all, for Poe, this will require some textual means of controlling the reader's responses, and the first order of business for Poe will be to place a material limit on the spatiotemporal experience of reading. To this end, Poe was an early advocate of the "genres" of the short story or the brief lyric poem, and his theory of these

---

[21] See, e.g. Tolkien, "On Fairy-Stories," 135.
[22] Jameson, *The Political Unconscious*, 106–7.

forms demonstrated both the highly practical and the aesthetic considerations that a writer must bear in mind. In his "Philosophy of Composition," as in his reviews of Hawthorne's *Twice-Told Tales*, Poe insisted that the extent or length of the work is crucial to its effectiveness as a work of art. Indeed, in Poe's view, the first real consideration of the poet when composing a new work is "that of extent." The reason, of course, has to do with Poe's famous theory of the single effect or the unity of effect, but what sometimes seems to be a lofty Romantic principle is based upon the physical exigencies of a reader's daily life. It has less to do with the truth and beauty to be found in contemplating Grecian urns, and far more to do with strategies for physically immobilizing one's audience, for keeping the reader's butt in the seat, and for making certain that no considerations other than the author's intended ones are available to the reader during the span in which the poem or story is being perused. For a poem or tale to achieve success, as Poe imagines it, the reader must be almost literally captivated.

In order to achieve that necessary unity of effect, a work must be comprehended as a whole. Poe's view holds that this totality can only be arrived at when the reader is physically, as well as mentally, engrossed in the work itself. If the reader starts reading, then gets up to make a sandwich, or goes to bed, returns the next day, and so forth, the "unity of impression" is broken and the effect of the tale or poem, which after all is the entire point of the work, is lost. "If any literary work is too long to be read at one sitting, we must be content to dispense with the immensely important effect derivable from unity of impression—for, if two sittings be required, the affairs of the world interfere, and every thing like totality is at once destroyed."[23] Poe notes that the long poem, so-called, is really just a series of short poems strung together, producing multiple effects along the way. Both epic and novel are objectionable for this reason, since they cannot produce that single effect in the reader. In his 1842 review of Hawthorne's *Twice-Told Tales*, Poe specifies the period suited to "one sitting" as a reading time lasting "from one half-hour to one or two hours," and Poe further explains that, as with the brief poem, the preservation of unity or totality is based primarily on the author's control over the body as well as the mind of the reader. "Worldly interests intervening during the pauses of perusal, *modify, annul,* or *counteract,* in a greater or less degree, the impression of the book. But simple cessation in reading would, of itself, be sufficient to destroy the true unity. In the brief tale, however, the author is enabled to carry out the fulness [*sic*] of his intention, be it what it may. During the hour of perusal the soul of the reader is at the writer's control. There are no external or extrinsic influences—resulting from weariness or interruption."[24] In order for piece of poetry or prose fiction to work from the perspective of this aesthetic theory, the reader must be held captive by the author. Not only does he require that the reader be under the author's spell, but Poe considers any potential breaking of the spell to be damaging

---

[23]   Poe, "The Philosophy of Composition," *Essays and Reviews*, 15.

[24]   Poe, "Nathaniel Hawthorne," ibid., 572, my emphasis. This quotation is from the review of *Twice-told Tales* published in *Graham's Magazine* in May 1842; Poe reviewed the same work alongside Hawthorne's *Mosses from an Old Manse,* using much of the same language but with a slightly more negative overall assessment, for *Godey's Lady's Book* in November 1847.

to the work of art itself, as the unleashed reader may modify, annul, or counteract the author's intended purposes. In some respects, the reader is thus the author's enemy, someone who, wittingly or otherwise, can damage the fruits of the writer's deliberate and meticulous labor.

As this makes clear, Poe's literary theory posits an almost antagonistic relationship between author and audience. This position may have been forged and strengthened by Poe's assessment of the literary marketplace, as presented in his 1835 letter to White. The author must attract readers in the first place by offering something intriguing, then the author must captivate them with the *types* of writing—again, "the ludicrous heightened into the grotesque: the fearful coloured into the horrible: the witty exaggerated into the burlesque: the singular wrought out into the strange and mystical"—that will hold readers spellbound, and the author must maintain this tenure and control over every reader through calculated compositional decisions over such matters as length and levels of detail, in order that the individual reader is less likely to (and, perhaps, actually cannot) undermine the author's own individual purpose. The reader is imagined as a kind of wild animal to be hunted, trapped, and held; perhaps given the brevity of this captivity, one might say that the successful author (or hunter) merely tags and releases back into the wild the wily and elusive reader. Remarkably, in this scenario, the reader seems to have the surplus of power. Only a really extraordinary work of art, one produced by a "skilful literary artist" who has "conceived, with deliberate care, a certain unique or single *effect* to be wrought out,"[25] can prevent the reader from, *at any time*, modifying, annulling, or counteracting the author's intentions. From this perspective, the author's purposive domination of the reader is itself an act of resistance. Poe's "skilful literary artist" can only hope for a mere hour or two in which to achieve his or her aims. After this brief period, if the artist is lucky and successful, he or she recedes into the shadows, and "worldly interests" take up their pre-eminence once more. The embattled author must strive only for such small, short-lived victories.

Poe's literary theory is rooted in a sense of self-possession and control that he wished to extend to the means of literary production themselves. As those familiar with his biography are well aware, Poe longed to produce his own magazine, one in which he could direct every aspect of the business, and in particular he coveted the power to determine editorial and literary content. In his 1843 prospectus for *The Stylus* (and using language quite similar to that employed in his prospectus for *The Penn Magazine*, which he had hoped to launch three years earlier), Poe cites his own experience as editor, but not owner, of two other successful magazines in order to make the case for the desideratum most "essential" to producing a successful magazine:

> The necessity for any very rigid definition of the literary character or aims of "The Stylus," is, in some measure, obviated by the general knowledge, on the part of the public, of the editor's connexion, formerly, with the two most successful

---

[25] Poe, "Nathaniel Hawthorne," *Essays and Reviews*, 572.

periodicals in the country—"The Southern Literary Messenger," and "Graham's Magazine." Having no proprietary right, however, in either of these journals; his objects, too, being, in many respects, at variance with those of their very worthy owners; he found it not only impossible to effect anything, on the score of taste, for the mechanical appearance of the works, but exceedingly difficult, also, to stamp, upon their internal character, that *individuality* which he believes essential to the full success of all similar publications. In regard to their extensive and permanent influence, it appears to him that continuity, definitiveness, and a marked certainty of purpose, are requisites of vital importance; and he cannot help thinking that these requisites are attainable, only where a single mind has at least *the general* direction of the enterprise. Experience, in a word, has distinctly shown him—what, indeed, might have been demonstrated *a priori*—that in founding a Magazine wherein his interest should be not merely editorial, lies his sole chance of carrying out to completion whatever peculiar intentions he may have entertained.[26]

Here, as in his earlier prospectus, Poe believes that combined ownership and editorship will enable him "to stamp" his individuality upon the publication, which alone can safeguard the "continuity, definitiveness, and a marked certainty of purpose" needed to achieve one's ends in the magazine industry. As with his theory of effective poetry and fiction, Poe's notion of what can make a magazine flourish boils down to the degree of control wielded by its producer over both its component parts and its audience. For Poe, literature, at least in part, is an activity of capture and control. The reader is held captive by the artfully crafted literary work, which maintains a "species of tenure" (as he will call it in his assessment of Catherine Maria Sedgwick's writing) proper to the author's own skills.

---

[26] Poe, "Prospectus of *The Stylus*," ibid., 1034; almost identical language can be found in Poe's 1840 "Prospectus of *The Penn Magazine*," ibid., 1024.

6

The Perverse Originality of Literature Proper

In his critical portrait of Catherine Maria Sedgwick in "The Literati of New York City" series, Poe made a rather fine distinction between the sort of materials this popular author had produced and "literature proper," a term not sufficiently defined in Poe's own day and still difficult to pin down in our era. Poe observed that, "[a]s the author of many *books*—of several absolutely bound volumes in the ordinary 'novel' form of auld lang syne, Miss Sedgwick has a certain adventitious hold upon the attention of the public, a species of tenure that has nothing to do with literature proper."[1] By the 1840s, the term *literature* had not yet acquired its more technical meaning, which would limit it to a particularly original, creative, and imaginative form of writing, often but not always referring particularly to fiction. However, this new meaning, which continues to dominate the marketing categories of booksellers today, was emerging during this period. Prior to the nineteenth century, *literature* could easily refer to almost any form of culturally valued writing, and it would have certainly included works that no longer as called literary, like philosophical treatises, scientific articles, historical accounts, political speeches, religious sermons, and so on. As Terry Eagleton has noted with some amusement, this "cultural value" did not necessarily extend to novels, which may have been considered too vulgar to merit the label "Literature" in the era when that term referred to "polite letters."[2] In Poe's assessment of Sedgwick, he appeared to narrow the scope of *literature* to specific kinds of writing that he did not see represented in the work of the popular novelist. This was at once a matter of classification and evaluation. For something to be literary, it had to not only fit within a certain type of writing but also maintain a certain level of worthiness, both of which involved aesthetic judgments.

Jonathan Arac, in his history of the emergence of literary narrative in nineteenth-century American prose, takes Poe's comment about Sedgwick to be a signal moment in the evolution of the conception of "literature." Although Hawthorne, both in his own time and in the following century, would become a more fitting exemplar of the literary writer, Arac asserts that "Edgar Allan Poe did more to put into place theories

[1] Poe, "Catherine M. Sedgwick," in "The Literati of New York City," *Essays and Reviews*, 1203.
[2] Eagleton, *Literary Theory*, 15.

and perspectives that have formed the twentieth-century notion of literature. [...] Poe vigorously supported this newly specialized sense of the word 'literature.'"[3] As Arac sees it,

> [b]y appealing to "literature proper," Poe was establishing a distinction between the mere fact of book publication and higher values that are essential rather than "adventitious." The values depend on spiritual facts rather than just on physical appearance in a familiar format. In fact, the familiar, "ordinary ... form of auld lang syne" is suspect. Literature proper apparently will be innovative, recognizable by its difference from, rather than its resemblance to, what has gone before. Yet there will necessarily be some problem with new work. It may require special talents to acknowledge it, to understand that the work in question is not a failed example of an old form but rather a uniquely innovative accomplishment.[4]

Poe's vision entails a kind of tenure that is imagined as essential or intrinsic to the literary work itself, which manages to seize and maintain the attention of the reader by virtue of the work's novelty and originality, qualities that only the talented author can provide. As this suggests, in advocating a particular form of literature Poe was also calling for a particular kind of reader.

Arac's broader argument about the development of a literary aesthetic and the shifting value placed upon originality, creativity, and innovation is well taken, but at least part of Poe's critique of Sedgwick's "adventitious hold upon the attention of the public" is rooted in the basic materiality of "absolutely bound volumes." As Poe continues the above-quoted sentence, the fact that Sedgwick is the author of *books* gives her "a very decided advantage, in short, over her more modern rivals whom fashion and the growing influence *of the want* of an international copyright law have condemned to the external insignificance of the yellow-backed pamphleteering."[5] Poe is certainly thinking of his own plight here, as he had found such difficulty in securing publishers for a number of book projects himself. Not only had his proposed *Tales of the Folio Club* been rejected, but his desire to amend and republish most of the *Tales of the Grotesque and Arabesque* under the preferred title, *Phantasy-Pieces*, had come to naught. In 1843, the first and, as it turned out, only volume of *The Prose Romances of Edgar Allan Poe* appeared, much in the form of "yellow-backed pamphleteering," it seems, since the "number" contained only two stories, "The Murders in the Rue Morgue" and "The Man that was Used Up," and sold for a mere 12½ cents. Throughout this period Poe had become increasingly agitated about the lack of international copyright protections, which not only cut into the potential profits of popular American writers but allowed the literary marketplace in the United States to be flooded with English and other European literature, delivered at cheap prices and in direct competition with work by Poe and other "magazinists." In his bitterly humorous essay, "Some Secrets of the Magazine Prison-House," written

---

[3] Arac, *The Emergence of American Literary Narrative*, 122.
[4] Ibid.
[5] Poe, "Catherine M. Sedgwick," in "The Literati of New York City," *Essays and Reviews*, 1203.

in 1845 (or about eighteen months before the Sedgwick piece), Poe posits that "the want of an International Copy-Right Law, by rendering it nearly impossible to obtain anything from the booksellers in the way of remuneration for literary labor, has had the effect of forcing many of our very best writers into the service of the Magazines and Reviews, which with a pertinacity that does them credit, keep up in a certain or uncertain degree the good old saying, that even in the thankless field of Letters the laborer is worthy of his hire."[6] It is always worth recalling that the material conditions of Poe's life, far from representing the circumstances his work wholly escaped from or transcended, clearly colored and constituted much of his theory and practice of literature.

Nevertheless, Poe's suspicion that Sedgwick held the adventitious advantage of book-binding was not the only thing which suggested that her novels' "species of tenure" had little to do with "literature proper." Poe goes on to apply his "critical judgment as it makes estimate of her abilities" expressly in the kinds of terms that Arac says typify the emergent, specialized sense of the *literary*. Referring to a number of contemporary female authors—some of whom, like Lydia Maria Child or Margaret Fuller, are still well known, while others (such as Emily Chubbuck or Mrs. A. M. F. Annan) are no longer household names—with whom he compares Sedgwick unfavorably, Poe asserts that she lacks the "vigor," "vivacious grace," "pure style," "classic imagination," "naturalness," and "thoughtful and suggestive originality" of these other writers. He concludes that Sedgwick "is an author of marked talent, but by no means of such decided genius as would entitle her to that precedence among our female writers."[7] The idea that one may have talent but lack genius is a remnant of the Romantic vocabulary, but the gist of Poe's critique is clear: "literature proper" will require more than mere evidence of being produced by someone with a talent for writing.

True originality

To return to Arac's point about the problem of original or innovative writing, how *does* one determine the difference between poorly executed imitation and well executed innovation? If Washington Irving could be lauded as the American Goldsmith, or James Fennimore Cooper as the American Scott, it was because their readers could recognize the degree to which the writings of these American authors approximated those of already acclaimed and beloved British ones. If Cooper's romances reminded the reader of Sir Walter Scott's historical novels, then that was all to the good, since this demonstrated Cooper's mastery of a popular form and his talent for extending it into new terrains. Originality, in the sense understood by Poe, Nathaniel Hawthorne, and later Herman Melville, was not required or even necessarily desirable. The valorization

---

[6] Poe, "Some Secrets of the Magazine Prison-House," ibid., 1036.
[7] Poe, "Catherine M. Sedgwick," in "The Literati of New York City," ibid., 1204.

of originality was part of the development of a redefinition of "literature" itself, although it largely remained a minority position throughout the antebellum period.

In "Hawthorne and His Mosses," a much less rhetorically restrained essay (as compared with Poe's reviews of Hawthorne), Melville also denigrated derivative or unoriginal writing. Combining a claim for universality (i.e., do not "cleave to nationality") with a kind of machismo ("write like a man"), Melville boldly announced that:

> it is better to fail at originality, than to succeed in imitation. He who has never failed somewhere, that man can not be great. Failure is the true test of greatness. [...] Without malice, but to speak the plain fact, they [these "smooth pleasing writers"] but furnish appendices to Goldsmith, and other English authors. And we want no American Goldsmiths; nay, we want no American Miltons. It were the vilest thing you could say of a true American author, that he were an American Thompkins. Call him an American, and have done; for you can not say a nobler thing of him. —But it is not meant that all American writers should studiously cleave to nationality in their writings; only this, no American writer should write like an Englishman, or a Frenchman; let him write like a man, for then he will be sure to write like an American. [...] Let us boldly contemn all imitation, though it comes to us as graceful and fragrant as the morning; and foster all originality, though, at first, it be crabbed and ugly as our own pine knots.[8]

As Melville suggested with this final line, greater originality carried risks for the author daring to produce original art. A truly original work might appear quite repulsive, for instance, particularly if the reader were expecting something resembling more closely prior, familiar models.

The original writer thus courted both honest misunderstanding and flat-out failure. What if the reader mistakenly assumes that the innovative author had actually intended to reproduce a familiar, formulaic narrative form? The reader thus misses the points of laudable originality in the work. For example, the reader of *Moby-Dick* who expected another relatively light personal narrative, along the lines of Melville's *Typee* and *Redburn*, might still enjoy the sprawling masterpiece, but that reader would likely have to overlook or actively ignore those elements that made *Moby-Dick* quite different from the sea-faring adventures of one Ishmael. Such, in any case, was Melville's own worry, as some reviewers found his extravagant treatment of the subject alarming. (It may also be telling that Melville was already working on the novel when he wrote "Hawthorne and His Mosses," so his defense of Hawthorne's originality might also be seen as a prophylactic measure intended to prepare a readership for the shocking originality of *Moby-Dick*.) Moreover, the original work may be viewed as a total failure if the writing veers too far from the familiar and comforting contours of recognizable genres. This appears to have been the case with Melville's subsequent novel, *Pierre, or, the Ambiguities*, which was presented as a sentimental romance of the type so extremely popular at the time, but which dissolved into a bizarre, grotesque parody of that form, while in it Melville may well have forged something else, some new form

---

[8] Melville, "Hawthorne and His Mosses," 247–8.

that many readers now perceive as proto-modernist, if not already modernist, and a possible precursor to James Joyce's *Portrait of the Artist as a Young Man*, among others. The originality that Poe embraced would have to contend with the specters of both misunderstanding and failure if he were to maintain "tenure" upon the minds of the reading public.

Unlike the Melville of 1850, however, Poe had had many years of success as a writer of magazine fiction. Even if his wallet did not bear witness to that success, Poe's general popularity in his own time is unquestionable.[9] In his second review of Hawthorne's *Twice-Told Tales* (now also reviewing *Mosses from an Old Manse*) from 1847, Poe offered another odd twist to the discussion of originality. Poe rather perversely distinguished between what he took to be the always popular *originality* and the frequently off-putting *peculiarity*. In his earlier review, Poe had heaped praise upon Hawthorne, precisely acknowledging his originality. "Mr. Hawthorne's distinctive trait is invention, creation, imagination, originality—a trait which, in the literature of fiction, is positively worth all the rest. [...] The inventive or original mind as frequently displays itself in novelty of *tone* as in novelty of matter. Mr. Hawthorne is original at *all* points."[10] But in revisiting that same work in 1847, Poe tries to account for Hawthorne's relative unpopularity—he is "*the* example, *par excellence*, in this country, of the privately-admired and publicly-unappreciated man of genius"—by the perverse argument that his work is not truly original, and indeed, going so far as to assert that Hawthorne "is *not* original in any sense."[11] Poe maintains that, contrary to the beliefs of most commentators, the truly original writer is *always* popular, as "the excitable, undisciplined and child-like popular mind [...] most keenly feels the original." In Poe's revised position, Hawthorne is not so much original as peculiar, a characteristic easily confused with originality but which actually is what deprives him "of all chance of popular appreciation."[12]

It is difficult to discern whether Poe's shifting views on this matter of Hawthorne's originality reflects a change in his own literary theory or a reassessment of a contemporary and a possible rival whom he no longer wishes to praise overmuch. The cynic might point out that, for example, with the immense success of "The Gold-Bug" (1843) and "The Raven" (1845) in the years after his first review of *Twice-Told Tales*, Poe may have wished to show how the truly original writer is also popular as a means of ensuring that he himself be appreciated for his own originality, not just for his popularity. Or perhaps the New England-based Hawthorne is a victim of the collateral damage from Poe's "Longfellow War," launched in 1845 and continuing for some months as Poe and defenders of Henry Wadsworth Longfellow sniped back and forth in the press, during which time Poe made a definitive break from the intellectual

---

[9] Melville specifically contrasted popular, unoriginal books that fill one's pocket with those unpopular, unoriginal books that "fail." In another famous letter written around the same time as "Hawthorne and His Mosses," Melville distinguishes books written merely for money and the sort of books that he wants to write: "So far as I am individually concerned, & independent of my pocket, it is my earnest desire to write those sort of books which are said to 'fail.'" See Melville, *Correspondence*, 139.

[10] Poe, "Nathaniel Hawthorne," *Essays and Reviews*, 574.

[11] Ibid., 578, 579.

[12] Ibid., 579, 582.

and literary culture of Boston, his native city and the one that he had begun referring to as "Frogpondium."[13] Whatever the extrinsic reasons for the modification, Poe no longer credited Hawthorne, whom he had once called "one of the few men of indisputable genius to whom our country has yet given birth,"[14] with that true originality he undoubtedly found in his own writings.

Poe's revised theory of originality is actually quite striking, partly through its own perverse, and perhaps deeply original, recasting of "true originality" as a phenomenon that employs elements of the familiar and well known while eschewing the "absolutely novel." Poe first states that "the element of the literary originality is novelty" and "the element of its appreciation by the reader is the reader's sense of the new." But he reasons that a kind of law of diminishing returns operates to the detriment of such originality. That is, a writer deemed original by a reader will begin to seem less so as one reads more and more of his or her work. A critic "who reads a single tale or essay by Hawthorne, may be justified in thinking him original; but the tone, or manner, or choice of subject, which induces in this critic the sense of the new, will—if not in a second tale, at least in a third and all subsequent ones—not only fail of inducing it, but bring about an exactly antagonistic impression." This makes a great deal of sense and could be seen even more in those authors who get "typecast," willingly or otherwise; the mythic view of the popular Poe in the twentieth century may provide an apt example, as many casual readers attempt to see the spooky or Gothic elements in even his clearly comedic writings. However, Poe goes on to make the astonishing claim that "true originality" in literature *cannot* involve "such combinations of thought, of incident, and so forth, as are, in fact, absolutely novel," because such novelty "tasks and startles the intellect," which causes the reader to be "excited, but embarrassed, disturbed, and in some degree even pained at his own want of perception." Rather, as Poe sees it, "the true originality—true in respect to its purposes—is that which, in bringing out the half-formed, the reluctant, or the unexpressed fancies of mankind, or in exciting the more delicate pulses of the heart's passion, or in giving birth to some universal sentiment or instinct in embryo, thus combines with the pleasurable effect of *apparent* novelty, a real egotistic delight." With the mere appearance of novelty, Poe continues, the reader's "pleasure is doubled. He is filled with an intrinsic and extrinsic delight. He feels and intensely enjoys the seeming novelty of the thought, enjoys it as really novel, as absolutely original with the writer—*and* himself. They two, he fancies, have, alone of all men, thought thus. They two have, together, created this thing. Henceforward there is a bond of sympathy between them—a sympathy which irradiates every subsequent page of the book."[15] In this view of originality, the author

---

[13] Poe refers to Boston as "Frogpondium" in a January 4, 1848, letter to George W. Eveleth, for example; see *The Letters of Edgar Allan Poe*, 354. In "X-ing a Paragrab," the buffoonish editor Mr. Touch-and-go Bullet-head is from Frogpondium; see *Poetry and Tales*, 918.

[14] Poe, "Nathaniel Hawthorne," *Essays and Reviews*, 569; this comes from a very brief notice, really almost an advertisement for the full review to come in the following issue, in the April 1842 issue of *Graham's Magazine*.

[15] Poe, "Nathaniel Hawthorne," *Essays and Reviews*, 579–81.

and the reader are no longer enemies, at loggerheads over the meaning of the text, but comrades and fellow travelers on the pleasant journey afforded by the literary work.

Assuming Poe is serious, which I do not think is always wise, this appears to be a real departure from his earlier position, in which the skilled artist captivates and dominates the reader, at least for the short time it takes to read the tale or poem. Are we now to understand the reader is not an enemy to be captured and detained, but an ally who cooperates with the author in making the work of art a successful enterprise? Not exactly. As the reference to the "undisciplined and child-like popular mind" would indicate, Poe does not view his reader as an equal partner in complex and nuanced project of literature proper. Rather, his revised theory of originality points to a more refined view of the same apparatus of capture imagined in his philosophy of composition. Here the aim is to trick or to con the reader into thinking she or he is a participant in order to more effectively attract, gain control over, and manipulate the reader. Poe is still thinking from the point of view of a professional magazine publisher, that is, by asking how to entice and to hold onto more paying customers, even as he elaborates his theory of what makes one a great literary artist by delineating those qualities that make for a great work of art. Poe, like his fictional alter ego C. Auguste Dupin, is always analyzing the situation, always calculating, always reading others while seeking his own best advantage. The reader, perhaps pleasurably enthralled by the tale, is nevertheless also the victim of Poe's machinations. We readers are like so many Fortunatos to his Montresor; we may think that we are being guided through the catacombs, and that we are helpfully accompanying the author in our shared quest for the prized meaning or effect, but in reality, Poe (like Montresor in "The Cask of Amontillado") has contrived all of this in an elaborate plot, and we are bound to be the victims of a practical joke.

There is that ever-present duality in Poe. He is simultaneously and at all times the canny, business-like, professional craftsman and the visionary, poetic artist. Poe's tales can function as practical jokes, whose victims or readers half-willingly participate in their own abuse, so enjoyable is the process and so fascinating the subject matter. In several of his critical essays, Poe's literary theory sometimes seems to amount to a technical manual for toying with the hearts and minds of a gullible public. Arac has pointed out that some contemporary readers envisioned Poe less as a Romantic artist or a *poète maudit*, as Baudelaire would present him, than as a lawyer, a figure that is "public, formal, cold, and insincere, even though also often inventive and mystifying. [...] And legal skills were associated with self-promotion, which, in contrast to the obscurity Hawthorne feared, offer the publicity Poe sought."[16] Poe's professional aspirations and aesthetic sensibilities fold together in his continuous effort to produce a variety of writings that can display his own genius, his own originality, and his own gift for obtaining a species of tenure over the public that has everything to do with literature proper.

---

[16] Arac, *The Emergence of American Literary Narrative*, 69–70.

Generic ambiguities

It may be, as Jameson suggests, that genre operates as a social contract between writer and reading public by which they agree to treat the text in a certain way. If so, Poe far more often than not reneges on the deal (or breaches his contract, perhaps) by producing what *appear* to be recognizable types of writing only to frustrate the reader's expectations or to blur the boundaries of those generic forms. Poe rightly valued what he thought of as his versatility, that is, his ability to write effectively across a range of genres and fields. In our time, a widespread literary critical establishment—be it composed of literature professors and students, booksellers and buyers, filmmakers and their audiences, or whatever other custodians of Poe's popular legacy—has managed to wedge Poe's writings into more-or-less well defined marketing genres, such as mystery, horror, or science fiction, which facilitate a certain easy, and perhaps distorted, understanding of his works. Consciously or not, such an approach directs one to apprehend the tales in a particular way in advance of reading them, imposing a certain interpretation or interpretive framework upon them beforehand. In Poe's own time, such marketing genres were not ready-made, nor had their prototypical elements yet crystallized into solid forms. The genres we now attribute to Poe were not so clearly defined in the 1830s and 1840s, and, with his multifarious literary productions cutting across a range of possible genres, his contemporary readers were frequently perplexed.

I have been arguing that Poe's *oeuvre* is best viewed as satirical critique, written in a fantasy mode. Many of Poe's tales are comparable to a sort of practical joking. This is not limited to those tales that we think of *as* hoaxes, satires, or burlesques. I believe that, underlying even Poe's most seemingly serious fiction and nonfiction, a spirit of prankishness or mockery prevails. To take just one example from a rather unlikely source, I find it hilarious that his prospectus for *The Stylus*, on the success of which so many of his personal and professional dreams depended, contains an epigraph attributed to "Launcelot Canning," a fictional author invented by Poe and used as part of a memorable scene in "The Fall of the House of Usher." In that story, Canning is purported to be the author of the "Mad Trist," a disconcertingly silly epic (or so it seems) whose plot points are neatly, and humorously, juxtaposed with the ominous and horrific happenings within the house of Usher. Poe's narrator even gives his opinion of the quality of Canning's epic, saying "in truth, there is little in its uncouth and unimaginative prolixity which could have had interest for the lofty and spiritual ideality" of Roderick Usher.[17] To include a line from an imaginary writer, best known, if at all, for his "uncouth and unimaginative prolixity," in a professional document like this, and to allow that particular fictional writer's words to serve as the gateway to Poe's own plea and rationale for financial support—well, this must have been an immensely funny private joke. In any case, there is something perverse about it. A spirit of the perverse, as Poe names it, seems to animate much of his own career, and one might speak of his artistic versatility and generic variety as manifestations of that perversity implicit in all of Poe's work.

---

[17] Poe, "The Fall of the House of Usher," *Poetry and Tales*, 332.

Aside from the more commonly understood genres like romance or realism, or even Poe's own labels in calling his tales "grotesque and arabesque," one can discern a basic ambiguity in nearly all of Poe's narratives that may be illustrated by thinking of the voices who tell the stories. In his famous analysis of Poe's narrators, James Gargano notes how distant Poe himself is from those individuals who serve as the narrative voices of his tales.[18] In almost every case, the narrator is very serious but also relates experiences and events that we are not accustomed to taking seriously. Frequently, as I have said, this introduces an element of absurdity into the tale, as with the calm, patient description, complete with an epigraph from a French play, in the first half of "MS. Found in a Bottle." The narrators of many of these short stories are extremely earnest, yet they cannot be considered wholly trustworthy. Arac has pointed out the "pseudoearnestness" of Poe's narrators, who so frequently recount their experiences with the utmost gravity and solemnity, even where the events of the plot are utterly unbelievable. This places the careful reader in an awkward position. Arac asks: "Was this pseudoearnestness the narrator's self-delusion, the author's wish to delude the reader, or a play in which all parties shared? Readers were confident in laughing at southwestern humor, and Hawthorne's complex ironies only emphasized his thoughtfulness, but Poe's work provoked fundamental uncertainty in response. Was he serious? Should his readers be serious? The problem is one of genre: What kind of work is this?"[19]

In a review of his 1845 *Tales*—a review likely written, at least in part, by Poe himself—Poe is praised for his meticulous clarity and the force of his short fiction, and for his "earnest" style. "There is often a minuteness of detail; but on examination it will always be found that this minuteness was necessary to the developement [*sic*] of the plot, the effects, or the incidents. His style may be called, strictly, an earnest one."[20] However, just as Poe's refined view of true originality required that the novel incidents not seem *too* original, so this earnestness derives, not from the actual sincerity or seriousness of the author, but from his ability to *simulate* earnestness. "A writer must have the fullest belief in his statements, or he must simulate that belief perfectly, to produce an absorbing interest in the mind of his reader. That power of simulation can only be possessed by a man of high genius."[21] This is what Arac means by Poe's "pseudoearnestness." Paradoxically, the mark of the writer's sincerity is his talent for pretending to be sincere. Maybe this is another way of saying that fiction is more capable of arriving at the truth than the mere recitation of facts, but it also suggests that the measure of a great artist, "a man of high genius," is his capacity to success-fully deceive others. The poetic spirit is here not the Byronic hero or the Baudelairean outcast, but the conniving card-sharp, the dexterous pick-pocket, the con artist on the make. It is a perverse image of the literary artist, but one that suits Poe's subversive and subterranean writing.

---

[18] See Gargano, "The Question of Poe's Narrators." For a view of the unreliability of Poe's narrators, see Amper, "Masters of Deceit: Poe's Lying Narrators."

[19] Arac, *The Emergence of American Literary Narrative*, 68.

[20] Poe, "Edgar Allan Poe," *Essays and Reviews*, 873.

[21] Ibid.

In such tales as "The Black Cat" and "The Imp of the Perverse," Poe identifies the spirit of perverseness as a general principle of the human mind and an internal instinct that causes us to act against our own best interests even, or especially, when we know we are doing so. Poe had alluded to the same psychological or philosophical impulse in a number of other works as well. For example, in *The Narrative of Arthur Gordon Pym*, Pym nearly plunges to his death while descending an Antarctic cliff, not because he slips but because, amid his tremendous fear of falling, he suddenly discovered that "my whole soul was pervaded with *a longing to fall*; a desire, a yearning, a passion utterly uncontrollable."[22] As Terence Martin has pointed out, the entire narrative is "sustained by the spirit of perverseness [...] Pym is the imp embodied," and his own name is itself an anagram of "ymp" or "imp."[23] In "The Imp of the Perverse," the narrator explains this vertiginous longing to fall, stating that "because our reason violently deters us from the brink, *therefore*, do we the more impetuously approach it."[24] And, to return to "The Raven" once more, the narrator of that poem—having figured out that his avian visitor will only answer the one word, "Nevermore," in response to any question—begins to ask pointed questions, the answer to which will cause him the most pain. As Poe puts it in "The Philosophy of Composition," he propounds "queries whose solution he has passionately at heart—propounds them half in superstition and half in that species of despair which delights in self-torture—propounds them not altogether because he believes in the prophetic or demoniac character of the bird (which, reason assures him is merely repeating a lesson learned by rote) but because he experiences a phrenzied pleasure in so modeling his questions as to receive from the *expected* 'Nevermore' the most delicious because the most intolerable of sorrow."[25] The list could go on, as many other tales and poems offer similar, if sometimes less obvious, versions of the same impulse.

In addition to the psychological perversity of characters in Poe's tales, one can detect a spirit of perverseness in the formal aspects of the narratives. Often, the narration itself seems to subvert the reader's expectations, to breach the social contract of generic expectations that the author and reader were to have agreed upon. Referring to what she calls "the aesthetics of shock and the poetics of the perverse," Dorothea E. von Mücke notes that the peculiar narrative break within Poe's "The Imp of the Perverse" serves to undermine "the basic conceptual grid that was to guide the nineteenth-century distinction between what was to be considered normal and natural and what was pathological."[26] In that tale, the narrator, who had at first seemed a disinterested, even scientific and objective, observer of psychological phenomena, reveals himself to be a murderer, and thus also transforms the tale itself into a lengthy confession. However, the psychologically inclined narrator's auto-analyzed *perversity* is disclosed, not in his crime, but in his perverse impulse to confess, which retroactively makes the entire narrative called "The Imp of the Perverse" a practical demonstration of the imp

---

22 Poe, "The Narrative of Arthur Gordon Pym of Nantucket," *Poetry and Tales*, 1170.
23 Martin, "The Imagination at Play: Edgar Allan Poe," 203.
24 Poe, "The Imp of the Perverse," *Poetry and Tales*, 829.
25 Poe, "The Philosophy of Composition," *Essays and Reviews*, 19.
26 Mücke, *The Seduction of the Occult and the Rise of the Fantastic Tale*, 106.

of the perverse. One could also say that, from the perspective of the reader, this radical break within the tale becomes a marked generic discontinuity as well, making it more difficult to understand just what is going on. This is a sort of calmly rational variation on the nightmare of the unknowable discussed in Chapter 4. As Mücke writes, "[i]f there is any shock involved, it is the surprise sprung on the reader whose generic expectations are radically questioned in this unexpected transition from the *I* of the neutral observer to the emphatic subjectivity of the criminal on death row."[27]

In "The Imp of the Perverse," the confession itself, and thus the whole narrative, turns out to be an enactment of the perverse impulse. As with the less rational, but otherwise similar narrators of "The Tell-Tale Heart" or, less directly, of "The Black Cat," this narrator's ultimately perverse action is the act of narrating. In "The Tell-Tale Heart," the narrator is wounded by what he takes to be the detectives' knowing mockery, and he shouts his confession, not out of any sense of guilt or even because of his madness *per se*, but because "anything was more tolerable than this derision" and "I could bear their hypocritical smiles no longer!"[28] And in "The Black Cat," it is a sense of pride or even braggadocio, what the narrator calls "the mere phrenzy of bravado," that causes him to thump the recently plastered wall and reveal the truth, against his intent but fully in keeping with that "spirit of perverseness" that had guided his murderous hand earlier in the tale.[29] So, too, in "The Imp of the Perverse," the narrator, in an effort to escape from perversely disclosing the truth, nevertheless attracts as much attention as possible, until "the long imprisoned secret burst forth from my soul."[30] From the reader's point of view, the real secret is now that the entire story has been one long, perversely delivered confession.

In Poe, then, the perverse is not merely the interior phenomenon that he or his narrators identify as a peculiar condition of the human mind, but a general comportment toward the world itself, and a crucial element of any narrative representation of that world. To the extent that genre serves as a means of making sense of the perplexing and often contradictory data—that is, of trying to comprehend the semic and sensual barrage of information pressing upon the reader and writer alike—Poe's perverse typologies loosen and destabilize genre, thus turning genre itself into another unknowable category. Note that this is not simply the case of a tale lacking definitive generic markers or crossing generic boundaries, as with a tale like "Ligeia," which combines romance, horror, fantasy (or witchcraft), psychological thriller, mystery, and so on. Poe's typologies of the perverse go further, suggesting the ways in which the categories employed to help us to make sense of things, the social contracts between the author and the reading public, are also wholly unreliable. Even in that more expansive genre of fantasy, which in its commitment to a radical alterity would seem

---

[27] Ibid.

[28] Poe, "The Tell-Tale Heart," *Poetry and Tales*, 559.

[29] Poe, "The Black Cat," ibid., 605. Susan Amper has provocatively argued that this narrator is not only unreliable, but actively deceiving the reader, and perhaps himself, with an elaborate ruse about the two black cats; in fact, Amper argues, the narrator killed and immured his wife long before the events occurred on the staircase where the narrator "accidentally" kills his wife while attempting to murder the cat. See Amper, "Untold Story: The Lying Narrator in 'The Black Cat.'"

[30] Poe, "The Imp of the Perverse," *Poetry and Tales*, 831.

to encompass other genres like science fiction, utopia or dystopia, and so on,[31] Poe's perverse approach is somewhat unsettling. As Mücke elaborates,

> [w]hereas the fantastic tale draws its central, defining feature from the funda-
> mental uncertainty of an observer position, from the observer's blind spot and the
> ultimate lack of control over the story, "The Imp of the Perverse" stages this blind
> spot and lack of control in a masterful execution of the compulsive confession.
> The reader of Poe's tale is thoroughly disoriented through the manner in which
> the text fuses the subjectivity of the participant's perspective with an initial
> speaking position that invokes the neutral subject of the scientific observer. What
> constitutes the basic uncertainty for the fantastic tale in Poe's text is assigned a
> definite place in a (pseudo-) scientific discourse. To the extent that this discourse
> parodies the phrenological paradigm and, in a more general sense, radically
> subverts the neutral, scientific-observer position, it also undermines the basic
> parameters of the map it proposes.[32]

This map is, of course, a sort of genre as well, and Poe's destabilization of the generic formulae and "social contracts" that assure, or at least promote, understanding turns out to be as grotesque or as arabesque as the subject matter of the tales or the style of the prose. As I mentioned earlier, we the readers have a creeping suspicion that Poe may not merely be captivating us for an hour or so, manipulating our responses, and producing in us the specific effects according to his authorial design, but laughing at us as well. In the perverse writings of Poe, the ultimate generic mode that unites the great variety of poetry, fiction, and criticism may turn out to be that of the practical joke.

Recognizing the force of Poe's combined aesthetic and business-like approach to the establishment of "literature proper" allows us to make better sense of what he was doing in his own time and of how his subterranean noises can speak to our own era, an epoch of globalization in which the interpenetration and cross-pollination of the artistic and commercial worlds seems total. The conscious or unconscious efforts by scholars, publishers, marketers, and simply fans of Poe to confine him to this or that genre (horror or mystery, say) or to limit his person to a particular type of character (such as the tortured poet or refined aesthete) have, as most scholars now recognize, delivered an image of the writer quite out of step with the reality. Poe's subversion of American literature also entails this ambiguity in persona, for the "lost soul" of American literature is as much an archetype, albeit a negative one, of American culture as the American Adam or the rugged individualist. For this, all can really be forgiven, as Poe himself was at least as much to blame in the creation of his own myth as the villainous Rufus Griswold who deliberately sullied Poe's reputation, or the chivalric Charles Baudelaire who championed Poe as the greatest writer of the age. One might say that the reputation formed around Poe in his various afterlives, as Scott Peeples calls them,[33] is itself a product of his own perverse literary theory and practice.

---

[31] See, e.g. China Miéville, "Cognition as Ideology: A Dialectic of SF Theory," 243–5.
[32] Mücke, *The Seduction of the Occult and the Rise of the Fantastic Tale*, 106.
[33] Peeples, *The Afterlife of Edgar Allan Poe*, ix.

However, just as he had stated in defense of "Berenice" back in 1835, Poe understood how to capture the attention of the reading public, how to produce novel effects in the reader, and how to offer such variety as to keep the earnest appearance of originality always in view. As with the gruesome "Berenice," Poe "approaches the very verge of bad taste," guiding the reader with him to the precipice; but in the end, the reader's own imp of the perverse determines whether to take the plunge.

7

The Cosmopolitan's Uncanny Duplicity

Poe's perverse literary theory and fantastic mode of writing may be connected to a peculiar double-consciousness that he maintains as a *littérateur* and critic. Poe is at all times performing a sort of metacommentary in his work, simultaneously creating and mapping his literary spaces. Poe's most memorable narrators are, in the main, somewhat detached observers who find themselves caught up in curious, bizarre, or terrifying circumstances or events. In the process, as we have seen in "MS. Found in a Bottle" and other tales, they frequently begin by presenting a largely dispassionate report on the people, setting, and atmosphere external to them, before shifting into an internal or psychological reflection on the ways that such happenstance affects them individually. The doubling of the observer and participant, with external and internal experience, enables Poe's narrators to be actively engaged in the narrative's events and to stand aloof from them at the same time. In some respects, Poe's archetypal narrative voice is that of the voyeuristic commentator who descries "the man of the crowd"; that narrator feigns to be a mere observer, but spends an entire day and night actively dogging the steps of his curious pedestrian. There is something both urban and urbane about such comportment, as one is isolated within the city's multitudes and obviously a constitutive part of them. Poe's double-takes are part of his cosmopolitanism, and even in those tales that do not necessarily take place in cities, Poe's urban sensibility obtains. In the perambulations of the *flâneur* and the man of the crowd, Poe discovers a form of the *Doppelgänger*, and the unsettling urban atmosphere clears the ground for unexpected comedy.

At sea in the city

It is, of course, not surprising that "The Man of the Crowd" is set in one of Poe's most thoroughly urban locales, the heart of the booming metropolis, London, the cultural geography of which is matched in size and complexity by only C. Auguste Dupin's contemporaneous Paris. Obviously, the premise of the tale requires a setting in which crowds are both present and moving, almost around the clock, so only a very large city would be suitable. But the metropolitan locale also exerts its influence on Poe's nightmare of the unknowable, as the city itself becomes a kind of barrier to under-standing and a scene of profound uncertainty. The perceptual barrage and a "world of strangers" makes the experience of the city, especially for the ingénue or the sensitive soul, somewhat like the experience of being "at sea," literally amidst and surrounded by an ocean of terrifying and unfamiliar imagery and sounds, and figuratively in the sense of being lost or adrift in this world.

The perceived liveliness that so animates a large city is closely connected to the strangeness of the sights and the people encountered. In his "Doings of Gotham," a series of letters published in *The Columbia Spy* in 1844 whereby Poe reported on his impressions of New York City for an audience in Philadelphia or even farther afield, Poe writes, "[t]he city is thronged with strangers, and everything wears an aspect of intense life."[1] This excitement is shared by the narrator of "The Man of the Crowd," who gazes upon "one of the principal thoroughfares of the city," which had been "very much crowded during the whole day." He finds fascinating the "dense and continuous tides of population rushing past the door," and states: "I had never before been in a similar situation, and the tumultuous seas of human heads filled me, therefore, with a delicious novelty of emotion."[2] Later, plunging into this "sea," the narrator comes face-to-face with the inscrutable text that so troubles him, and that perhaps troubles the reader as well.

As I discussed in the Introduction, Charles Olson's distinction between Melville and Poe, which establishes these writers as opposing poles and as the two contra-dictory approaches to the "space" of American life and literature, is really a vision of two types of alternatives to American civilization, not alternatives within it. Melville and Poe are engaged in very different projects, of course, but they share a profound uneasiness with their native land, with its increasingly dominant national ideology, an ideology enunciated, on some level, in the philosophical reflections of a Ralph Waldo Emerson, whom both Melville and Poe criticize, if not outright despise. Both Melville and Poe are also dismayed over what they perceived as the sort of literature that authors in the country produced and that readers valued, even though each made more-or-less successful sallies into the literary marketplace of the era. Both writers were "at sea," lost in the culture in which they operated but in which they were not fully integrated. If one wished to dramatize the distinction between Melville and Poe, one could choose to set the scene as a sea-scape versus a city-scape. This is what Olson himself does when, in continuing (and then abruptly ending) his comparison between the two, he argues that Melville "had the sea of himself in a vigorous, stricken way, as Poe the street."[3] If the street is to Poe what the sea is to Melville, it is worth pointing out that both are far from the rustic ideals of the archetypically "American" landscape, whether in the frontier imagery of the early and mid-nineteenth century or in the equation of heartland and homeland, where "real Americans" live (at least, according

---

[1] Poe, "Doings of Gotham," Letter II.
[2] Poe, "The Man of the Crowd," *Poetry and Tales*, 388–9.
[3] Olson, *Call Me Ishmael*, 12–13; this is the last time Poe is mentioned at all in Olson's text.

to the rhetoric still popular and balefully effective in political discourse in the twenty-first century). Whereas the dominant national image seeks ever to be grounded in a native soil, Poe, like Melville, is forever at sea in the city.

The sea is "the 'forgotten space' of our modernity," as Allan Sekula and Noël Burch put it: "nowhere else is the disorientation, violence and alienation of contemporary capitalism more manifest."[4] Ironically, this disorientation, violence, and alienation have also been traditionally associated with that most "remembered" space of modernity: the city. The emblematic figurative space of capitalist modernity, the large city or metropolis can resemble the sea in its expansiveness, its shifting currents of commerce and humanity, and its quotidian unpredictability. The cosmopolitan character of the modern world and in particular the growth of cities, as Marx and Engels famously put it, "rescued a considerable part of the population from the idiocy of rural life."[5] The defining aspects of life in those cites produce not only sociological, economic, or political effects, but also psychological ones. The profound differences between being at sea and being on the land, of which Melville made so much in works like *Typee* or later *Moby-Dick* and *Pierre*,[6] have their terrestrial counterparts in the imaginary divide between city and country. I mean *country* in both senses: the difference is not only between urban and rural, but between a mode of existence that is not representative of "America" and one that is or is thought to be. Just as Melville had discovered an alternative to the national narrative in the transnational or postnational space of the ocean, Poe found in this emergent space of the city a radical departure from the national culture that was coalescing in the public imagination of his era, and Poe used the peculiarities of this urban experience to redefine both the art and the craft of his literature. If Jonathan Arac finds Poe's short fiction to be "local," it is not because of any "well-established regional residence" or because his writings "draw upon local history, lore, and customs," but because "Poe strove to make his art a world of its own, a place beyond locality or even nationality."[7] Most often this atmosphere, if not the setting, was urban and strange.

Poe's nomadic life and writings were made possible, perhaps even necessary, by the radical transformation of social experience in the United States. Perhaps the most visible aspect of this transformation is the rapid increase in urbanization. As Arac notes, "Poe's career depended on a primary fact of modern American life: the growth of cities. New York, Philadelphia, and Baltimore were the nation's three largest cities, and from 1820 to 1860 their population increased some sixfold. In the United States only 6 percent of the population lived in cities in 1810 and 1820, but by 1860, nearly 20 percent did. Urban population increased over 90 percent in the 1840s, growing almost three times as fast as total population."[8] Not only did those major cities in

---

[4] Sekula and Burch, "The Forgotten Space," *New Left Review* 69 (May–June 2011).
[5] Marx and Engels, *The Communist Manifesto*, 55.
[6] For an interesting take on the ocean itself as a sort of character in *Moby-Dick*, see Sarah Youree's "The Immense, the Wild, the Watery, the Unshored: The Ocean as Heterotopia in *Moby-Dick*," 73–89.
[7] Arac, *The Emergence of American Literary Narrative*, 62–3.
[8] Ibid., 70–1.

which Poe dwelled for a few years at a time dramatically increase in size, with respect to both population and physical geographical boundaries. It was also the case that more and more small towns were becoming urbanized, as the basic demographics of the country began to shift from rural to urban. For example, in 1820 there were only 12 cities in the United States with a population of 10,000 or more, but by 1860 there were 101 such cities; during the same period the number of cities containing 100,000 or more persons jumped from two to eight, with New York surpassing 1,000,000.[9] Although these facts are not really disputed, the ideology of the American national identity, which was and is frequently reinforced through various forms of national self-representation that include pastoral images of a Virgin Land, Jeffersonian yeoman farmers, or the still constantly invoked "heartland," has remained committed to a rustic ideal, and Poe's very urbanity amounts to another somewhat "anti-American" characteristic. In reality, of course, Poe's city-dwelling placed him well within the dominant trend of American social life in the 1830s and 1840s, but it placed him well outside of the "national imaginary," both within his era and especially in twentieth-century American Studies, which continued to find representative national figures in rustics confronting some sort of frontier.[10]

Poe's peripatetic life, along with the frequent peripeties in his life story, ensured that his sensibilities remained non-regional but still somewhat local, only the "locale" in question was less a particular place than a kind of space: the urban. The romantic vision of Poe as a homeless wanderer, forever and in vain seeking a home for himself in the world, is only about half right. Poe also carved out for himself a real place that is not an imaginary homeland like the nation, nor strictly speaking a realm of the literary imagination, but a place in the world of the business of letters that required energy, industry, and a great deal of savvy. If Poe did not belong to one particular place in the world, that does not mean he was not thoroughly worldly.

In response to the sometimes churlish debates about where Poe really "belongs," and particularly addressing the often good-natured contests among Poe scholars or fanatics in Richmond, Baltimore, Philadelphia, New York, or Boston, among other cities, to determine which city gets to claim Poe for its own, Scott Peeples has suggested that we ought to view Poe as a kind of "nowhere man." By this, Peeples does not mean Poe belongs to a utopian, otherworldly, or ethereal realm of Platonic forms or transcendent ideas, "out of place, out of time," as some critics have suggested. Rather, he argues that Poe's very groundedness in the urban milieu and his nearly constant movement among the major Atlantic coast cities made him a true "cosmo-politan." Peeples names Poe a "connoisseur of cities," who feels, as it were, right at

---

[9] See Miller, *The Urbanization of Modern America: A Brief History*, 31–2.

[10] In *Truth's Ragged Edge: The Rise of the American Novel*, Philip F. Gura has demonstrated the degree to which twentieth-century American literary studies largely ignored the vast majority of popular (and representative) nineteenth-century fiction in the United States, in order to present the exceptional as somehow representative. In so doing, American Studies established Natty Bumppo, Hester Prynne, Ishmael, and Huckleberry Finn—extraordinary characters operating in unfamiliar places and with exotic experiences—as emblematically American figures, whereas the vast majority of characters in nineteenth-century novels, like their readers, led rather different, increasingly urban, lives.

home in these spaces. I have already discussed how the biographical and geographical trajectory of Poe's early life may have helped to form his nomad thought and overall nomadism within American literature, and his peripatetic life, moving from city to city, certainly contributed to the urbanity or cosmopolitan aspect of his worldview. Peeples notes that the many "removals" of Poe's adulthood instilled, or reinforced, this cosmopolitanism:

> Consider the frequent removals that characterize Poe's life from age 17 until his death at age 40: Charlottesville, Richmond, Boston, Sullivan's Island, Old Point Comfort (Virginia), West Point, Baltimore, Richmond, Manhattan, Philadelphia, Manhattan, the Bronx. We can compare the lengths of time Poe lived in each of these places, but what strikes me is the frequency of the moves, his not living in one city for more than five years. As an enlisted man, Poe went where he was sent, and after that, quite reasonably, he went where he thought he could find work and advance his career. Moving in hopes of making a better life is an old phenomenon, but I believe Poe's relocations are a sign of something more modern. I see him as a kind of cosmopolitan without money, someone who understood city life and appreciated it even though he lacked the income to enjoy many of the pleasures we associate with cosmopolitan life, like good meals, social drinking that doesn't lead to blackouts and debilitation, leisure travel, and so on. It is tempting to associate Poe—in this regard—with Auguste Dupin, a man whom we can only imagine operating in a city, or the narrator of "The Man of the Crowd," a scholar of the urban environment who, in the first half of that story, can categorize everyone who walks by the window of his café and is drawn almost magnetically to the man who seems to embody the urban crowd itself, in all its complexity and paradox.[11]

Referring to Poe's journalistic "Doings of Gotham" pieces in particular, but arguing for the more general characterization, Peeples writes that Poe presents himself "as something of a connoisseur of cities, alone but somewhat at home in the anonymous urban environment."[12]

From his own personal experiences with poverty, not to mention his keen sense of the appetites of urban readers, Poe knew better than most the lurid details and "mysteries of the city" that made for such compelling critiques of metropolitan social life in the nineteenth century. Although he dabbles in the rhetoric of the urban exposé, particularly in the more sensational aspects of the form, which provide much of the excitement in tales like "The Murders in the Rue Morgue" or "The Mystery of Marie Roget," Poe does not write as a social reformer (like Charles Dickens) or as an anti-urban romantic (like William Wordsworth), but very much as an indigenous and well adapted city-dweller. As Peeples puts it, "Poe rarely criticizes New York or addresses social problems, but instead writes as someone who understands and accepts the

---

[11] Peeples, "Nowhere Man," 89.
[12] Ibid., 90.

modern city on its own terms."[13] The terms were those of his fiction as well, in which uncertainty and illegibility are frequently the norm.

Poe's canniness with respect to the city is a product of his own urbanity, here understood in a strongly geographic sense, but the knowledge of the city is not only a critical awareness of its differences from non-urban spaces. It also involves a clear sense of the different forces and effects of a city, and these are often rendered most evident through observing urban populations. Demographic knowledge is nearly as crucial as geographic knowledge, and in Poe's explorations of the city in the sea—the real places in which he dwelt, not the fanciful "doomed" city of sin in his poem, "The City in the Sea"—the dynamic psychology of metropolitan populations is a key aspect of Poe's poetics of descent. Poe takes to the streets, scouting out the "urban island, a sea within the middle of the sea," and he eschews the more comprehensive vision afforded by the narrative overview, the perspective of a "Solar Eye," as Michel de Certeau termed it.[14] Georg Simmel, in his famous essay on "The Metropolis and Mental Life," points out that "the psychological basis of the metropolitan type of individuality consists in the *intensification of nervous stimulation* which results from the swift and uninterrupted change of outer and inner stimuli."[15] That is, the perceptual bombardment of mobile and protean phenomena that characterizes daily life in the big city alters a given individual's fundamental physiological and cognitive processes. Poe's man of the crowd, as well as the narrator who unsuccessfully attempts to understand him, become representative figures of this intensification, and in constantly walking in the city, they are fundamentally *displaced* at all times. As Certeau puts it, "[t]o walk is to lack a place."[16]

The symbol and avatar of Certeau's pedestrian "poet of cities" must surely be Charles Baudelaire's *flâneur*, who became for Walter Benjamin the representative figure of modernity itself.[17] In "The Painter of Modern Life," Baudelaire characterizes the *flâneur* as a man of the crowd; however, as I will discuss shortly, although Baudelaire's model may derive from Poe's tale, it is not the title character, but the narrator, who really fits the bill. Referring specifically to the French artist, Constantin Guys, Baudelaire also presents a broader explanation of the *flâneur*'s definitive characteristics.

> The crowd is his element, as the air is that of birds and water of fishes. His passion and his profession are to become one flesh with the crowd. For the perfect *flâneur*,

---

[13] Ibid., 89–90.
[14] Certeau, *The Practice of Everyday Life*, 91–2. In this chapter ("Walking in the City"), Certeau distinguishes between the street-level view of the pedestrian or window-shopper from the panoptic overview afforded by looking down upon the city from a great height, his example of which is the observation deck of the then newly constructed World Trade Center. In Certeau's view, the latter vantage point creates a god's-eye view that presumes to *know* the city, whereas the pedestrian actually *writes* the city in "a long poem of walking."
[15] Simmel, "The Metropolis and Mental Life," 409–10.
[16] Certeau, *The Practice of Everyday Life*, 103.
[17] See, e.g. Benjamin, "Paris, Capital of the Nineteenth Century," 156–8. For an excellent discussion of the figure of the *flâneur* in the American context, with particular reference to Benjamin, Baudelaire, and Poe, see Dana Brand, *The Spectator and the City in Nineteenth-Century American Literature*.

for the passionate spectator, it is an immense joy to set up house in the heart of the multitude, amid the ebb and flow of movement, in the midst of the fugitive and infinite. To be away from home and yet to feel oneself everywhere at home; to see the world, to be at the centre of the world, and yet to remain hidden from the world—such are a few of the slightest pleasures of those independent, passionate, impartial natures which the tongue can but clumsily define. The spectator is a *prince* who everywhere rejoices in his incognito. The lover of life makes the whole world his family, just like the lover of the fair sex who builds up his family from all the beautiful women that he has ever found, or that are—or are not—to be found; or the lover of pictures who lives in a magical society of dreams painted on canvas. Thus the lover of universal life enters into the crowd as though it were an immense reservoir of electrical energy. Or we might liken him to a mirror as vast as the crowd itself; or to a kaleidoscope gifted with consciousness, responding to each one of its movements and reproducing the multiplicity of life and the flick-ering grace of all the elements of life. He is an "I" with an insatiable appetite for the "non-I," at every instant rendering and explaining it in pictures more living than life itself, which is always unstable and fugitive.[18]

Poe's own varied works also present a kind of kaleidoscopic image of the world, with the strange blended with the beautiful in often grotesque and arabesque patterns. The "world" thus represented is not really a world to be known, but a plenum to be experi-enced in various, often unsettling ways.

Baudelaire understood immediately that the key aspect of Poe's genius lay not in discovering a hitherto unknown entity, but in approaching reality from a particular point of view and thereby seeing things very differently. For Baudelaire, the novel way of seeing is artistic, yes, but it is also far more than that. It requires what Baudelaire calls "a *man of the world* [...] a man who understands the world and the mysterious and lawful reasons for all of its uses." Baudelaire cites Poe's "Man of the Crowd" to make his point. Notably, Baudelaire focuses attention on the narrator of that story, not the fugitive figure of "man of the crowd" himself, to define the type of artist that can really be the man of the world. As Baudelaire summarizes,

Do you remember a picture (it really is a picture!), painted—or rather written— by the most powerful pen of our age, and entitled *The Man of the Crowd*? In the window of a coffee-house there sits a convalescent, pleasurably absorbed in gazing at the crowd, and mingling, through the medium of thought, in the turmoil of thought that surrounds him. But lately returned from the valley of the shadow of death, he is rapturously breathing in all the odours and essences of life; as he has been on the brink of total oblivion, he remembers, and fervently desires to remember, everything. Finally he hurls himself headlong into the midst of the throng, in pursuit of the unknown, half-glimpsed countenance that has, on an instant, bewitched him. Curiosity has become a fatal, irresistible passion.[19]

---

[18] Baudelaire, "The Painter of Modern Life," 9–10.
[19] Ibid., 7.

The man of the world is not, therefore, the man of the crowd. The man of the world, here represented by Poe's convalescent and exceedingly curious narrator, is a "passionate spectator." This kaleidoscope equipped with consciousness is not, however, the social scientist that the narrator had imagined himself to be at the beginning of the tale, but an uncertain, mobile registrar of the unknowable.

With Poe, inscrutability is the constant, lurking menace, confounding the sense of sense-making and troubling one's confidence in knowing at all. Like the purloined letter, the text and its desired meaning dangle right before our eyes, without our being able to comprehend it in any definitive way. Or, like Poe's narrator in "The Man of the Crowd," we can marvel at the enigma before us, but we cannot understand. That narrator begins his tale by noting that men "die with despair of heart and convulsion of throat, on account of the hideousness of mysteries that will not *suffer themselves* to be revealed."[20] But, by the end of his long, dark night of fruitlessly investigating the mysterious "man of the crowd," the narrator changes his tune. Given what greater terrors might be found if we truly could look into those inscrutable mysteries, "perhaps it is but one of the great mercies of God that *er lässt sich nicht lesen.*"[21] Maybe this reasonable and comforting thought will allow him to sleep, but as Goya so memorably depicted it, the sleep of reason breeds monsters. Yet, in his own comical doubling, as one who has spent the night being himself a sort of man of the crowd (by following the other), the narrator's final revelation comes across as vaguely comical. He himself is a book that does not permit itself to be read, least of all by himself. An unwitting *Doppelgänger*, the man of the world faces his mirror image, but cannot quite recognize him.

The *Doppelgänger*'s mirror image

Although he remains best known for tales of Gothic horror or mystery, Poe's overall *oeuvre* is suffused with a tone of satire, prankishness, and humor. Indeed, one might characterize Poe's work as essentially comic, and the violence and terror associated with so many of his best known tales are frequently part of the joke, although the joke may most likely be on us, the readers, rather than on any of the characters in the tales. So it is with Poe's paradigmatic *Doppelgänger* story, "William Wilson," in which the narrator who has seemingly been plagued by his mysterious double at last stabs his enemy with a rapier. Upon expiring, Wilson—or is it the narrator himself?—declares that, in the image of his death, the murderer can see "how utterly thou hast murdered thyself."[22] As in the comedian's slang phrase, "I kill myself," this may indicate the risibility of the scene, as the *peripeteia* of a murder-that-turns-out-to-be-a-suicide is really a kind of practical joke. The reader may not be laughing, but perhaps Poe is.

As a master of the forms of Gothic sensationalism, Poe expertly blends the comically absurd with the most gut-wrenchingly violent imagery, as when the narrator

---

[20] Poe, "The Man of the Crowd," *Poetry and Tales*, 388.
[21] Ibid., 396.
[22] Poe, "William Wilson," ibid., 357.

of "Berenice" extracts the teeth from his still-living but prematurely interred love, to take a particularly gruesome example. As we have seen, Poe was also an adept at gauging the public appetites for such fare; in response to his editor's dismay at how "horrible" the tale was, Poe argued that those magazines which were successful published work "similar in nature" to "Berenice," and that such nature consisted in "the ludicrous heightened into the grotesque: the fearful coloured into the horrible: the witty exaggerated into the burlesque: the singular wrought out into the strange and mystical."[23] In each of these elements, Poe makes clear that *excess*—perhaps *doubling* the initial sensation to produce ever greater effects in the reader—is the key to successfully capturing the attention of the audience. As I discuss in the following chapter, Poe gleefully ventures *extra moenia flammantia mundi*, away from simplicity and the cant of the day, into a fantastic literary extravagance. Poe's doubling down on the perceived limit of "good taste" in many of his most famous stories, and in many more of his lesser known ones, is a mark of his own comic sensibilities, as the laughter with which one encounters a transgression is only possible once one has identified, and then crossed over, the boundary.

Poe also frequently invokes the popular figure of the *Doppelgänger*, most directly visible in "William Wilson," but also throughout his *oeuvre*. One thinks of the double-characterization of Roderick and Madeleine Usher, for instance, or the ghostly doublings in "Morella" or "Ligeia," or again the strange relationship between the narrator and his man of the crowd. Amid the horror of these tales, Poe also seems to be having some fun with the reader, and I would argue that his use of the "double" and his literary practice of "doubling" is a means of intensifying the comic aspects of his violent and terrifying work.

"William Wilson," which was initially written in response to the great humorist Washington Irving's invitation to complete "An Unwritten Drama of Lord Byron," provides an exquisite case study. In Irving's sketchy plot summary, a masked man haunts the footsteps of the increasingly agitated protagonist; at the climactic moment, the protagonist stabs his persecutor and, removing the mask, discovers his own face staring back at him. Irving concludes that story by inviting "a poet or dramatist of the Byron school" to pen a complete version of the tale, an invitation Poe clearly accepted, as he notes in a letter to Irving, in which he enclosed a copy of "William Wilson," in 1839. Given this pre-history, one might say that the story is already a doubling of a tale that may have been known to others in Poe's original audience, at least to those who had seen Irving's "Unfinished Drama" in the August 1835 issue of *The Knickerbocker; Or, the New York Monthly Magazine*. Furthermore, the reference to Byron adds another double, in so far as the narrator or William Wilson is already suggestive of the Byronic hero or villain, whether in view of the poet's creative works or with respect to his infamous biography. The redoubled duplication involving Irving's own retelling of a Spanish drama by a British poet makes the narrative itself a kind of garden of forking paths, in which all possibilities seem open, but where any truly ascertainable meaning seems foreclosed in advance.

[23] Poe, "Letter to Thomas W. White" (April 30, 1835), *The Letters of Edgar Allan Poe*, 57.

In Poe's version of the tale, "William Wilson" presents itself as an inscrutable phantasmagoria in which the reader is made to feel perplexed from the outset. Beginning with the dual identification and non-identification of the narrator, who declines to give his real name and provisionally introduces himself with a pseudonym, the obscuring of personal identity in the tale continues to mystify by oscillating between at least two identities, those of the two William Wilsons. This actually raises the question of a double-*Doppelgänger*, since the reader is invited to associate the narrator with the "real" William Wilson who is plagued by his double, but the reader is also made aware of the inconsistencies in the narrator's story, allowing one to doubt exactly who is the double and who is the original. Indeed, as I suggest below, the *mise en abyme* of the tale renders the narrative a kind of text that does not allow itself to be read.

"William Wilson" begins rather inauspiciously. The narrator's two introductory paragraphs seem to provide a rationale for the storytelling, by explaining why *this* narrator would want to tell *this* story, but these lines also serve to obscure the presentation of a truly accessible "reality" even further. Paradoxically, the very paragraphs that would establish the authority of the narrator and commend the reader to believe the tale are the ones that begin to undermine the truth-value of the narrative. As in "The Tell-Tale Heart," in which the obviously insane narrator pleads with the reader to recognize his sanity, the narrator of "William Wilson" undermines his own narrative authority even as he establishes his narrative voice, as one can discern in the opening lines: "Let me call myself, for the present, William Wilson. The fair page lying before me need not be sullied with my real appellation."[24] First, by invoking and then providing a false name, the narrator introduces deceit from the very beginning of the tale. The name *William Wilson* is thus a sign, but one that signifies an absence in the text. The "real" person who would appear to be relating important events from his own biography remains cloaked. Moreover, since this narrative is intended to solicit the reader's belief, the unreliability of the narrator becomes part of the joke. In simultaneously inviting and rebuffing the audience's credulity, Poe is toying with the reader. "William Wilson," it appears, is not just a tale of a double, but also a tale of duplicity.

The overall plot of "William Wilson" may be summarized briefly. The narrator endeavors to explain the origin of his "later years of unspeakable misery, and unpardonable crime," and, although he will not describe any aspect of that "turpitude," he explains his desire to expose its source. In this untrustworthy narrative, the reader is urged to understand that the source of the narrator's apparently notorious, but ever unknown, bad behavior lies in an event which will be revealed only in the closing lines of the story. The main body of the tale, which elaborates the narrator's morally questionable early life and his eerie encounters with a mysterious *Doppelgänger*, is really all prologue to the real criminal enormities left unexposed. Hence, even the confessional form of the story is a joke; the narrator does not confess anything, but rather weaves a tale that will explain in advance those mortal sins that must remain unknown. This represents yet another doubling, where the meaning of the "turpitude"

---

[24] Poe, "William Wilson," *Poetry and Tales*, 337.

is forever deferred or displaced, or perhaps located in a parallel world just outside of the text itself.

Famously, the narrator is plagued by the appearance at his school of another boy who coincidentally shares his name, his date of birth, his approximate height and build ... in other words, this second William Wilson appears to be his exact double. Perplexingly, however, the narrator concedes that no one else at his school noticed the resemblance, so the reader is placed in a position of uncertainty and doubt from the start. Does this *Doppelgänger* even exist, or if the boy is himself real, is he really a "double"? The narrator is vexed by a sense of Wilson's superiority, but his "real feelings towards him [...] formed a motley and heterogeneous admixture—some petulant animosity, which was not yet hatred, some esteem, more respect, much fear, with a world of uneasy curiosity."[25] One night, the narrator creeps into Wilson's bedchamber to execute some malicious practical joke when he is struck by Wilson's apparently identical aspect to his own, and he flees both the room and the academy forever. In the course of the remainder of the story, we see three key incidents in which Wilson reappears in time to thwart the narrator's desires. First, as a student at Eton, the narrator is interrupted by Wilson's mysterious appearance just as he was engaged in some wild debauchery. Then, at Oxford, while the narrator is trying to cheat in a card game, Wilson's ghostly voice reveals the truth of the deception, forcing the narrator to flee the outraged company of his intended victims. Now on the continent, the narrator briefly mentions a number of similar episodes before describing the final scene, in which he attempts to seduce a nobleman's wife at a masquerade ball in Rome, when a masked Wilson once more interferes. Dragging Wilson into a cloakroom, the furious narrator stabs his persecutor. For a slight moment, confusing what seems to be a mirror image with the scene before him, the narrator is alarmed by his own bloody countenance, but discovers that Wilson, now unmasked, is indeed his identical double. Wilson gets the final word before dying, however, by stating that his death is really the narrator's own: "*In me didst thou exist—and, in my death, see by this image, which is thine own, how utterly thou hast murdered thyself.*"[26]

For the reader, an initial confusion persists throughout the story, calling into question almost the entire plot of "William Wilson." If nobody else at Dr. Bransby's school or elsewhere notices the second Wilson, or notices him *as* the narrator's double or even as a rival, then is all of this merely in the narrator's head? Is the second Wilson simply a metaphor, the personification of the narrator's conscience, and not a real human being? Could this story be another practical joke, a prank upon the too gullible audience of the day? Susan Amper has suggested that this tale, like such murderer's narratives as "The Tell-Tale Heart," "The Black Cat," or "The Imp of the Perverse," is in fact an example of a lying (or duplicitous?) narrator, one who has in fact killed someone back at Dr. Bransby's Manor School and who has been at large, on some sort of crime spree, ever since.[27] Is this not an otherworldly mystery, but a more

---

[25] Ibid., 343.
[26] Ibid., 357.
[27] See Amper, "Masters of Deceit," 170–211.

straightforward tale of a violent psychopath, who seeks to cover his tracks with an outlandish alibi? Or is "William Wilson" a send-up of the Gothic *Doppelgänger* genre?

An apt figure for the overall narrative game being played upon the reader in "William Wilson" might be found in the narrator's curious description of Dr. Bransby's school itself.

> But the house! — how quaint an old building was this! — to me how veritably a palace of enchantment! There was really no end to its windings — to its incomprehensible subdivisions. It was difficult, at any given time, to say with certainty upon which of its two stories one happened to be. From each room to every other there were sure to be found three or four steps either in ascent or descent. Then the lateral branches were innumerable — inconceivable — and so returning in upon themselves, that our most exact ideas in regard to the whole mansion were not very far different from those with which we pondered upon infinity. During the five years of my residence here, I was never able to ascertain with precision, in what remote locality lay the little sleeping apartment assigned to myself and some eighteen or twenty other scholars.[28]

The mysteriously unmappable place might be said to represent the narrative space of the tale itself, since the reader is forced to chart the contours and discernible features of a story which the narrator, and perhaps author, seems intent on obscuring. One finds a mixture of humor and terror in the image of a schoolboy who gets lost in his own school. Not knowing where he is at any given moment, the boy must project an imaginary cartography in order to acquire the desired orientation and to realistically know his place. In performing this kind of cognitive mapping, the narrator calls upon not so much spatial analysis (which, in any case, is lacking in the text itself) as a kind of moral geography, in which his own actions can be situated in a recognizable environment of good and bad, right and wrong. But, notwithstanding this astonishing passage concerning the uncharitable space of the Manor House, the boy in question in "William Wilson" navigates the space quite well, as he notes by describing his ability to steal effortlessly "through a wilderness of narrow passages" to find Wilson's bedroom, where he intended to commit "one of those ill-natured pieces of practical wit."[29] So it is not really the narrator, but the reader, who is comically, and terrifyingly, lost in the tale's cosmopolitan wilderness.

The appearance of the mirror in the final scene causes another momentary confusion, and it adds to the overall sense that "William Wilson" is itself one of Poe's practical jokes. After repeatedly stabbing Wilson with his sword, the narrator briefly turns away to lock the door; then, looking upon the scene afresh, he sees himself, bloody and staggering toward him. "The brief moment in which I averted my eyes had been sufficient to produce, apparently, a material change in the arrangements at the upper or farther end of the room. A large mirror—so at first it seemed to me in my confusion—now stood where none had been perceptible before; and, as I stepped

---

[28] Poe, "William Wilson," *Poetry and Tales*, 340.
[29] Ibid., 346.

up to it in extremity of terror, mine own image, but with features all pale and dabbled in blood, advanced to meet me with a feeble and tottering gait."[30] The insertion of the mirror into the "arrangements of the room" would be almost comical, even in its macabre depiction of the gory self-image lurching toward the murderer, but for its illusoriness. The notion of the infinite regression of identical images, the *mise en abyme*, is raised in the narrator's vision of himself at this moment and of himself at the story, as the narrator doubles himself in the narration, and the reader cannot be certain of who is who at any given moment. But, of course, there is no mirror. The narrator continues: "Thus it appeared I say, but was not."[31] This reintroduces the *Doppelgänger* story, allowing a physically identical Wilson to address the narrator, but the line also speaks for the story as a whole. "Thus it appeared I say, but was not" is a caveat applicable to "William Wilson" in general. Here is a seemingly final duplicity, a doubling that renders the most violent scene of the tale a comical one as well, as Poe plays a last trick upon the reader.

One might observe an additional perversity detectible in the tale. In his playful use of the double, Poe also doubles himself, presenting another "Poe" who becomes a means of satire. The Poe who takes pride in his talents, the "poet or dramatist of the Byron school" capable of successfully meeting Irving's challenge, is also an avatar or a sign representing more than the biographical person born on January 19, 1809 in Boston, et cetera. (And, naturally, few readers fail to notice that Poe gave both the narrator of "William Wilson" and the Wilson-*Doppelgänger* Poe's own birth date, along with his own named "elementary school" in Dr. Bransby's.) Poe's presumably deliberate doubling in this story dramatizes the double-consciousness of the author. One thinks of Jorge Luis Borges's fable, "Borges and I," depicting the eerie uncertainties of a writer seeking to avoid himself, discovering that "my life is a flight and I lose everything and everything belongs to oblivion, or to him."[32] Borges concludes this parable by saying that "I do not know which of us has written this page,"[33] a haunting return to a situation not unlike that of the narrator of "William Wilson." In both his fictional doubles and his own doubled self, Poe offers a combination of comedy and terror that satirizes both, while also promulgating new literary forms and novel approaches to understanding them.

As I have suggested, this double-Poe reveals itself in Poe's work in the form of a practical joke. Or, to use an even more precise term from Poe's *corpus*, a "diddle." In "Diddling Considered as One of the Exact Sciences," Poe notes that the final and essential element of every diddle (that is, prank, swindle, or confidence game) is the grin: "Your *true* diddler winds up all with a grin. But this nobody sees but himself." Poe concludes, "a diddle would be *no* diddle without a grin."[34] At the end of the comically eerie *Doppelgänger* tale of "William Wilson," it may be Poe who wears the diddler's grin, while the readers are left to scratch their heads.

[30] Ibid., 356.
[31] Ibid.
[32] Borges, *Labyrinths*, 246.
[33] Ibid., 247.
[34] Poe, "Diddling Considered as One of the Exact Sciences," *Poetry and Tales*, 609.

Poe's urbane and urban writing exemplifies the mysterious and sometimes humorous uncertainties of nineteenth-century social experience in the United States. The rapid population growth and urbanization, establishing among many citizens for the first time a "world of strangers," undoubtedly created novel opportunities for encountering bizarre eccentrics and uncanny look-alikes, inscrutable men of the crowd and curious doubles. As a "connoisseur of cities," Poe recognized and exaggerated the urban types, and in his satirical critique of contemporary culture he exploited the fantastic mode to brilliant effect. His mode of urbane fantasy was not merely that of Dickens, in which the most quotidian experiences are made enchanting by the powers of "MOOR EEFFOC." Referring to "that elvish kind of realism Dickens adopted everywhere," G. K. Chesterton recounts how a young Charles Dickens discovered these seemingly magical words by seeing the sign "Coffee Room" from the other side of a glass door. Chesterton concludes that "it is the masterpiece of the good realistic principle—the principle that the most fantastic of all is often the precise fact."[35] In his own experiences, Poe did not stand in awe of the merely eccentric, but allowed himself as a writer to venture beyond the flaming walls of the world in producing his satirical critique.

---

[35] Chesterton, *Charles Dickens*, 47–8.

8

Extra Mœnia Flammantia Mundi: Satire, Fantasy, and the Critic's Laughter

The subterranean noises emanating from the crypt in Poe's writings are typical of his underground satire, fantasy, and critique of the burgeoning national culture in the nineteenth-century United States. Poe's poetics of descent counters the lofty pretentions and rhetoric of ascent of the prevailing ideologies of the era, pronounced in that optative mood with Emersonian self-assurance, and proleptically punctures the self-inflated, triumphalist, secular religion of an American Studies in the twentieth century, which would attempt to shape those earlier ideologies into a mythic national identity and mission. Poe makes a mockery of such national ideals. In his life and work, Poe contests the popular frontier ethic of settlement in favor of unsettling movement, rebuffs the domesticating comforts of home while proposing irreversible descent into the unknowable, denies the epistemic claims of both social science and narrative while evoking the terrors of an unmappable space, and disputes the moral and patriotic value of literature. At the same time, Poe re-imagines the project of literature as a perverse, conflicted activity that entails captivity, control, and perplexity. The worldliness of the author and of his own sense of literary production comports well with the increasing urbanization and immigrations, early instances of the overall movement toward globalization that Marx had identified as the foundation for a world literature. Just as Marx and Engels had noted that, with the development of the world market, "[n]ational one-sidedness and narrow-mindedness become more and more impossible, and from the numerous national and local literatures, there arises a world literature," Poe also makes clear that no "true literature *could be* 'national' " and that "the world at large" is "the only proper stage for the literary *histrio*."[1] But Poe's objection to national narrative is less in the interest of unifying literary workers of the world than in undermining the narrow-minded "literary America" coming into being in the 1840s. In his criticism and reviews, Poe makes a mockery of the aims and effects of this national project, and the resounding traces of Poe's presence in the American literary tradition are the echoes of his laughter.

Poe's risible, subterranean noises represent a sort of counter-movement to the clear voice of a nationalist American Studies. To the jeremiads of this or that generation of

---

[1] Marx and Engels, *The Communist Manifesto*, 55; Poe, "Exordium to Critical Notices," *Essays and Reviews*, 1027.

apologists, to those who proclaim a quasi-sacred national mission or lament that "we" have lost our way, Poe starkly unveils the ghastly materiality of the earthly perspective from which one discerns no grand national mission and no American way, but merely the swirling circulation of bodies in motion. Poe's laughter punctures the ludicrously solemn enterprise that would sanctify a handful of century-old products of mass culture and of a vicissitudinous marketplace, turning them into sacred texts of a providentially chosen people on an errand into the wilderness. With the emergence of the disciplinary field of American literature, these nineteenth-century writings—at least the ones that can be made to fit into the mythic, national image repertoire—have often been subsumed within the larger project of American Studies. This is how such eccentric literary figures as Hester Prynne, or a person called "Ishmael," or even the picaresque Huckleberry Finn suddenly find themselves, in the twentieth century, to be anthropomorphic embodiments of the nation itself. It is not surprising that, as David Shumway has put it, just when the United States has attained a level of supremacy among the nations of the world, it "discovered" that it had a unified and coherent national literature. The job of American literature scholars was "to explain how the canonized writers fit together in a literary tradition or cultural pattern," and, as a result, "the effect of the collective work of the discipline of American literature was to celebrate American civilization."[2] In large part, the formal study of American literature emerges concurrently with a discourse of the "American Century," to use the term that Henry Luce introduced in 1941, the same year as F. O. Matthiessen's field-establishing *American Renaissance*. But Poe is already somehow "post-American" or, perhaps, simply anti-American. In Poe, there is no such representative avatar of American thought, but a series of pranksters who, like Hop-Frog, would delight in dressing these haughty personages as buffoons and setting them aflame. Or worse, a number of Poe's characters *are* representative American types, like "The Business Man" Peter Pendulum (a.k.a. Peter Proffit), but they are fools to be mocked, not part of any "community of saints" to be admired.[3] Poe's writings have little truck with the literary nationalism of his or the following century's, and the most clearly audible strain in his work comes from a thoroughly sardonic voice, satirical and otherworldly, from below.

Much of Poe's work appears to be grounded in an aggressively satirical mode, but, as Tom Quirk has argued, this does not necessarily mean that Poe's humor is funny.[4] Poe's mockery may not be entirely as mean-spirited as Quirk supposes, although his barbs at the literati of New York and, more pointedly, at the popular philosophers of "Frogpondium" are rather sharp at times. However, Poe's laughter also carries with it the jubilation of the critic, a kind of delight in sending up the self-satisfied or uncritical assumptions permeating the mainstream culture of those places, while also laden with a small tinge of melancholy at the recognition that such satirical critique is all-too-needed in one's own world. It is the laughter of Friedrich Nietzsche, who writes in the

---

[2] David Shumway, *Creating American Civilization*, 299, 319, 339.
[3] The phrase "community of saints" is Lionel Trilling's, who applied it to the relationship between Huck and Jim in *The Adventures of Huckleberry Finn*; see Trilling, *The Liberal Imagination*, 108.
[4] See Quirk, *Nothing Abstract*, 53–63.

opening lines of *The Twilight of the Idols* that "maintaining cheerfulness in the midst of a gloomy affair, fraught with immeasurable responsibility, is no small feat; and yet, what is needed more than cheerfulness? Nothing succeeds if prankishness has no part in it."[5] Poe's is a prankish sort of criticism, a jocular kind of underground rumbling, that can remind readers of alternative ways of looking at the American literature and culture frequently taken for granted. The subterranean noises of Poe's work are like that strange music, faintly heard, emanating from another, seemingly fantastic world, but helping us think differently about our own real world.

As discussed in the previous chapters, Poe's versatility and eclectic sensibility, along with his ambiguous tone and penchant for sarcasm, make any global statements about him untenable. Just as Poe's writings did not quite fit in Jonathan Arac's classifications of nineteenth-century narrative forms, so too does Poe's work resist the generic limits of horror, mystery, science fiction, comedy, or farce. If called upon to name one, I would say that the genre that most ably encompasses Poe multifaceted *oeuvre* is fantasy, a term more or less synonymous with Poe's usage of grotesque and arabesque, and which establishes *alterity* as its fundamental characteristic.[6] Indeed, Poe himself seems to have favored the term, as evidenced by his desire to issue a revised and expanded version of *Tales of the Grotesque and Arabesque* under the title *Phantasy-Pieces*. By claiming that Poe is essentially a fantasist, I do not in any way mean to suggest that he is no longer the satirist, the hoaxer, the mocking critic, or the playful prankster. On the contrary, I find Poe's satirical critique to be all the more forceful when considered in the fantastic mode. For fantasy is not, as is sometimes supposed, an escape from reality, a flight of fancy away from the exigencies of the real world. Rather, in the radical alterity and sheer weirdness of the mode, fantasy maintains a directly critical function, presenting alternative realities as a positive means of calling into question the often false or distorted aspects of the apparently "real" world in which we live. Poe's literary voyages "beyond the flaming walls of the world," I argue and conclude, do not seek to transcend the material realities of his time and place, but to bring his reader back to earth, grounding the reader in the truer reality revealed through the satirical and fantastic works. As in the horror or the comedy of Poe's premature burials, the re-emergence of the subterranean presence changes the way we see the narrative as a whole, as well as the ways we see the world that such narratives fitfully and uncertainly represent.

Poe's alterity can be seen partly in his supposed "outsider" status with American literature and his rather *outré* perspective on the cultures of the United States. Poe is a thoroughly worldly figure, adept at coping with and exploiting the commercial and social realities of the nineteenth-century United States, and, at the same time, he is an otherworldly presence, an underground man whose mocking laughter and practical joking troubles the main currents of American thought. Charles Baudelaire understood him as a "man of the world," and yet Poe also manages to stand apart from that

---

[5] Nietzsche, *The Twilight of the Idols*, 465.
[6] Of course, Poe is well known as a fantasist, both in his own work and as the precursor to later writers of fantasy. For an overview of Poe and fantasy, see Kent Ljungquist, "The Short Fiction of Poe"; see also Brian Attebery, *The Fantasy Tradition in American Literature*.

world, not as an ethereal presence rising above it but as the sharp-eyed observer and prankster. Poe's otherworldliness carries with it the aura of satire, and thus critique, and the fantastic elements of Poe's writings are intimately tied to the humorous ones, often overlapping to a degree that makes any generic boundaries between them rather indistinct. Poe's reputation and skills as a humorist are well known, even if he is still predominantly viewed as a writer of horror, mystery, and suspense, but the combination of satirical and fantastic modes in Poe's overall corpus suggests another perspective. Poe's fantastic or otherworldly satire, mobilized in the service of his general critique of the American literary and national culture, might be thought of as his "last laugh."

Phantasy-pieces

In his portrait of Nathaniel P. Willis in "The Literati of New York City" series, Poe includes a lengthy and philosophical footnote in which he explains the definitions and interrelations among four mental faculties, each and all of which bear on Poe's own writing. It is worth quoting at length:[7]

> Imagination, fancy, fantasy and humour, have in common the elements combination and novelty. The imagination is the artist of the four. From novel arrangements of old forms which present themselves to it, it selects such only as are harmonious; the result, of course, is *beauty* itself—using the word in its most extended sense and as inclusive of the sublime. The pure imagination chooses, *from either beauty or deformity,* only the most combinable things hitherto uncombined; the compound, as a general rule, partaking in character of sublimity or beauty in the ratio of the respective sublimity or beauty of the things combined, which are themselves still to be considered as atomic—that is to say, as previous combinations. But, as often analogously happens in physical chemistry, so not unfrequently does it occur in this chemistry of the intellect, that the admixture of two elements will result in a something that shall have nothing of the quality of one of them—or even nothing of the qualities of either. The range of imagination is thus unlimited. Its materials extend throughout the universe. Even out of deformities it fabricates that *beauty* which is at once its sole object and its inevitable test. But, in general, the richness of the matters combined, the facility of discovering combinable novelties worth combining, and *the absolute "chemical combination"* of the completed mass, are the particulars to be regarded in our estimate of imagination. It is this thorough harmony of an imaginative work which so often causes it to be undervalued by the undiscriminating, through the character of *obviousness* which is superinduced. We are apt to find ourselves asking *why it is that these combinations have never been imagined before.*

Poe is here reiterating his long-standing position, disputing Samuel Taylor Coleridge's distinction between fancy and the imagination, which had held that "fancy

---

[7] Poe, "N. P. Willis," in "The Literati of New York City," *Essays and Reviews*, 1126–7.

combines—imagination creates." In Poe's view, the mind does not *create* at all, techni-cally, since "[t]he mind of man can imagine nothing which does not really exist; if it could, it would create not only ideally but substantially, as do the thoughts of God." But Poe goes on to characterize the differences between the imagination and fancy, as well as between these and fantasy or humor, as differences in degree and in kind. In other words, these are different genres that partake of the same spirit and substance, but involve highly nuanced, yet seemingly natural, responses to various combinations of imagery.

In delineating the contours of the four modes, Poe points out their subtle differ-ences, but he also makes clear that each is the result of the same basic literary process, which is to say, *combination*. As Poe continues from the lines previously quoted above,

> Now, when this question *does not occur,* when the harmony of the combination is comparatively neglected, and when, in addition to the element of novelty, there is introduced the sub-element of *unexpectedness*—when, for example, matters are brought into combination which not only have never been combined, but whose combination strikes us as a *difficulty happily overcome,* the result then appertains to the fancy, and is, to the majority of mankind, more grateful than the purely harmonious one—although, absolutely, it is less beautiful (or grand) for the reason that *it is* less harmonious.
>
> Carrying its errors into excess—for, however enticing, they *are* errors still, or nature lies—fancy is at length found infringing upon the province of fantasy. The votaries of this latter delight not only in novelty and unexpectedness of combi-nation, but in the *avoidance* of proportion. The result is, therefore, abnormal, and, to a healthy mind, affords less of pleasure through its novelty than of pain through its incoherence. When, proceeding a step farther, however, fancy seeks not merely disproportionate but incongruous or antagonistic elements, the effect is rendered more pleasurable by its greater positiveness; there is a merry effort of truth to shake from her that which is no property of hers, and we laugh outright in recognizing humour.
>
> The four faculties in question seem to me all of their class; but when either fancy or humour is expressed to gain an end, is pointed at a purpose—whenever either becomes objective in place of subjective, then it becomes, also, pure wit or sarcasm, just as the purpose is benevolent or malevolent.

Not all would agree with Poe's theory of humor, tied as it is to the primacy of sarcasm in its usage. Poe's sense of humor can sometimes seem a bit more mean-spirited than good-natured, but that is perhaps unsurprising in one who reveled in hoaxes. However, the crucial aspect of Poe's aesthetic theory is laid bare in this perverse notion of art as *combinatoire*, and Poe's almost sacred power of the imagination can be seen mingling with the most profane and pedestrian, earthy or street-level humor.

If the fancy produces inharmonious combinations that are unexpected, the power of fantasy lies in the intentional "avoidance of proportion." The artist operating in a fantastic mode thus intentionally causes some "pain" through the purposed incoherence of the work. Yet, as Poe explains, the same basic incoherence becomes all the more pleasurable for the reader when pushed a step further, where the fantastic is no longer weird or "disproportionate" but actually antagonistic, at which point fantasy becomes humor. Thus the fantastic mode also incorporates the satirical, humorous, or comical force that animates so much of Poe's overall corpus. In this sense, Poe's laughter really is otherworldly, but it is directed, positively and pointedly, at our own world.

Owing to his own use of the terms in the first collection of short stories he was able to publish, much has quite rightly been made of Poe's tales of the *grotesque* and *arabesque*. However, as noted previously, it is misleading to think of these as clearly defined genres in themselves. In any event, Poe's work cannot be limited to these two, unless they be understood as encompassing an exceptionally broad range of writings. I believe one could in fact make this case, but only if *grotesque* and *arabesque* are conceived as merely alternative ways of referring to the fantastic mode itself, a mode of radical alterity. Of the many genres in which Poe wrote—or, rather, into which Poe's multifarious compositions might be placed—Poe himself designated one as the title of a book he never published, *Phantasy-Pieces*. In a hand-written title page for a new collection which would include "all the author's late tales with a new edition of the 'Grotesque and Arabesque,'"[8] Poe subtly elevates "phantasy" to a preferred status, and in re-presenting nearly all of his prose fiction under the guise of "phantasy-pieces," Poe attempts to re-evaluate, if not undermine entirely, the traditional valuation of more purely mimetic art, as I discuss below. The epigraph, quoting Goethe and written in German, also in Poe's handwriting, reads:

Seltsamen tochter Jovis,
Seinem schosskinde,
Der *Phantasie*.

It is a dedication, "to the strange daughter of Jove, his best-loved child, Phantasy." The poem from which these lines are extracted goes even further, and the title alone shows how Goethe—and perhaps more so, Poe—felt about this strange daughter of Jove. The first stanza of "Mein Göttin" ("My Goddess") asks, then answers: "Which immortal deserves the highest praise? With none I contend, but I will give it to the ever-moving, always new, strange daughter of Jove, his best-loved child, Phantasy."[9] The peripatetic nomad in a land of settlers and tireless crier on behalf of a true originality, Poe too was ever-moving, always new, and, more often than not, strange. Poe almost certainly copied Goethe's lines from another source, as was his custom,[10] but his use of this of all possible epigraphs suggests that his commitment to fantasy extends more deeply than it would appear from those handful of tales that might today be placed in the

---

[8] A facsimile of the title page, as well as the table of contents, appears on the indispensable website of the Edgar Allan Poe Society of Baltimore, http://www.eapoe.org. Poe's two-volume *Tales of the Grotesque and Arabesque*, which had used the same Goethe quotation as an epigraph, had appeared in 1840, and it is likely that its tepid sales made it difficult for Poe to find a publisher for a revised and expanded edition.

[9] Goethe, "Mein Göttin," 63, translation modified.

[10] Mabbott notes that Poe probably read the lines in George Bancroft's "The Life and Genius of Goethe" in the *North American Review* in 1924; see Poe, *Complete Poems*, 118.

marketing genre or subgenre that is labeled "fantasy." Poe's handwritten table of contents discloses that he planned to include almost all of his tales and sketches under this banner of *phantasy*, as the collection would lead off with such diverse works as "The Murders in the Rue Morgue," "The Man That Was Used Up," "Descent into the Maelstrom," and so on.

Poe's sense of fantasy obviously differed from that of many contemporaries. Poe's well known labels, *grotesque* and *arabesque*, were almost certainly borrowed from Sir Walter Scott, who used these terms, but did not necessarily distinguish between them, twice in his 1827 essay "On the Supernatural in Fictitious Composition." Nominally an extensive review of several works by E. T. A. Hoffmann, Scott's essay provides a foundational text for a debate about the suitable proportion of fantasy and reality in literature, a debate that continues to elicit heated responses to this day, particularly among those who question the distinctions between so-called "literary" and "genre" fiction.[11] At one point, Scott casually delineates the contours of this battlefield, and thus, perhaps inadvertently, he also constructs the framework in which Poe's own sense of the literary and of genres will emerge. Scott first quotes the concluding paragraph of Hoffmann's *The Entail*, a story not entirely dissimilar to some of Poe's "phantasy-pieces," in which a frightfully supernatural occurrence concludes with a calm, somewhat revelatory but still eerie explanation. Scott then offers a critical elaboration and assessment:

> The passage which we have just quoted, while it shows the wildness of Hoffmann's fancy, evinces also that he possessed power which ought to have mitigated and allayed it. Unfortunately, his taste and temperament directed him too strongly to the grotesque and fantastic,—carried him too far "extra mœnia flammantia mundi," too much beyond the circle not only of probability but even of possibility, to admit of his composing much in the better style which he might easily have attained. The popular romance, no doubt, has many walks, nor are we at all inclined to halloo the dogs of criticism against those whose object is merely to amuse a passing hour. It may be repeated with truth, that in this path of light literature, "tout genre est permis hors les genres ennuyeux," and of course, an error in taste ought not to be followed up and hunted down as if it were a false maxim in morality, a delusive hypothesis in science, or a heresy in religion itself. Genius too, is, we are aware, capricious, and must be allowed to take its own flights, however eccentric, were it but for the sake of experiment. Sometimes, also, it may be eminently pleasing to look at the wildness of an Arabesque painting executed by a man of rich fancy. But we do not desire to see genius expand or rather exhaust itself upon themes which cannot be reconciled to taste; and the utmost length in which we can indulge a turn to the fantastic is, where it tends to excite agreeable and pleasing ideas.
>
> We are not called upon to be equally tolerant of such capriccios as are not only startling by their extravagance, but disgusting by their horrible import.[12]

---

[11] See Hume, *Fantasy and Mimesis.*
[12] Scott, "On the Supernatural in Fictitious Composition," 247.

Here Scott seems to anticipate, several years earlier, Thomas W. White's less philo-sophical but still pertinent judgment that Poe's "Berenice" was "far too horrible" and that "it approaches the very verge of bad taste."[13] It may be noteworthy that Scott is willing to forgive literature that extends "beyond the flaming walls of the world" (to translate the Latin phrase) so long as it can "excite agreeable and pleasant ideas." Poe would, of course, push through the disagreeable and unpleasant ideas to get to whatever lay beyond such walls.

Scott, who by practically inventing the historical novel also laid the foundation for nineteenth-century national narrative, exerted a profound influence over generations of writers and critics.[14] This review is itself a key text in the history of fantasy writing. The French maxim Scott paraphrases is already familiar; it is Voltaire's assertion that all genres are good except the boring ones, a view that Poe and his intended readership would probably embrace. The Latin expression that Scott quotes does not derive from a work of fantasy, nor does the phrase carry any negative connotation in the original. In fact, in its original usage, the phrase signifies a great achievement, a sign of the intellectual courage of the scientific or philosophical mind willing to go beyond the superstitious chimeras of religion in order to seek the truth "beyond the flaming walls of the world." The famous line from Lucretius' *De Rerum Natura* refers to Epicurus, the atomist and materialist Greek philosopher whose "victory," according to Lucretius, brought religion down under our feet and placed human beings on a level with heaven.[15] It is remarkable that, in its original context, the movement *extra mœnia flammantia mundi* is not an escape from the real world into a false one, but a brave discovery of precisely that really real world that had been hidden and veiled by the false realities of superstition and religion. In its oddly tortuous philological journey from the first century to the nineteenth century, the phrase as used by Scott has come to contain nearly its opposite meaning. However, in what might be considered one more turn of the screw or yet another dialectical reversal, one can argue that Scott's own use or abuse of the phrase as a means of criticizing fantasy reveals the power of fantasy as a device for social and literary critique.

In Poe's writings, the fantastic mode is frequently used in such a way as to allow readers to perceive the world and the things in it more clearly than they would if they were limited to the all-too-mimetic or realistic modes favored by certain critics. Of course, that world remains inscrutable and perplexing, but that is at least in part because the world is itself inscrutable and perplexing, and the fantastic presentation of such a world comports well with the underlying "reality" presented in Poe's work. Part of the desirability of the fantastic mode for Poe unquestionably relates to his desire for autonomy and control over the manner and the materials of his aesthetic production. Like Nathaniel Hawthorne's famous apologia concerning "romance" in the preface to

[13] These words are Poe's, in response to White's apparent criticisms of the lurid tale. See Poe, "Letter to Thomas W. White" (April 30, 1835), *The Letters of Edgar Allan Poe*, 57, 58.

[14] On Scott's influence on the development of American national narrative, and especially his influence on Cooper, see Arac, *The Emergence of American Literary Narrative*, 6–8. For a more general treatment of Scott's development of the form, see Lukács, *The Historical Novel*.

[15] See Lucretius, *On the Nature of the Universe*, 29.

The House of the Seven Gables, Poe would certain wish to "claim a certain latitude" in his writing, to avoid being limited "not merely to the possible, but to the probable and ordinary course of man's experience," and to reserve "a right to present [the] truth under circumstances, to a great extent, of [his] own choosing or creation."[16] Poe not only wishes to remain unfettered by any restraints of unimaginative, fact-based realism in order to preserve his rights as an artist, however. He also suggests that the "truth" of the subject to be represented, or even perceived in the first place, is arrived at by indirect means. The overly minute inspection of details can lead to a blindness to the real matter at hand.

This is the premise of "The Purloined Letter," for example. Dupin is a poet, which is to say, the sort of person that the Prefect takes to be "only one remove from a fool." Dupin's poetic sensibility presumably allows him to see what the police—whom Dupin concedes are "persevering, ingenious, cunning, and thoroughly versed in the knowledge which their duties seem chiefly to demand"—cannot, which is how he so easily discovers the purloined letter which they had missed.[17] In explaining his method, Dupin uses the analogy of a parlor game that involves reading a map.

> There is a game of puzzles [...] which is played upon a map. One party playing requires another to find a given word—the name of a town, river, state or empire—any word, in short, upon the motley and perplexed surface of the chart. A novice in the game generally seeks to embarrass his opponents by giving them the most minutely lettered names; but the adept selects such words as stretch, in large characters, from one end of the chart to the other. These, like the over-largely lettered signs and placards of the street, escape observation by dint of being excessively obvious; and here the physical oversight is precisely analogous with the moral inapprehension by which the intellect suffers to pass unnoticed those considerations which are too obtrusively and too palpably self-evident.[18]

Dupin's example of a reader who is unable to see that which is far too obvious is somewhat akin to the generalized cartographic anxiety associated with the urban milieu, which has its own relationship to fantasy and satire. But here the argument hinges upon a particular way of seeing. Dupin, or Poe, suggests that detail-seeking eyes of the meticulous realist will miss what the abstract, blurrier vision of the fantasist can detect. Dupin's critical acumen is tied to his ability to see things *not* as they are in reality, which is the perfected mode of perception of the Prefect, but from an imaginative, fanciful, or fantastic vantage. Such a perspective might be considered ironic or even humorous, in Poe's sense of the mind's trajectory from the imagination to humor, and Dupin frequently seems to be toying or joking with the narrator, the Prefect, and (in "The Purloined Letter") the Minister who is perpetrating the crime. In this way, Dupin is consistently able to get the last laugh.

---

[16] Hawthorne, *The House of the Seven Gables,* 1.
[17] Poe, "The Purloined Letter," *Poetry and Tales,* 684, 688.
[18] Ibid., 694.

The laugh of Edgar Allan Poe

Poe had used a similar argument, again rather playfully, much earlier in his career. Poe's Dupin is actually enunciating a principle that a young, brash poet named Edgar A. Poe had stated in 1831, while criticizing the profundity of Coleridge ("a giant in intellect and learning") and arguing for the greater power of inexactitude and blurred vision. As Poe puts it in his "Letter to Mr. — —," Coleridge "goes wrong by reason of this very profundity, and of his error we have a natural type in the contemplation of a star. He who regards it directly and intensely sees, it is true, the star, but it is the star without a ray—while he who surveys it less inquisitively is conscious of all for which the star is useful to us below—its brilliancy and its beauty."[19] Poe's concern for knowledge here, in so far as it is "useful to us below" rather than being merely and uninterestingly accurate in an astronomical way, betrays a somewhat romantic blend of art and science, but Poe also establishes the fantastic as the preferred mode of representing reality.

One could argue that, at bottom, this conception may be linked to the old cliché of fiction's being able to present the greater truth, a sentiment that claims for the artist and the imagination a power unavailable to the mere philosopher and the faculty of reason. The more intriguing aspect of Poe's view is not the critique of scientific enquiry or rationalism, itself already a cliché among a number of romantics, but rather the critique of *knowing* at all. As with his tales of terror and the nightmare of the unknowable, Poe explicitly calls into question the epistemic bases for apprehending the truth of the mysteries surrounding us. However, the poetic vision afforded by perceiving and representing the world in a fantastic mode allows one to engage with it, critically and with good humor, in order to make it imaginatively inhabitable. For Poe, this fantastic mode offers the opportunity to see differently, to apprehend reality not in the arrogant sense of the amateur social scientist, such as the narrators of "MS. Found in a Bottle" or "The Man of the Crowd," but as fantasists who can better grasp an alternative to the images held up before one's eyes in order to call them into question. Such fantasists are also better able to see the absurdity in the solemn claims of the unimaginative realist and the cliché-spouting traditionalist. Perhaps this is the source of the frequent temptation to laugh at them. As in the long footnote from "The Literati of New York City" essay on Willis, Poe's satirical fantasy extends itself to the point of humor, and the voice of the critic merges neatly with the laughter of court jester.

In a letter to fellow writer Beverley Tucker in 1835, Poe responds to Tucker's complaint that levity or humor has no place in criticism. As Poe explains,

> [t]he distinction you make between levity, and wit or humour (that which produces a smile) I perfectly understand; but that levity is unbecoming the chair of the critic, must be taken, I think, cum grano salis. Moreover — are you *sure* Jeffrey was never jocular or frivolous in his critical opinions? I think

---

[19] Poe, "Letter to Mr. — —," *Poetry and Tales*, 13–14.

I can call to mind some instances of the purest *grotesque* in his Reviews — downright horse-laughter. Did you ever see a *critique* in Blackwood's Mag: upon an Epic Poem by a cockney tailor? Its chief witticisms were aimed not at the poem, but at the goose, and bandy legs of the author, and the notice ended, after innumerable oddities in — "ha! ha! ha! — he! he! he! — hi! hi! hi! — ho! ho! ho! — hu! hu! hu"! Yet it was, without exception, the most annihilating, and altogether the most effective Review I remember to have read. Of course I do not mean to palliate such indecency. The reviewer should have been horsewhipped. Still I cannot help thinking levity *here* was indispensable. Indeed how otherwise the subject could have been treated I do not perceive. To treat a tailor's Epic seriously, (and such an Epic too!) would have defeated the ends of the critic, in weakening his own authority by making himself ridiculous.[20]

In his own criticism, as in his poetry and tales, Poe issues forth his own "horse-laughter," and his often ferocious mirthfulness brings together the fantastic and satirical elements of his overall literary and critical project. To avoid laughter in one's criticism for the sake of propriety is to recuse oneself from criticism entirely, Poe seems to suggest. To suffer fools too gladly is to reveal one's own foolishness. Similarly, to write works that fear to tread beyond the flaming walls of the world is to give up on the critical project inherent to literature itself. In his poetics of descent, Poe gleefully drags the highfalutin and lofty pretensions of his age down to the street-level, where what had previously seemed sacred or pure now looks rather ridiculous. Through his nomad thought or subterraneous noises, Poe does not hesitate, therefore, to ridicule it.

In an early farce, "The Duc De L'Omelette," Poe himself employs the same silly laughter spoofed in the letter to Tucker, the giggles that run through the vowels like a musician practicing scales. Thomas Ollive Mabbott described this tale as "one of the few stories involving humor in which Poe seems to me to be wholly successful."[21] The tale recounts details of the untimely death (and, hence, premature burial?) of the titular aristocrat who, when confronted with the Devil, laughs at the suggestion that he belongs in such a place. "I have sinned—*c'est vrai*—but, my good sir, consider!—you have no actual intention of putting such—such—barbarous threats into execution." One thinks of Poe himself in the worthy Duke's place, astonished to find himself in some hell of an American nationalist literary tradition, where barbaric presentations and interpretations are executed upon his corpus. The Duke challenges the Devil to a game of cards, wagering his own soul so that, if he loses, he shall be "doubly-damned." Upon winning, he politely assures his satanic majesty that, were he not the Duc De L'Omelette, he would have no objection to being the Devil.[22] Perhaps Poe, too, in subverting the national literary traditions to which he has so often been consigned, either as a canonical exemplar or more often as an outsider within the tradition, would

[20] Poe, "To Beverley Tucker" (December 1, 1835), *The Letters of Edgar Allan Poe*, 77.
[21] Mabbott, in Poe, *Tales and Sketches*, 31.
[22] Poe, "The Duc De L'Omelette," *Poetry and Tales*, 143, 146.

be gracious in victory, but it would be difficult to detect his true sentiments from beneath the peals of laughter, "a live voice that still eludes the tomb of the text," the jester's final jest.[23]

---

[23] Certeau, "The Laugh of Michel Foucault," 194; Poe, "Hop-Frog," *Poetry and Tales*, 908.

Conclusion: Premature Burials

In the final moments of "The Cask of Amontillado," Montresor pauses before setting into place that last stone of the wall behind which his victim is chained. From within, a "sad voice, which I had difficulty recognizing as that of the noble Fortunato," suddenly erupts with laughter: "'Ha! ha! ha!—he! he!—a very good joke indeed—an excellent jest. We will have many a rich laugh about it at the palazzo—he! he! he!—over our wine—he! he! he!" Fortunato is correct. This is a perverse joke, but the joke is on him, and he will not be able to yuck it up with Montresor over a glass of Amontillado in the future. Just before the final immurement of his rival, Montresor checks to see whether the now silent Fortunato is still conscious. Calling out his name in vain, Montresor then thrusts his torch through the small hole in the almost finished wall. "There came forth in return only a jingling of the bells."[1] The harlequin's motley with the conical hat and bells worn by Fortunato offer the only response to the inquisitor, and the premature burial is complete. Another laughing "jingle man" is neatly stowed away in this final resting place.

Poe himself was famously dismissed as a "jingle man" by perhaps the leading literary intellectual of his lifetime, Ralph Waldo Emerson, and Poe has subsequently been buried from time to time by the guardians of the American national literary culture in the century and a half since. Like a Fortunato, Poe remains a permanent fixture in the canonical catacombs of American literature, but he sometimes appears to be an unwilling and forlorn presence there. By this jest I do not really mean to claim that Poe has been *buried* by an American literary tradition in which he scarcely belongs, but of which he remains inescapably a part. However, just as several of his various characters experience this or that form of living interment, Poe has been subjected to numerous premature burials and resurrections, both during his life and in the afterlife of his literary reputations. Even in the early days of his career, Poe experienced the ups and downs of literary renown, and in the decades and centuries that followed, the roller-coaster trajectory has continued. Poe's subterranean noises, first issued as a mocking critique of contemporary culture, still resonate in American and world literature today.

[1] Poe, "The Cask of Amontillado," *Poetry and Tales*, 853–4.

Premature burial, a recurrent theme in many of Poe's tales, also stands as an apt figure for understanding Poe's career, in his own lifetime and in his afterlife as a literary figure and "cultural signifier" in our own era.[2] The horror of the actual phenomenon of premature burial is suitably registered in those stories that depict it, but Poe also invokes this image again and again for what are essentially comedic purposes. As I have argued, Poe's principal mode is fantastic, but his fantasy is almost always put to satirical, comedic, hoaxing, or prankish ends. Accordingly, Poe's descriptions of premature burials in his writings are, as often as not, part of the practical joke played on the audience and, more generally, on the culture at large. Just as in "Loss of Breath," in which the republished treatise on "the nature and origin of subterranean noises" turns out to make a mockery of the mania for scientific and political supremacy in the United States, Poe uses a wholly fantastic story for the purposes of his satirical critique. Even in those tales that include what appear to be more serious or terrifying versions, such as in "Berenice," "The Fall of the House of Usher," "The Cask of Amontillado," or *The Narrative of Arthur Gordon Pym*, Poe's grotesque and burlesque treatment of the subject makes one suspect that he might be poking fun. Poe or his reviewer, if not both at the same time, once stated that the thesis of "The Fall of the House of Usher" is "the revulsion of feeling consequent upon discovering that for a long period of time we have been mistaking sounds of agony for those of mirth or indifference."[3] I would suggest that something like the reverse is happening when one considers Poe in the light of his subversion of American literature: What we had thought of as Gothic gloom or psychological horror or eerie mystery turns out to be laughter, hearty and loud, and rather uncomfortably aimed in our direction.

Premature burial was less a physical danger to Poe than a threat to his career in literature. Two documents from an early stage of that career might serve as illustrations of the risk. The first is a letter from the committee that awarded Poe's "MS. Found in a Bottle" the top prize in the *Baltimore Saturday Visiter* [sic] contest, thus effectively launching Poe's career as a professional writer. The second is a rejection letter from the publisher Harper and Brothers, declining the opportunity to publish Poe's manuscript for *Tales of the Folio Club*, thus potentially retarding the development of Poe's career as a professional writer. Both letters make an express case for enhancing the reputation of Poe, and both argue that his reputation ought to be of paramount concern for the young author. By juxtaposing these two "secondary" texts, one finds the damned-if-you-do, damned-if-you-don't frustrations attendant upon Poe's early efforts to establish his literary reputation.

A portion of the letter from John Pendleton Kennedy and the other *Baltimore Saturday Visiter* judges was quoted in an editorial comment in the August 1835 issue of the *Southern Literary Messenger*:

> Among the prose articles offered were many of various and distinguished merit; but the singular force and beauty of those sent by the author of the *Tales of the Folio Club*, leave us no room for hesitation in that department. We have

---

[2] See Peeples, *The Afterlife of Edgar Allan Poe*, especially 125–54.
[3] Poe, "Edgar Allan Poe," *Essays and Reviews*, 870.

accordingly awarded the premium to a Tale entitled *MS. Found in a Bottle*. It would hardly be doing justice to the writer of this collection to say that the Tale we have chosen is the best of the six offered by him. We cannot refrain from saying that *the author owes it to his own reputation*, as well as to the gratification of the community, to publish the entire volume, (the Tales of the Folio Club.) These Tales are eminently distinguished by a wild, vigorous, and poetical imagination—a rich style—a fertile invention—and varied and curious learning.[4]

Poe was just beginning work as an editorial assistant and writer for the *Messenger*, so in reprinting the letter from Kennedy et al., the magazine was also advertising its newly acquired literary talent. The editorial notice also implies that the opinions of these eminent persons should themselves alone serve as sufficient answer to those who had found some of Poe's already published work objectionable. The reprinting of this letter is thus a defensive act, but one that allows Poe to go on the offensive, using the reputations of his patrons to bolster his own.

Although Poe may have, in the judges' words, owed it to his reputation to publish his *Tales of the Folio Club* in book form, a prominent publisher disagreed. In a letter of June 1836 to Poe from Harpers and Brothers, the publishers flatly rejected the manuscript, which by this point included 16 stories, and offered a three-part rationale for their decision:

> The reasons why we declined publishing them were threefold. First, because the greater portion of them had already appeared in print. Secondly, because they consisted of detached tales and pieces; and our long experience has taught us that both these are very serious objections to the success of any publication. Readers in this country have a decided and strong preference for works, (especially fictions) in which a single and connected story occupies the whole volume, or number of volumes, as the case may be; and we have always found that republications of Magazine articles, known to be such, are the most unsaleable of all literary performances. The third objection was equally cogent. The papers are too learned and mystical. They would be understood and relished only by a very few—not by the multitude. The number of readers in this country capable of appreciating and enjoying such writings as those you submitted to us is very small indeed. We were therefore inclined to believe that it was for your own interest not to publish them. It is all important to an author that his first work should be popular. Nothing is more difficult, *in regard to literary reputation*, than to overcome the injurious effect of a first failure.[5]

An undoubtedly disappointed Poe did take the publisher's advice, for soon thereafter he wrote *The Narrative of Arthur Gordon Pym*, a book-length work that was indeed published by Harper and Brothers. But his plan for the *Tales of the Folio Club*, like his later attempt to publish *Phantasy-Pieces*, came to naught. As I mentioned in Chapter 6, one can view Poe's comments regarding Catherine Maria Sedgwick's "adventitious"

[4] See Thomas and Jackson, *The Poe Log*, 169, my emphasis.
[5] Ibid., 212, my emphasis.

hold over the public's attention in the light of the fact that he had trouble finding a publisher willing to produce "absolutely bound volumes" of his work.

Remarkably, both the letter from the Baltimore judges and the one from the New York publishers emphasize the importance of Poe's reputation, yet they arrive at opposite conclusions. In the first case, Poe's work is considered too *little known*, since it has been buried in the various magazines; Kennedy and the others suggest that the tales need to be exhumed and presented in a single book so that the author's well deserved good reputation can be shared with others, and his prematurely buried stories can appear in the public light of day. In the second example, Poe's work is already too *well known*, in the sense that it has been "previously published"; the tales are also disjointed and arcane, and to publish them in a single book would amount to another premature burial of the young author, who might be unable to emerge from the pauper's grave of a bad reputation at some later date. Harper and Brothers contend that whatever good reputation Poe could hope to have would be buried by his inevitable "first failure." So, within a year in which he labored furiously as a writer of fiction and poetry, as well as an editor and book reviewer for *The Southern Literary Messenger*, Poe learns that, in the interest of his reputation, he *must* publish his tales in book form but also that he *must not* risk his potential reputation by doing so. This situation might be described as perverse.

During his career and since his death, Poe's protean critical and popular reputation has been subject to various premature burials. Interred and exhumed again and again, Poe's reputation waxed and waned throughout his career. At his death, Rufus Griswold's hatchet job damaged Poe's personal reputation even as it elicited vociferous defenses from Poe's admirers. In France, Charles Baudelaire's translations and his re-presentation of Poe as a lost soul, a *poète maudit* too beautiful for the base world that values only the "making-money author," a phrase the poet contemptuously writes in English, as if it were too distasteful or even impossible to render into proper French, are intended as laudatory, but the characterization transformed Poe into a stereotype, a mannequin for a Goth brand of marketable counter-culture, a figure well adapted to replicate the dominant culture through self-parody. In this respect, both his detractors and his champions had a hand in burying Edgar Allan Poe. They consigned him to either a potter's field or an ornately decorated sepulcher, but each is a kind of premature burial. From these tombs, however, Poe periodically cries out, claiming a place among the living. At times this voice from the crypt crackles with laughter or contempt, as when Mr. Lackobreath emerges from his tomb or when those sailors roughly shout down and manhandle the bewildered narrator of "The Premature Burial." At other times, Poe's return may seem as horrific as Madeline Usher's, a ghastly spectacle in which the repressed terrors of oblivion and the unknown return to haunt those who had considered themselves "in the know." Sometimes the voice from beyond the tomb can be indecipherable or mysterious, like Ligeia pressing her way through the hallucinatory mists of the reader's perceptions. At still other moments, the revenant may be but a dream, like "the rare and radiant maiden whom the angels name Lenore— / Nameless here for evermore."[6] Occasionally, there is only the voiceless jingling of the bells or some other subterranean noises, all the more unsettling in their apparent senselessness.

---

[6] Poe, "The Raven," *Poetry and Tales*, 82.

Poe makes great use of the evocative and terrifying image of premature burial throughout his career. Premature burials, of various types, ranging from the farcical to the tragic and sublime, appear in at least a dozen tales.[7] Among his earliest stories, "Loss of Breath" depicts an absurdly satirical premature burial, as the narrator's literal breathlessness causes him to be mistaken for a corpse. Grotesque living inhumation is the fate of Berenice, and perhaps Morella, as well as of Madeline of the House of Usher. Ligeia's return from beyond the grave offers a variation on the theme. The black cat with its peculiar gallows-markings and the ill-fated Fortunato in "The Cask of Amontillado" are entombed while living, and the narrators of *The Narrative of Arthur Gordon Pym*, "The Pit and the Pendulum," and "A Premature Burial" all find themselves nearly buried alive. The inscriber of the manuscript found in a bottle is buried alive in another way, just as the man who descended into the maelstrom almost succumbs to that fate. And so on. There is even the inversion of this process, as when Monsieur Valdemar keeps talking well past his expiration date; his burial is not so much not premature as long overdue.

Part of the terror of the premature burial lies in the inability of the still-living subject to speak; or, just as troubling, if this victim can still speak, he or she can no longer be heard. Those prematurely buried quite literally have no say in the proceedings that most certainly and directly affect them. This situation is exploited by Poe to ludicrous and exaggerated effect in "Loss of Breath," whose narrator loses his breath while yelling at his wife, then gets mistaken for a corpse, is dissected by a medical student, and winds up eventually being buried in a crypt, before he discovers another corpse, Mr. Windenough, whose surfeit of breath makes possible a contractual exchange between them to set things right. (As it turns out, Mr. Windenough had managed to "catch" the very breath that Mr. Lackobreath has lost, so this insubstantial but decidedly crucial property was restored to its rightful owner.) As J. Gerald Kennedy has pointed out, however, it is not really a lack of *breath* that leads to Mr. Lackobreath's premature burial, but his lack of *speech*. Unable to speak for himself, he is taken for a dead man, even when flailing his limbs or giving other such "signs of life." Some of Poe's other victims of premature burial appear not to have had this luxury of speech in the first place. Madeleine Usher is completely silent, ever ghost-like, gliding sound-lessly through the house of Usher. Berenice, who certainly did have a voice, was apparently unable to make herself heard, as her tormenter was too focused on the materially dental "ideas" to take notice of any immaterial words also issuing from her mouth at the time. In any event, with premature burials, one who still has something to say can no longer speak or be understood.

But writing, reducing thoughts to symbols and extending one's presence through words, even in one's physical absence, allows a writer to speak for himself or herself long after death. The visible trace, as Jacques Derrida has made so famous, allows the presence of the author to linger long after his or her disappearance from the world. Writing is thus a hedge against the silence of death, but it is no safeguard for one's reputation, for the "failure" of the written word may linger on as much as its "success,"

---

[7] See, e.g. Kennedy, *Poe, Death, and the Life of Writing*, 32–59.

as Harper and Brothers warned Poe in 1836, and a person's reputation lives or dies long after the funeral.

The ups-and-downs of Poe's literary reputation are, of course, well known. In his own generation and those immediately following, the reviews of his value as a writer were decidedly mixed. The work of a "jingle man" in Emerson's dismissive opinion, Poe's poetry is, for Baudelaire, "finely wrought, pure, correct, and brilliant as a crystal jewel." At the turn of the century, William Butler Yeats admitted "his fame always puzzles me," and, aside from a few pieces, "the rest of him seems to me vulgar and commonplace." Yet George Bernard Shaw can say, a few years later, that Poe is "the most legitimate, the most classical, of all writers"; Shaw also notes, paradoxically, that Poe's "supremacy"—that is, his superiority to all other American writers—"has cost him his reputation. This is a phenomenon which occurs when an artist achieves such perfection as to place himself *hors concours*."[8] Although Poe's work remained popular throughout the century, opinion as to its literary merit was all over the place, as virulent opponents of Poe were met on the field of honor by his enthusiastic supporters, in the United States and abroad.

In the wide world of literary fandom, Poe unquestionably maintains a place of honor, and he remains one of the most popular writers of the nineteenth century. With the advent of academic American literary studies in the mid-twentieth century and since, Poe's value has been enthusiastically asserted, ensuring his place in an American literary canon. At the same time, among some detractors, Poe's presence in "the Western Canon" has also been begrudged as unavoidable, if rarely denied entirely.[9] To cite the famous example of Matthiessen's *American Renaissance* once more, Poe was omitted from this canon-forming (or, at least, canon-reinforcing) study nominally because his life and career fell outside the primary historical window that Matthiessen's study examined in detail, the period between 1850 and 1855, and Poe, of course, died in October 1849. However, Matthiessen felt compelled to justify this exclusion further, by noting that Poe's "value, even more than Emerson's, is now seen to consist in his influence rather than in the body of his own work," and his "stories, less harrowing upon the nerves as they were, seem relatively factitious when contrasted with the moral depth of Hawthorne and Melville."[10] More recently Jonathan Arac, referring to Poe's short stories, called Poe "an engineer of sensations, his craft neither the 'purest art' to which it aspired or the 'literature' against which modern readers judge it."[11] Of course, a powerful line of criticism, especially psychoanalytic in orientation and often French in nationality, following Marie Bonaparte's groundbreaking study and

---

[8] These quotations may be found in Tally, volume ed., *Edgar Allan Poe (Bloom's Classic Critical Views)*, 53, 88, 94, 92.

[9] Notably, except for two passing slights, Edgar Allan Poe is not discussed in Harold Bloom's *The Western Canon*. Bloom's rationale is summed up in the first of these slights, stating that "Poe is too universally accepted around the world to be excluded, though his writing is almost invariably atrocious" (269). See also note 13 below.

[10] Matthiessen, *American Renaissance*, xii, note 3; in fairness, it should also be recalled that Matthiessen wrote the largely laudatory entry on Poe in the 1948 *Literary History of the United States*, Robert Spiller et al. (eds).

[11] Arac, *The Emergence of American Literary Narrative*, 75.

Jacques Lacan's seminar on "The Purloined Letter," among other interventions, has greatly enhanced Poe's reputation, not just in Europe but back in the United States. Nevertheless, in 2008, it is still possible for perhaps the United States' best known literary critic, Harold Bloom, to write that Poe is "the worst" American writer, as I discuss below. I do not mean to overstate this case, however. Poe is about as canonical a writer as the United States has produced, and, as teachers of American literature can easily confirm, his popularity with students remains extraordinarily high, even as fewer students seem likely to read so-called "classics" for pleasure. But, then, as in the famous line from Henry James, stating that "to take [Poe] with more than a certain degree of seriousness is to lack seriousness oneself,"[12] there is always the *haut couture*'s riposte to Poe's apparently immortal popularity. Poe's glowing reputation among so many readers is a matter of great perturbation among those whose opinions differ.

To cite a more comical example, Bloom, one of the most imminent and influential literary critics in the United States, is somewhat notorious for his loathing of Poe. In his introduction to a recent volume published in a series of studies aimed at high school and college students, Bloom reiterates a long-held view of Poe, effectively castigating the implied "majority of critics" who clearly value Poe's work for their lack of perspicacity or critical acumen in dealing with that *oeuvre*, and also dismissing the throngs of fans who have made Poe likely the world's most popular writer born in the United States. As Bloom puts it,

> [t]ogether with Walt Whitman, Poe continues to be the most influential of American writers on a worldwide basis, eclipsing even Eliot and Faulkner. For me, this constitutes a considerable irony, since I regard Whitman as the greatest of New World writers and Poe as the worst (among those of repute, obviously). Though I am in the minority of critics on Poe, the plain badness of Poe's various styles, in prose and in verse, is merely palpable. Emerson dismissed Poe as "the jingle man," and the Gothic tales were accurately represented (even a touch improved) by the series of horror movies starring Vincent Price.[13]

Bloom's citation of Emerson's off-hand critique, itself reported only second-hand by William Dean Howells in his *Literary Friends and Acquaintance*, is cutting, but the reference to the delightfully dreadful B-grade films of Vincent Price, works that were utterly and unabashedly untrue to the source material in Poe (or Hawthorne for that matter),[14] is the unkindest cut of all, and the insult is frankly beyond the pale. Such a comment can only be intended to wound, not Poe, who is far beyond the reach of such criticism, but all of those who enjoy Poe's writing or take it seriously. Bloom's pointed observation is an act of good-natured aggression, and a charitable reading of it might

---

[12] James, "Charles Baudelaire," 154.

[13] Harold Bloom, "Introduction," *Edgar Allan Poe (Bloom's Classic Critical Views)*, xi.

[14] Vincent Price also appeared in 1963's ghastly "adaptation" of *Twice-Told Tales*—the parts of which were *very* loosely based on "Dr. Heidegger's Experiment," "Rappaccini's Daughter," and *The House of the Seven Gables*—using plots so different from those of the original texts that few scholars of American literature would recognize them, with much certainty, as Hawthorne's.

consider Bloom's anti-Poe stance as somewhat akin to the sort of pose struck by Poe in his role as the critical "tomahawk man."

Regarding Emerson's even more famous "jingle man" brush-off, I would point out rarely if ever do critics note the context in which Howells reports it. Howells is recalling a conversation with Emerson on the subject of Hawthorne, whose final novel, *The Marble Faun*, Emerson called "a mere mush." Indignantly, it seems, Howells writes that "this great man was no better equipped to judge an artistic fiction than the groundlings who were then crying out upon the indefinite close of *The Marble Faun*." Howells goes on to say that "Emerson had, in fact, a defective sense as to specific pieces of literature," explaining that "he praised extravagantly, and in the wrong place, especially among the new things, and he failed to see the worth of much that was fine and precious beside the line of his fancy."[15] The "jingle man" line follows from Howells's admission that he only knew the work of William Ellery Channing through Poe's critical reviews of the poet. For Howells, Emerson's "jingle man" comment was less a critique of Poe than of Howells himself, and, although he adds that he was not really an admirer of Poe, he feels slighted by the remark. "I do not think I could have been more abashed," writes Howells. "Perhaps I felt an edge of reproof, of admonition, in a characterization of Poe which the world will hardly agree with."[16] Coming directly on the heels of Howells's critique of Emerson's own abilities as a literary critic, the "jingle man" assessment cannot be taken as a critical evaluation of a famous author, but only as an unkind and insulting remark directed toward an aspiring one. In other words, one of the most well known dismissals of Poe's literary value comes from a writer who had "a defective sense" when it came to literature and was perfectly willing to belittle any others whose sense of literary value differed from his own. Emerson here is not above a bit of mean-spirited, intellectual intimidation. Both Emerson and Bloom, it seems, attack Poe primarily in order to denigrate the literary or critical judgments of Poe's admirers.

Of course, Emerson's casual dismissal of Poe's importance, like Bloom's, fits with a certain tradition within American literature or American Studies which sees Poe as fundamentally unworthy of, or perhaps unsuitable for, inclusion on the grounds that his writings either lack the requisite aesthetic quality or are simply un-American. In fact, as Shaw had suggested, his actual popularity with some critics and with a mass of readers may stem precisely from his lack of fit in what the more rebellious readers might view as the mainstream of American culture. Even Poe's most ardent supporters within the United States do not claim that he ought to stand as the representative writer of the national literature, in the way that a Melville or a Twain have been viewed by many of their more nationalistic champions. Poe has always been most popularly seen as an outsider in that American tradition, a nomad crossing the paths of national settlers, homeless and displaced. This is part of what his fans like about him. Or so it seems.

One could argue, to the contrary, that Poe's materialism, his marketplace savvy, his irreverence, his showmanship, his inventiveness and practical joking, all make Poe out

---

[15] William Dean Howells, *Literary Friends and Acquaintance*, 62.
[16] Ibid., 63–4.

to be *more* American than a lot of the nineteenth-century writers. This image of Poe as confidence man places him squarely in a tradition that includes such representative national figures as P. T. Barnum, Thomas Edison, and Mark Twain (at least, before Twain was somewhat dubiously sanctified as a prophet of racial equality by American Studies scholars like Lionel Trilling or Leslie Fiedler in the 1940s and 1950s).[17] Poe's satirical mode and leg-pulling philosophy would make him a neat fit for a certain kind of American type, the hustler, the showman, or the grifter. To be sure, this is not the figure best suited to the imagery of an American Adam on an Errand into the Wilderness across a Virgin Land,[18] but it does offer another distinctive, national type.

However, the question is really not whether Poe is truly American, un-American, or anti-American in his own life and work. These categories could be adjusted to make Poe fit into each, just as Poe's own personal characteristics could be interpreted to make him suit the preferred category. Poe's writings have certainly been interpreted in ways that could allow a good case to be made for each. I maintain that Poe's work runs athwart an image of the "America" formed through mid-twentieth-century American Studies and maintained in various forms even in the revisionary approaches that have emerged in the late twentieth- and early twenty-first-century scholarship and criticism. Poe's place in American literature is well established, but it is established as a place not entirely *of* that literature. The satirical, fantastic, and critical force of his writings set Poe apart from the national culture of the United States during his lifetime, even as these modes of satire, fantasy, and critique were developed and honed precisely because of Poe's worldly perceptions of his culture. However, even moving beyond the mythic, Baudelairean image of Poe the wandering mystic, "out of place and out of time," Poe's worldliness sets him apart from many of his well regarded literary contemporaries. For example, Terence Whalen's *Edgar Allan Poe and the Masses* makes the powerful case for Poe's being very much of his time and place. But Poe's intimate familiarity with the material, quotidian conditions of that world—a world many other writers were sheltered from, economically and culturally, as Poe bitterly noted of some of his Bostonian contemporaries—also contributed to Poe's literary theory and practice. Buried in the rising ash-heaps of capitalism, urbanism, and an emerging culture industry, Poe is able to speak from the heart of the historical moment.

For all these reputational shifts within his lifetime and in the years since, Poe offers another version of that "one sepulchral Idea" of premature burial,[19] the flipside in fact: Not the image of the living man reduced to silence by the untimely grave, but the image of the dead man empowered to speak, the revenant power of words from beyond the grave. This voice from below is also a voice from athwart, antagonizing the hallowed rhetoric of the living and of the dead alike. In seeking to bury Poe prematurely, one finds Poe speaking still. In opening the crypt in search of the "nature and origin of subterranean noises," one finds it empty, but for the echoes of a sardonic laugher. "Ha! ha! ha! — he! he! — a very good joke indeed—an excellent jest."

[17] On the critical transformation of Twain from a querulous outsider into a representative figure of a national literary tradition, see especially Arac, *Huckleberry Finn as Idol and Target*.

[18] See Donald E. Pease, "National Identities, Postmodern Artifacts, and Postnational Narratives," 4.

[19] Poe, "The Premature Burial," *Poetry and Tales*, 674.

Or perhaps one detects a mocking tone of a grotesque harlequin, clad in the jester's motley, like a Hop-Frog chortling as he escapes through the ceiling following his "last jest." Maybe it is a mischievous voice like that of the Foucauldian persona who springs forth in unexpected places, playfully crying out, "no, no, I'm not where you are lying in wait for me, but over here, laughing at you."[20] Poe's ultimate subversion of American literature may be found in this spirit of mockery, this satirical fantasy, and this critical rejection of the national literary tradition itself.

---

[20] Poe, "The Cask of Amontillado," ibid., 854; Poe, "Hop-Frog," ibid., 908; and Foucault, *The Archaeology of Knowledge*, 17.

Bibliography

Ackroyd, Peter. *Poe: A Life Cut Short*. New York: Doubleday, 2008.

Allen, Hervey. *Israfel: The Life and Times of Edgar Allan Poe*. New York: Farrar & Rinehart, 1934.

Allen, Michael. *Poe and the British Magazine Tradition*. Oxford: Oxford University Press, 1969.

Amper, Susan. "Masters of Deceit: Poe's Lying Narrators." Ph.D. dissertation, Fordham University, 2001.

—"Untold Story: The Lying Narrator in 'The Black Cat.'" *Studies in Short Fiction* 29 (Fall 1992): 475–85.

Anderson, Douglas. *Pictures of Ascent in the Fiction of Edgar Allan Poe*. New York: Palgrave Macmillan, 2009.

Arac, Jonathan. *Commissioned Spirits: The Shaping of Social Motion in Dickens, Carlyle, Melville, and Hawthorne*. New York: Columbia University Press, 1989.

—*The Emergence of American Literary Narrative, 1820–1860*. Cambridge, MA: Harvard University Press, 2005.

—"F. O. Matthiessen: Authorizing the American Renaissance." *The American Renaissance Reconsidered*. Walter Benn Michaels and Donald E (eds). Pease. Baltimore: Johns Hopkins University Press, 1985. 90–112.

—*Huckleberry Finn as Idol and Target: The Functions of Criticism in Our Time*. Madison: University of Wisconsin Press, 1997.

—*Impure Worlds: The Institution of Literature in the Age of the Novel*. New York: Fordham University Press, 2010.

—"Narrative Forms." *The Cambridge History of American Literature, Volume 2: 1820–1860*. Sacvan Bercovitch, ed. Cambridge: Cambridge University Press, 1995. 605–777.

—"The Politics of *The Scarlet Letter*." *Ideology and Classic American Literature*. Sacvan Bercovitch and Myra Jehlen (eds). Cambridge: Cambridge University Press, 1986. 247–66.

—"'A Romantic Book': *Moby-Dick* and Novel Agency." *boundary 2: A Journal of Cultural and Critical Studies* 17.2 (1990): 40–59.

Aristotle. *Poetics*. Trans. Malcolm Heath. New York: Penguin, 1996.

Attebery, Brian. *The Fantasy Tradition in American Literature: From Irving to LeGuin*. Bloomington: Indiana University Press, 1980.

Baudelaire, Charles. "Edgar Allan Poe: His Life and Works." *The Painter of Modern Life and Other Essays*. Trans. and ed. Jonathan Mayne. London: Phaidon Press, 1964. 69–92.

—"The Painter of Modern Life." *The Painter of Modern Life and Other Essays*. Trans. and ed. Jonathan Mayne. London: Phaidon Press, 1964. 1–40.

Beaver, Harold. "Doodling America: Poe's 'MS. Found in a Bottle.'" In *A Centre of Excellence: Essays Presented to Seymour Belsky*. Robert Druce, ed. Amsterdam: Rodolphi, 1981. 15–27.

Benjamin, Walter. "On Some Motifs in Baudelaire." *Illuminations: Essays and Reflections.*
  Trans. Harry Zohn. New York: Schocken Books, 1985. 155–200.
—"Paris, Capital of the Nineteenth Century." *Reflections: Essays, Aphorisms,*
  Autobiographical Writings. Peter Demetz, ed. Trans. Edmund Jephcott. New York:
  Schocken Books, 1978. 146–62.
Bercovitch, Sacvan. *The American Jeremiad.* Madison: University of Wisconsin Press,
  1978.
—*The Puritan Origins of the American Self.* New Haven: Yale University Press, 1975.
—*The Rites of Assent: Transformations of the Symbolic Construction of America.* London:
  Routledge, 1993.
Bloom, Harold. "Introduction." *Edgar Allan Poe (Bloom's Classic Critical Views).* Volume
  ed. Robert T. Tally Jr. Harold Bloom, ed. New York: Chelsea House, 2008. xi–xii.
—*The Western Canon: The Books and Schools of the Ages.* New York: Riverhead, 1995.
Borges, Jorge Luis. *Labyrinths: Selected Stories and Other Writings.* New York: New
  Directions, 1964.
Brand, Dana. *The Spectator and the City in Nineteenth-Century America.* Cambridge:
  Cambridge University Press, 1991.
Brown, Marshall. *The Gothic Text.* Palo Alto: Stanford University Press, 2005.
Budd, Louis J., and Edwin H. Cady (eds). *On Poe.* Durham, NC: Duke University Press,
  1993.
Cagle, Jeremey. "Reading Well: Transcendental Hermeneutics in Poe's 'The Man of the
  Crowd.'" *The Edgar Allan Poe Review* IX.2 (Fall 2008): 17–35.
Casarino, Cesare. *Modernity at Sea: Marx, Melville, and Conrad in Crisis.* Minneapolis:
  University of Minnesota Press, 2002.
Certeau, Michel de. "The Laugh of Michel Foucault." *Heterologies.* Trans. Brian Massumi.
  Minneapolis: University of Minnesota Press, 1986. 193–8.
—*The Practice of Everyday Life.* Trans. Steven Rendall. Berkeley: University of California
  Press, 1984.
Chesterton, G. K. *Charles Dickens: A Critical Study.* New York: Dodd Mead and Co.,
  1906.
Coleridge, Samuel Taylor. *Biographia Literaria.* James Engell and W. Jackson Bate (eds).
  Princeton: Princeton University Press, 1983.
Cooper, James Fenimore. *The Pioneers.* New York: Signet Classics, 2007.
Dayan, Joan. *Fables of Mind: An Inquiry into Poe's Fiction.* Oxford: Oxford University
  Press, 1987.
Deleuze, Gilles. *Difference and Repetition.* Trans. Paul Patton. New York: Columbia
  University Press, 1994.
—*Expressionism in Philosophy: Spinoza.* Trans. Martin Joughin. New York: Zone Books,
  1990.
—*Nietzsche and Philosophy.* Trans. Hugh Tomlinson. New York: Columbia University
  Press, 1983.
—"Nomad Thought." Trans. David B. Allison. *The New Nietzsche.* David B. Allison, ed.
  Cambridge, MA: The MIT Press, 1985. 142–9.
—*Spinoza: Practical Philosophy.* Trans. Robert Hurley. San Francisco: City Lights, 1988.
Deleuze, Gilles, and Félix Guattari. *A Thousand Plateaus.* Trans. Brian Massumi.
  Minneapolis: University of Minnesota Press, 1988.
Deleuze, Gilles, and Claire Parnet. *Dialogues.* Trans. Hugh Tomlinson and Barbara
  Habberjam. New York: Columbia University Press, 1987.

Derrida, Jacques. "The Purveyor of Truth." Trans. Alan Sheridan. *The Purloined Poe: Lacan, Derrida, and Psychoanalytic Reading.* John P. Muller and William J. Richardson (eds). Baltimore: Johns Hopkins University Press, 1988. 173–212.

Douglass, Frederick. *Narrative of the Life of Frederick Douglass, Written by Himself.* New York: Dover, 1995.

Eagleton, Terry. *Literary Theory: An Introduction*, 2nd edn. Minneapolis: University of Minnesota Press, 1996.

Eddings, Dennis, ed. *The Naiad Voice: Essays on Poe's Satiric Hoaxing.* Port Washington, NY: Associated Faculty Press, 1983.

Emerson, Ralph Waldo. "History." *Selected Essays.* Larzer Ziff, ed. New York: Penguin, 1982. 149–73.

—"The Poet." *Selected Essays.* Larzer Ziff, ed. New York: Penguin, 1982. 263–4.

—"Self-Reliance." *Selected Essays.* Larzer Ziff, ed. New York: Penguin, 1982. 175–203.

Erkkila, Betsy. "Perverting the American Renaissance: Poe, Democracy, Critical Theory." In *Poe and the Remapping of Antebellum Print Culture.* J. Gerald Kennedy and Jerome McGann (eds). Baton Rouge: Louisiana State University Press, 2012. 65–100.

Fisher, Benjamin. "Playful 'Germanism' in 'The Fall of the House of Usher': The Storyteller's Art." *The Ruined Eden of the Present: Hawthorne, Melville, and Poe.* G. R. Thompson and Virgil L. Lokke (eds). West Lafayette, IN: Purdue University Press, 1981. 355–74.

Foucault, Michel. *The Archaeology of Knowledge.* Trans. A. M. Sheridan Smith. New York: Pantheon, 1972.

—*Maurice Blanchot: The Thought from Outside.* Trans. Brian Massumi. New York: Zone Books, 1990.

—"Theatrum Philosophicum." *Language, Counter-Memory, Practice.* Donald F. Bouchard, ed. Trans. Donald F. Bouchard and Sherry Simon. Ithaca: Cornell University Press, 1977. 165–96.

Galloway, David, ed. *The Other Poe: Comedies and Satires.* New York: Penguin, 1983.

Gargano, James. "The Question of Poe's Narrators." *College English* 25.3 (December 1963): 177–81.

Goethe, Johann Wolfgang von. "Mein Göttin." *Selected Verse.* Trans. and ed. David Luke. New York: Penguin, 1986. 63–6.

Greeson, Jennifer Rae. "Poe's 1848: *Eureka,* the Southern Margin, and the Expanding U[niverse] of S[tars]." In *Poe and the Remapping of Antebellum Print Culture.* J. Gerald Kennedy and Jerome McGann (eds). Baton Rouge: Louisiana State University Press, 2012. 123–40.

Gurl, Philip F. *Truth's Ragged Edge: The Rise of the American Novel.* New York: Farrar, Straus, & Giroux, 2013.

Hanţiu, Ecaterina. "Humor and Satire in Edgar Allan Poe's Absurd Stories." *The Edgar Allan Poe Review* 11.2 (Fall 2010): 28–35.

Hawthorne, Nathaniel. *The House of the Seven Gables.* New York: Penguin, 1981.

—*The Scarlet Letter.* New York: Penguin, 1983.

Hayes, Kevin J. *Poe and the Printed Word.* Cambridge: Cambridge University Press, 2000.

Heidegger, Martin. *Being and Time.* Trans. John Macquarrie and Edward Robinson. New York: Harper and Row, 1962.

Hoffman, Daniel. *Poe, Poe, Poe, Poe, Poe, Poe, Poe.* New York: Vintage, 1985.

Howells, William Dean. *Literary Friends and Acquaintance: A Personal Retrospect of American Authorship.* New York: Harper and Brothers, 1911.

Hume, Kathryn. *Fantasy and Mimesis: Responses to Reality in Western Literature.* New York: Methuen, 1984.

Hutchisson, James. *Poe.* Oxford, MS: University Press of Mississippi, 2005.

Irving, John T. *American Hieroglyphics: The Symbol of Egyptian Hieroglyphics in the American Renaissance.* Baltimore: Johns Hopkins University Press, 1980.

Irving, Washington. "The Legend of Sleepy Hollow." *The Legend of Sleepy Hollow and Other Writings from the Sketch-Book.* New York: Signet, 2006. 338–69.

James, Henry. "Charles Baudelaire." *Literary Criticism,* vol. 2. New York: Library of America, 1984. 152–8.

Jameson, Fredric. *The Modernist Papers.* London: Verso, 2008.

—*The Political Unconscious: Narrative as a Socially Symbolic Act.* Ithaca, NY: Cornell University Press, 1981.

—*Postmodernism, or, the Cultural Logic of Late Capitalism.* Durham, NC: Duke University Press, 1991.

Kant, Immanuel. *Critique of Pure Reason.* Trans. Norman Kemp Smith. London: Macmillan, 1933.

Kennedy, J. Gerald. "Edgar Allan Poe, 1809–1949: A Brief Biography." *A Historical Guide to Edgar Allan Poe.* J. Gerald Kennedy, ed. Oxford: Oxford University Press, 2001. 19–59.

—"Introduction." *The Portable Edgar Allan Poe.* J. Gerald Kennedy, ed. New York: Penguin, 2006. ix–xxx.

—*Poe, Death, and the Life of Writing.* New Haven: Yale University Press, 1987.

—ed. *A Historical Guide to Edgar Allan Poe.* Oxford: Oxford University Press, 2001.

Kennedy, J. Gerald, and Jerome McGann (eds). *Poe and the Remapping of Antebellum Print Culture.* Baton Rouge: Louisiana State University Press, 2012.

Ketterer, David. *The Rationale of Deception in Poe.* Baton Rouge: Louisiana State University Press, 1979.

Lacan, Jacques. "Seminar on 'The Purloined Letter,'" trans. Jeffrey Mehlman. *Yale French Studies* 48 (1973): 39–72.

Lathrop, George Parsons. "Poe, Irving, Hawthorne." *Scribner's* (April 1876): 799–808.

—*A Study of Hawthorne.* Boston: James R. Osgood and Co., 1876.

Lawrence, D. H. *Studies in Classic American Literature.* New York: Viking, 1964.

Lenz, William E. *The Poetics of the Antarctic: A Study in Nineteenth-Century American Cultural Perceptions.* New York: Garland, 1995

Levin, Harry. *The Power of Blackness: Hawthorne, Poe, Melville.* Athens, OH: Ohio University Press, 1989.

Levine, Stuart. "Poe and American Society." *Canadian Review of American Studies* 9.1 (1978): 16–33.

Lewis, R. W. B. *The American Adam: Innocence, Tragedy, and Tradition in the Nineteenth Century.* Chicago: University of Chicago Press, 1955.

Leyda, Jay. *A Melville Log: A Documentary Life of Herman Melville, 1819–1891.* New York: Harcourt, 1951.

Ljungquist, Kurt. "The Short Fiction of Poe." *Survey of Modern Fantasy Literature.* Vol. IV. Englewood Cliffs, NJ: Salem Press, 1983. 1665–78.

Lofland, Lyn H. *A World of Strangers: Order and Action in Urban Public Space.* New York: Basic Books, 1973.

Lukács, Georg. *The Historical Novel.* Trans. Hannah and Stanley Mitchell. Lincoln, NE: University of Nebraska Press, 1983.

Lucretius. *On the Nature of the Universe*. Trans. Ronald Latham. New York: Penguin, 1951.

Martin, Terence. "The Imagination at Play: Edgar Allan Poe." *The Kenyon Review* 28.2 (March 1966): 194–209.

Marx, Karl. *The Eighteenth Brumaire of Louis Bonaparte*. Trans. anon. New York: International Publishers, 1963.

Marx, Karl, and Friedrich Engels. *The Communist Manifesto*. Trans. anon. New York: Penguin, 1998.

Matthiessen, F. O. *American Renaissance: Art and Expression in the Age of Emerson and Whitman*. Oxford: Oxford University Press, 1941.

—"Edgar Allan Poe." *The Literary History of the United States*. Robert E. Spiller et al. (eds). New York: Macmillan, 1948. 321–32.

McGill, Meredith L. *American Literature and the Culture of Reprinting, 1834–1853*. Philadelphia: University of Pennsylvania Press, 2003.

Melville, Herman. *Correspondence*. Harrison Hayford, Alma A. MacDougall, G. Thomas Tanselle, et al. (eds). Evanston and Chicago: Northwestern University Press and the Newberry Library, 1987.

—"Hawthorne and His Mosses." *The Piazza Tales and Other Prose Pieces, 1839–1860*. Harrison Hayford, Alma A. MacDougall, G. Thomas Tanselle, et al. (eds). Evanston and Chicago: Northwestern University Press and the Newberry Library, 1987. 239–53.

—*Mardi, and A Voyage Thither*. Harrison Hayford, Hershel Parker, and G. Thomas Tanselle (eds). Evanston and Chicago: Northwestern University Press and the Newberry Library, 1970.

—*Moby-Dick, or, the Whale*. Harrison Hayford, Hershel Parker, and G. Thomas Tanselle (eds). Evanston and Chicago: Northwestern University Press and the Newberry Library, 1988.

—*Pierre, or, the Ambiguities*. Harrison Hayford, Hershel Parker, and G. Thomas Tanselle (eds). Evanston and Chicago: Northwestern University Press and the Newberry Library, 1995.

—*Redburn: His First Voyage*. Harrison Hayford, Hershel Parker, and G. Thomas Tanselle (eds). Evanston and Chicago: Northwestern University Press and the Newberry Library, 1969.

—"A Thought on Book-Binding." *The Piazza Tales and Other Prose Pieces, 1839–1860*. Harrison Hayford, Alma A. MacDougall, G. Thomas Tanselle, et al. (eds). Evanston and Chicago: Northwestern University Press and the Newberry Library, 1987. 237–8.

—*Typee: A Peep at Polynesian Life*. Harrison Hayford, Hershel Parker, and G. Thomas Tanselle (eds). Evanston and Chicago: Northwestern University Press and the Newberry Library, 1968.

—*White-Jacket, or, the World in a Man-of-War*. Harrison Hayford, Hershel Parker, and G. Thomas Tanselle (eds). Evanston and Chicago: Northwestern University Press and the Newberry Library, 1970.

Meyers, Jeffrey. *Edgar A. Poe: His Life and Legacy*. New York: Scribners, 1992.

Miéville, China. "Cognition as Ideology: A Dialectic of SF Theory." *Red Planets: Marxism and Science Fiction*. Mark Bould and China Miéville (eds). Middletown, CT: Wesleyan University Press, 2009. 231–48.

—"Editorial Introduction." Symposium: Marxism and Fantasy. *Historical Materialism* 10.4 (2003): 39–49.

Miller, Perry. *Errand into the Wilderness*. New York: Harper and Row, 1956.

—*The Raven and the Whale: The War of Words and Wits in the Era of Poe and Melville.* New York: Harcourt, Brace, and Co., 1956.

Miller, Zane. *The Urbanization of Modern America: A Brief History.* New York: Harcourt Brace Jovanovich, 1987.

Mooney, Stephen L. "The Comic in Poe's Fiction." *On Poe.* Louis J. Budd and Edwin H. Cady (eds). Durham, NC: Duke University Press, 1993. 133–41.

Morrison, Toni. *Playing in the Dark: Whiteness and the Literary Imagination.* Cambridge, MA: Harvard University Press, 1992.

Mücke, Dorothea E. von. *The Seduction of the Occult and the Rise of the Fantastic Tale.* Palo Alto: Stanford University Press, 2003.

Negri, Antonio. *The Savage Anomaly: The Power of Spinoza's Metaphysics and Politics.* Trans. Michael Hardt. Minneapolis: University of Minnesota Press, 1991.

Nietzsche, Friedrich. *Twilight of the Idols.* In *The Portable Nietzsche.* Trans. and ed. Walter Kaufmann. New York: Penguin, 1982. 462–563.

Olson, Charles. *Call Me Ishmael.* San Francisco: City Lights, 1947.

Parrington, V. L. *Main Currents of American Thought.* 3 vols. New York: Harcourt, Brace, and Company, 1927.

Pease, Donald E. "National Identities, Postmodern Artifacts, and Postnational Narratives." *National Identities and Post-Americanist Narratives.* Donald E. Pease, ed. Durham, NC: Duke University Press, 1994. 1–13.

—*Visionary Compacts: American Renaissance Writings in Cultural Context.* Madison: University of Wisconsin Press, 1987.

Peeples, Scott. *The Afterlife of Edgar Allan Poe.* Rochester, NY: Camden House, 2004.

—"Nowhere Man: The Problem of Poe and Place." *Nexus: Publication of the Asociación Española de Estudios Anglo-Norteamericanos* 2009.1 (2009): 85–90.

—" 'To Reproduce a City': New York Letters and the Urban American Renaissance." In *Poe and the Remapping of Antebellum Print Culture.* J. Gerald Kennedy and Jerome McGann (eds). Baton Rouge: Louisiana State University Press, 2012. 101–22.

Poe, Edgar Allan. *Complete Poems.* Thomas Ollive Mabbott, ed. Urbana and Chicago: University of Illinois Press, 2000.

—"Doings of Gotham." *The Columbia Spy* (1844). Available online at http://www.eapoe.org (accessed 16 August 2013).

—*Essays and Reviews.* Ed. G. R. Thompson. New York: Library of America, 1984.

—*The Letters of Edgar Allan Poe.* John Ward Ostrom, ed. Cambridge, MA: Harvard University Press, 1948.

—*Poetry and Tales.* Patrick F. Quinn, ed. New York: Library of America, 1984.

—*Tales and Sketches.* 2 vols. Thomas Ollive Mabbott, ed. Urbana and Chicago: University of Illinois Press, 2000.

Pollin, Burton. "Poe's Use of Material from Bernardin de Saint-Pierre's Études." *Romance Notes* 12 (1971): 331–8.

Pratt, Mary Louise. *Imperial Eyes: Travel Writing and Transculturation.* London: Routledge, 1992.

Quinn, Arthur Hobson. *Edgar Allan Poe: A Critical Biography.* New York: D. Appleton-Century Co., 1941.

Quinn, Patrick F. *The French Face of Edgar Poe.* Carbondale, IL: Southern Illinois University Press, 1957.

Quirk, Tom. *Nothing Abstract: Investigations in the American Literary Imagination.* Columbia, MO: University of Missouri Press, 2001.

Renza, Louis A. *Edgar Allan Poe, Wallace Stevens, and the Poetics of American Privacy.* Baton Rouge: Louisiana State University Press, 2002.

Reynolds, David S. *Beneath the American Renaissance: The Subversive Imagination in the Age of Emerson and Melville.* New York: Knopf, 1988.

Ridgely, Joseph. "Tragical-Mythical-Satirical-Hoaxical: Problems of Genre in *Pym.*" *American Transcendental Quarterly* 24 (Fall 1974): 4–9.

Scott, Sir Walter. "On the Supernatural in Fictitious Composition." *Sir Walter Scott on Novelists and Fiction.* Ed. Ioan Williams. London: Routledge, 1968. 222–51.

Sekula, Allan, and Noël Burch. "The Forgotten Space." *New Left Review* 69 (May–June 2011).

Shumway, David. *Creating American Civilization: A Genealogy of American Literature as an Academic Discipline.* Minneapolis: University of Minnesota Press, 1994.

Silverman, Kenneth. *Edgar A. Poe: A Mournful and Never-ending Remembrance.* New York: HarperCollins, 1991.

Simmel, Georg. "The Metropolis and Mental Life." *The Sociology of Georg Simmel.* Trans. and ed. Kurt H. Wolff. New York: The Free Press, 1950. 409–24.

Smith, Henry Nash. *The Virgin Land: The American West as Symbol and Myth.* Cambridge, MA: Harvard University Press, 1950.

Spanos, William V. *The Errant Art of Moby-Dick: The Canon, the Cold War, and the Struggle for American Studies.* Durham, NC: Duke University Press, 1995.

Spark, Clare L. *Hunting Captain Ahab: Psychological Warfare and the Melville Revival,* 2nd edn. Kent, OH: Kent State University Press, 2006.

Tally, Robert T., Jr., vol. ed. *Edgar Allan Poe (Bloom's Classic Critical Views).* Harold Bloom, ed. New York: Chelsea House, 2008.

—*Melville, Mapping and Globalization: Literary Cartography in the American Baroque Writer.* London and New York: Continuum, 2009.

Tocqueville, Alexis de. *Democracy in America.* 2 vols. Phillips Bradley, ed. Trans. Henry Reeve. New York: Vintage, 1990.

Thomas, Dwight, and David K. Jackson. *The Poe Log: A Documentary Life of Edgar Allan Poe, 1809–1849.* Boston: G. K. Hall and Company, 1987.

Thompson, G. R. "Edgar Allan Poe." *The Dictionary of Literary Biography.* Vol. 3. Detroit, MI: Gale Research, 1979. 249–97.

—*Poe's Fiction: Romantic Irony in the Gothic Tales.* Madison: University of Wisconsin Press, 1973.

Todorov, Tzvetan. *Genres in Discourse.* Trans. Catherine Porter. Cambridge: Cambridge University Press, 1990.

Tolkien, J. R. R. "On Fairy-Stories." *The Monsters and the Critics and Other Essays.* Christopher Tolkien, ed. New York: HarperCollins, 2006. 109–61.

Trilling, Lionel. *The Liberal Imagination.* New York: Harcourt, 1950.

Voltaire. *L'Enfant Prodigue.* Paris: Chez Praut fils, 1738.

Whalen, Terrence. *Edgar Allan Poe and the Masses: The Political Economy of Literature in Antebellum America.* Princeton: Princeton University Press, 1999.

Wilbur, Richard. "The House of Poe." *The Recognition of Edgar Allan Poe.* Eric W. Carlson, ed. Ann Arbor: University of Michigan Press, 1966. 255–77.

Youree, Sarah. "The Immense, the Wild, the Watery, the Unshored: The Ocean as Heterotopia in *Moby-Dick.*" *Teaching American Literature: A Journal of Theory and Practice* 4.1 (Fall 2010): 73–89.

Zimmerman, Brett. *Edgar Allan Poe: Rhetoric and Style.* Montreal: McGill-Queen's University Press, 2005.

Index